IN SEARCH OF THE DARK AGES

IN SEARCH OF
THE DARK AGES

Michael Wood

Checkmark Books®

An imprint of Facts On File, Inc.

For my mother and father

IN SEARCH OF THE DARK AGES

Checkmark Books
An imprint of Facts On File, Inc.
11 Penn Plaza
New York, NY 10001-2006

Library of Congress Cataloging-in-Publication Data

Wood, Michael.
    In Search of the Dark Ages.

    Bibliography: p.
    Includes index.
    1. Great Britain—History—To 1066. 2. England—Civilization—To 1066. 3. Anglo-Saxons. I. Title.
DA135.W83   1987   942.01   86–19839
ISBN 0-8160-4702-2

Cover design by Cathy Rincon

Printed in Great Britain

10 9 8 7 6 5 4 3 2 1

CONTENTS

Acknowledgements

I must first thank the staffs of the following libraries for their kindness and helpfulness, without which this book would not have been possible: Corpus Christi College Cambridge, Jesus College Oxford, the Bodleian Library Oxford, the Cathedral Library Durham, the British Library, Worcester Cathedral Library, the Public Record Office, and the British Museum Coin Room.

I am indebted to Bob Meeson at Tamworth, Robin Brown at Saham Toney and Paul Sealey at Colchester Museum, who were all kind enough to let me use their unpublished researches. In Caen Michel de Boüard was unstintingly helpful to an unrepentant Anglo-Saxonist, and in Oxford John Griffiths generously gave his advice and provided me with a photograph of the Florentine manuscript of Tacitus: to both go my warm thanks. In particular I must express my gratitude to two friends: Phil Barker for his encouragement and criticism, and David Hill whose conversation always throws out new insights into Anglo-Saxon England. My editor, Sheila Ableman, has had to work on a nightmare of a typescript; without her constructive criticism this book would have been much the poorer; a special thanks to her. Finally, I must thank the producer of the *In Search of . . .* films, Derek Towers, and the cameraman, Richard Ganniclifft, both of whose special talents gave so much to the series, and the executive producer, Roger Laughton.

INTRODUCTION

The modern British are a nation of immigrants. This book spans a period of a thousand years of their history. Its framework is the gradual transformation of mainland Britain under the impact of various invading people. The Iron Age inhabitants, the Celtic-speaking Britons (ancestors of today's Welsh), were overcome by the Romans after AD 43. There was initial, bitter resistance, culminating in the savage revolt of Boudica in 60–61, but for over three centuries Britain was a relatively prosperous province of the Roman Empire.

Between AD 400 and 500, the period traditionally known as the Fall of the Roman Empire, the Romano-British society in lowland Britain which had lasted over 300 years was invaded and partially conquered by Anglo-Saxon immigrants who came from Denmark and Saxony. These fifth-century invasions form the background of the period to which later traditions assign the wars of King Arthur in which he defended British society against the invading English. (Today we often use the terms 'British' and 'English' indiscriminately, but, historically, the British were the original islanders and the English the Anglo-Saxon newcomers, and this distinction is used throughout this book.)

In the ninth and tenth centuries Britain was swept by new waves of invaders from Scandinavia – the Vikings. They came for plunder, but most of all for land to settle and farm. At this time a number of Anglo-Saxon kingdoms flourished in what was to become known as England. Most were destroyed by the invaders. The careers of the three greatest Anglo-Saxon kings, Offa (757–96), Alfred the Great (871–99) and Athelstan (924–39) were all touched by the Vikings – to Offa they were a shadow on the horizon; to Alfred they were enemies in a life and death struggle; Athelstan was their conqueror and assimilator. The course of the Viking invasions left Wessex the chief power in Britain, and by 939 'England' existed in roughly the same geographic terms as it does today. But in the eastern and northern parts of England the Vikings had settled permanently, irrevocably changing the character of the society. The heavy settlement of a Scandinavian free peasantry and warrior class in the Midlands and East Anglia meant that the Anglo-Saxon kings had to be an effective power there to outface Viking kings from overseas. At first the English succeeded, for example procuring the downfall of Eric Bloodaxe, the last king of an independent Viking Northumbria in

954. But failure to maintain this influence by Ethelred the Unready (978–1016) led to the fall of the English monarchy and a generation of Danish rule under Canute and his successors. Although the line of Alfred was restored in 1042 in the person of Edward 'the Confessor', the royal house had lost its vigour. When Edward died childless in January 1066, a powerful earl with no great claim to the throne, Harold Godwinson, became king, only to fall in battle at Hastings the same year fighting one of his rivals, Duke William of Normandy, 'the Conqueror'. The Norman Conquest signifies the end of Anglo-Saxon England, though the English people still speak an Anglo-Saxon language, and their social and political organisation has its roots in the society founded in this island by Germanic invaders 1500 years ago.

As might be expected, the sources for such a long period are not only diverse but variable in quantity and quality. We can divide them into three main categories: narrative history (chronicles, annals, histories), documentary records (laws, charters, wills, writs, *Domesday Book*), and material sources (coinage, metalwork, sculpture, manuscripts, embroideries, etc). In the last category we might also include the whole range of archaeological evidence. Other kinds of sources appear in these pages, particularly literary compositions – poems, letters, saints' lives, royal biographies – but it is perhaps the chronicles and charters which require a brief explanation.

Chronicles are year-by-year notes recording important events – accessions, battles, deaths, and so on. They are not shaped works which interpret history in the manner of the classical historians. They were perhaps originally jottings set down by monks in calendars and tables used to calculate the date of Easter. At first they might be as simple as 'Day dark as night' (*Annals of Wales* AD 447); gradually they give more detail: 'In this year Aldfrith king of Northumbria passed away on 14 December at Driffield' (*Anglo-Saxon Chronicle* AD 705).

In 731 the first great work of English historical writing was published by a monk called Bede at the monastery of Jarrow in Northumbria. The *Ecclesiastical History of the English People* transformed the bare framework of annals into a true historical synthesis with vision and style. Bede's work was to remain the framework for much that followed – for instance, he was the first to use dating by the Incarnation – AD – for historical purposes, and his book became the international best seller of the early Middle Ages. Bede's sources were mainly oral, though he had access to documents from some of the English churches, notably in Kent.

The classical tradition of historical writing was still known. For example, although Tacitus' works were not rediscovered until the Renaissance, Suetonius' biographies of the Roman emperors were very influential; they gave barbarian kings an idea of what a ruler should be, and they were also a model for a shaped work of history with a 'message' which could serve the interests of a royal dynasty. These ideas grew stronger after the reign of Charlemagne in Francia (modern France) from 768 to 814, the epoch we now call Carolingian after him. Charlemagne's forceful and glamorous kingship was an ideal for later kings like Alfred the Great. Accordingly a work like the *Anglo-Saxon Chronicle*, though based on earlier West-Saxon monastic annals, becomes expansive in the Frankish style in the reign of Alfred in a way which suggests that it was compiled under Alfred's personal supervision in order to advertise the success of his own dynasty. Copies of the chronicle (handwritten of course) were then disseminated to churches throughout England, and it survives in several somewhat different versions. (Generally I have not distinguished between them in my text.)

The later a chronicle is written after the events it describes, the less value it has. But that is not to say that some later chronicles do not sometimes preserve valuable material from sources now lost. For instance, early thirteenth-century chroniclers from the great history school at St Albans record what look like genuine fifth- and sixth-century Mercian traditions, and one of these writers, Roger of Wendover, is alone in preserving details of the death of Eric Bloodaxe in 954 from a now lost northern chronicle. The value of all such works depends on a combination of the circumstances of their composition and the sources and bias of their author. The most important cases are discussed in the relevant chapters – what makes Tacitus trustworthy on Boudica, the *Annals of Wales* unreliable on King Arthur, the *Anglo-Saxon Chronicle* ambivalent on Ethelred, and so on.

Charters are a quite different kind of source. They are title deeds, the records of land transactions, such as the gift of an estate by a king to a monastery. They may sound dry but they tell us a lot about the king's power and pretensions. They show us where kings did or did not possess land; they give us clues as to how they managed the royal estates; they enable us to trace the rise of the great families and the lesser military aristocracy. Charters can even give us insight into character: Offa's hard-nosed grasp of the workings of kingship, Athelstan's love of high-flown titles, Ethelred's self-justifying ineffectiveness. Anglo-Saxon charters date from before the period of systematic governmental archives and were preserved in the muniments rooms of the local bishoprics. They were often copied and recopied, and most only survive in later copies which are often tampered with and usually corrupt. But charters are one of the prime sources by which modern historians have been able to build a picture of the fabric of Anglo-Saxon society.

There is now debate about the roots of English and British identity. This book centres on the emergence of the English state and an English identity during the Dark Ages. The nature of this legacy is now of interest to all inhabitants of the British Isles – and indeed, to a wider world.

GENEALOGIES OF
THE EAST ANGLIAN,
MERCIAN, AND
WEST SAXON
DYNASTIES c500—955,
INCLUDING THE
MYTHOLOGICAL
EARLY PARTS OF
THEIR PEDIGREES.

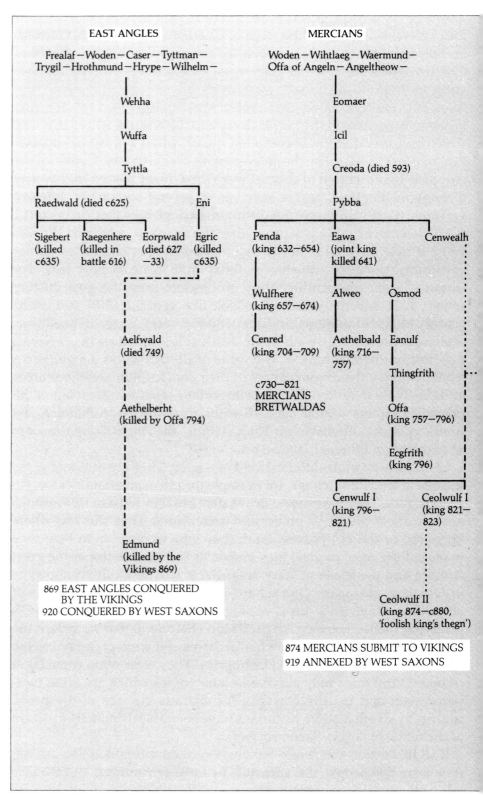

EAST ANGLES

Frealaf — Woden — Caser — Tyttman —
Trygil — Hrothmund — Hrype — Wilhelm —

Wehha

Wuffa

Tyttla

Raedwald (died c625)　　　　Eni

Sigebert (killed c635)　Raegenhere (killed in battle 616)　Eorpwald (died 627 —33)　Egric (killed c635)

Aelfwald (died 749)

Aethelberht (killed by Offa 794)

Edmund (killed by the Vikings 869)

869 EAST ANGLES CONQUERED
BY THE VIKINGS
920 CONQUERED BY WEST SAXONS

MERCIANS

Woden — Wihtlaeg — Waermund —
Offa of Angeln — Angeltheow —

Eomaer

Icil

Creoda (died 593)

Pybba

Penda (king 632—654)　Eawa (joint king killed 641)　Cenwealh

Wulfhere (king 657—674)　Alweo　Osmod

Cenred (king 704—709)　Aethelbald (king 716—757)　Eanulf

c730—821
MERCIANS
BRETWALDAS

Thingfrith

Offa (king 757—796)

Ecgfrith (king 796)

Cenwulf I (king 796—821)　　Ceolwulf I (king 821—823)

Ceolwulf II (king 874—c880, 'foolish king's thegn')

874 MERCIANS SUBMIT TO VIKINGS
919 ANNEXED BY WEST SAXONS

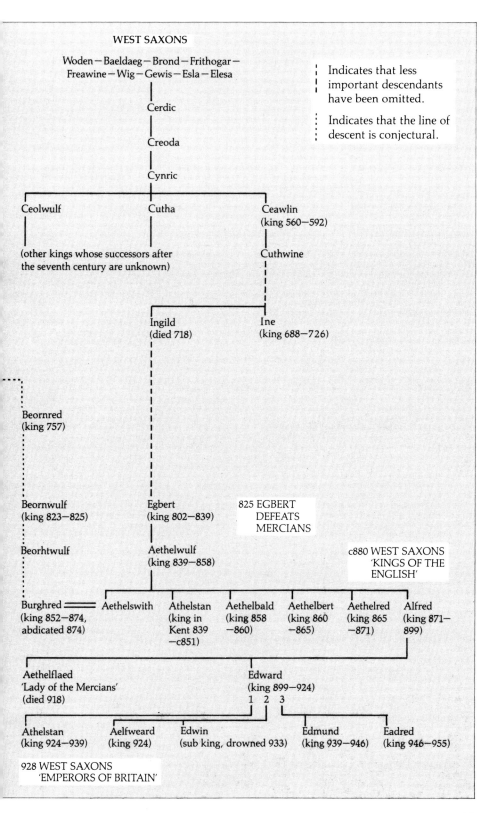

WEST SAXONS

Woden — Baeldaeg — Brond — Frithogar —
Freawine — Wig — Gewis — Esla — Elesa

Cerdic

Creoda

Cynric

Ceolwulf   Cutha   Ceawlin
                                 (king 560—592)

(other kings whose successors after   Cuthwine
the seventh century are unknown)

                 Ingild   Ine
                 (died 718)   (king 688—726)

Beornred
(king 757)

Beornwulf   Egbert   825 EGBERT
(king 823—825)   (king 802—839)   DEFEATS
                                     MERCIANS

Beorhtwulf   Aethelwulf   c880 WEST SAXONS
                 (king 839—858)   'KINGS OF THE
                                     ENGLISH'

Burghred === Aethelswith   Athelstan   Aethelbald   Aethelbert   Aethelred   Alfred
(king 852—874,   (king in   (king 858   (king 860   (king 865   (king 871—
abdicated 874)   Kent 839   —860)   —865)   —871)   899)
                           —c851)

Aethelflaed   Edward
'Lady of the Mercians'   (king 899—924)
(died 918)   1 2 3

Athelstan   Aelfweard   Edwin   Edmund   Eadred
(king 924—939)   (king 924)   (sub king, drowned 933) (king 939—946) (king 946—955)

928 WEST SAXONS
    'EMPERORS OF BRITAIN'

Indicates that less
important descendants
have been omitted.

Indicates that the line of
descent is conjectural.

CHAPTER 1

BOADICEA

She was very tall, the glance of her eye most fierce; her voice harsh. A great mass of the reddest hair fell down to her hips. Around her neck was a large golden necklace, and she always wore a tunic of many colours over which she fastened a thick cloak with a broach. Her appearance was terrifying.

Dio Cassius *Roman History*

Boadicea has a place of her own in British folk history. The warrior queen who fought her terrible, unavailing struggle against the might of Rome. Her story is so strange and dramatic it is odd that Hollywood has not seized on it. These days the virago on the scythed chariot is so ingrained in the popular imagination that cartoonists could portray the British Prime Minister, Margaret Thatcher, as Boadicea immediately after her election victory, knowing that everyone would get the point.

Boadicea first became known to the British public in the reign of Elizabeth I, but fittingly enough it was under that other great queen, Victoria, that she really became enshrined in popular myth, a myth symbolised by the famous colossal group on the Thames embankment next to Big Ben and the Houses of Parliament. In fact it was Prince Albert himself who sponsored the statue. It was created at the height of the British empire, a period of romantic obsession with myths of free democratic peoples: the Britons, who were free before they fell beneath the Romans, the Anglo-Saxons, who lost their liberty to the Normans.

To the Victorians Boadicea was a patriotic queen, a freedom fighter who died defending the liberty of her country against a ruthless and alien power. 'Regions Caesar never knew thy posterity shall sway,' reads the inscription on the group: for an Edwardian Englishman the message was clear enough. But the statue encapsulates a nineteenth-century myth, not first-century reality.

The queen's name was not Boadicea (a spelling mistake in an influential Renaissance manuscript) but Boudica, which means 'Victoria', 'Victory'. Her chariots were light, springy, wicker vehicles, not armoured carts (nor, in all probability, did they have scythes on their wheels). As for Boudica herself, whatever she may have looked like – Dio's description which heads this chapter was written in the second century – she

Thomas Thornycroft's statue of Boudica on the Embankment. The 'regions Caesar never knew' were of course the British Empire, which Victorians saw as a historical fulfilment of the Roman Empire.

BOADICEA.

did not look like Isadora Duncan. However, the evidence that archaeologists are finding suggests a far more strange and complex story than Prince Albert could have imagined. It is the story of the bitterest war ever fought in Britain; a desperate colonial war between a backward, underdeveloped 'Third World' people and a remorseless, highly organised and 'civilised' imperial power; a war of terrible atrocities; a war which saw the destruction of the largest Roman towns yet planted in Britain, and the deaths of 70,000 colonists and untold numbers of Britons. None of these things was new to the Roman conquerors; what made this war exceptional was that they had to fight for their lives against a woman.

Britons and Romans

This book covers a period when society in Britain was changed by several waves of invaders – Celtic, Roman, Anglo-Saxon, Viking and Norman – all of whom settled and permanently altered life here. In the period from the arrival of the Romans to the Norman Conquest, Britain lay outside the Mediterranean world around which classical civilisation had grown, 'like frogs around a frogpond' as Plato said. Britain was felt to be at the edge of the world itself, not just of the Euro-Asian landmass.

It was 'at the outermost edge, almost into the whirlpools'. Roman writers refer to its remoteness, 'set apart in the boundless ocean' with its inaccessible shores, treacherous tides and wintry climate, 'another world' as a panegyric to the emperor Constantius calls it. It is clear that the islands were often visited by traders, as they had been since early Greek times, and there was frequent contact between the Celts of Gaul and Britain. But when Julius Caesar landed in 55 and 54 BC it was not a successful venture for the Romans. The British Isles were still not very well known to them. A famous passage in the *Annals* of the Roman historian Tacitus, on the wreck of a Roman fleet in the North Sea in AD 16, is a classic example of sailors' tall stories: those survivors who were swept across to Britain came back with tales which lost nothing in the telling: 'terrible hurricanes, unknown birds, creatures half man and half beast – all of which they had seen, or believed they had seen, in their fear'. It was well known, adds Tacitus, that this ocean was 'more stormy than any other sea in the world'.

Throughout its history Britain has been a refuge or a goal for tribes pushing westwards, and the successive immigrants have left their mark, shaping landscape, culture and language over 5000 years. The first people in Britain were nomadic hunters, food gatherers, who were followed in around 3500 BC by settlers who first cultivated land and raised crops. These people were of Celtic stock and spoke a Celtic language, the distant ancestor of today's Welsh, Cornish and Breton. The Iron Age civilisation which the Romans conquered seems to have diffused westwards from the Alpine region during the late second millennium and the early first millennium BC, bringing with it the characteristic feature of Iron Age culture – metalworking, wheeled vehicles and horsemanship. They are also responsible for the great fortified hilltop forts and settlements which were all over southern Britain.

In about 75 BC a new wave of settlers invaded Britain. We call them the Belgae, as the Romans did. They came from a part of France called by the Romans Gallia Belgica. They were great metalworkers and produced gold, silver, bronze and iron ornaments of marvellous work-manship; they also revolutionised agriculture by inventing a new, heavy plough. At this time the process of clearing the heavily wooded valleys of the south-east started, and has gone on ever since. This was the period when the south-east first began to be exploited properly by man, and the Belgic field systems can still be seen there on the high ground. Grain was the staple – wheat, spelt and barley; and the native vegetables – turnip, cabbage and parsnip.

The Belgic tribes conquered south-east Britain, but not East Anglia where the Iceni lived in what is now Norfolk. The Iceni were Boudica's tribe, and they seem to have been relatively isolated and culturally

15

backward. The Belgic peoples were more 'modern' than the Celtic; they minted coins on Roman models with Latin inscriptions; they traded with the Romans, who by then had made Gaul (France) part of their empire; they bought luxury goods in exchange for slaves won in war. The Belgic tribes also fought each other, and the original native tribes, for dominance. During the period around the birth of Christ the Catuvellauni and the Trinovantes under King Cunobelinus extended their control over much of what is now south-eastern England. Colchester was their chief centre. It was then called Camulodunum, a vast Iron Age settlement surrounded by a massive and complex series of defensive earthworks whose focal point was a 700-acre site two miles southwest of the centre of modern Colchester; it is now called the Gosbecks and is as yet only known through aerial photography of crop marks. It included a large ditched enclosure, an extensive system of trackways and dykes, and a temple precinct within a walled area; later additions built after the Roman Conquest were a Roman fort, a theatre and a road linking the site with the Roman colony to the north-east where Colchester now stands.

Until excavation, the full significance of this huge Belgic site will be unclear, but it represents a late Iron Age site which probably only waned after Boudica's revolt in AD 60–61. Camulodunum has been called the most outstanding late Iron Age – early Roman site in the country. It was the centre of the most powerful overlordship which had yet arisen in Britain, something of a parvenu monarchy with Roman tastes, but nevertheless possessed of wealth and influence. Cunobelinus, who ruled from AD 10 at Camulodunum, issued fine coinages on a vast scale in bronze and silver from there and from Verulamium (St Albans). Some coins were made in the native Celtic fashions, others were based on Roman coins and showed a sphinx instead of the Celtic horse. The golden age of Cunobelinus ended around AD 40, on the eve of the emperor Claudius' invasion of Britain.

The Roman invasion

Into this Celtic-speaking, essentially backward country, the Romans came with their legions in AD 43. We do not know why they invaded Britain: perhaps for its precious metals, its corn, wool, and other natural resources: maybe just 'because it was there' as a young British imperialist said of another kind of conquest. Most likely the reason was simply *la gloire*; an imperial triumph for Emperor Claudius, who needed all the martial publicity he could get. He proclaimed himself 'first to bring the barbarian peoples across the ocean under the sway of the Roman people' and he was, in effect, extending the empire to the western limits of the known world.

Many tribes, especially those with strong trading contacts, welcomed the Romans, or at least submitted without a fight. These included many enemies of the overking Cunobelinus. Others fought and were defeated. The Iceni of Norfolk were among those who submitted quietly, and the Romans were able to celebrate their triumph within a matter of months while their armies fanned out northwards and westwards. As we shall often see in these stories, conquerors always make a grand show to demonstrate their supremacy and their ideology, and none were better at this than the Romans. As soon as the military situation in the south-east was safe, the Emperor Claudius himself hastened to Britain and held a great ceremony at Camulodunum. The Britons were overawed with a display of Roman dazzle and majesty and they formally submitted to the invaders. These events were recorded on a triumphal arch in Rome and the inscription can still be seen in the Palazzo Barberini:

'Victory over the Britons': a Roman coin, celebrating Claudius' conquest of AD 43. On a triumphal arch the mounted emperor receives the British submission.

> To Tiberius Caesar Germanicus . . . Father of the State and the People of Rome, because without any mishap he received in unconditional surrender eleven conquered British kings, and for the first time reduced the barbarians beyond the sea under the power of the Roman people.

It was, for the Romans, a great day, that day at Camulodunum: the emperor and his retinue on their dais with the commander-in-chief, the high-ranking officers and the praetorian guard, pennons flapping, watching Roman might parade past with elephants (a nice touch to impress the vanquished, most of whom would never have even heard of such an animal).

Then Claudius supervised the formal surrender in which the British kings placed themselves under the protection of the Roman people. Among those kings was Prasutagus of the Iceni, and in the circumstances of Prasutagus' deal with the Romans lies the origin of the great revolt of AD 60–61. For Prasutagus' wife was Boudica.

Iceni

Prasutagus' people, the Iceni, were isolated, cut off behind the forests of Suffolk and Norfolk from the Romanised tribes of Essex and the south-east. As yet very little is known about their tribal organisation. In his *Commentaries* Caesar speaks of the *Ceni Magni*, implying that there was a 'lesser' as well as a 'greater' Icenian tribe, and small clues from chance archaeological finds do indeed seem to indicate that the group did not have one nucleus. In fact a threefold division is suggested by the finds of coins and metalwork, and it may be that there were three different royal clans to go with them, with three distinct royal centres. At present we

A silver coin of the Iceni from the period of the Roman Conquest. Like all Celtic art it displays an extraordinary gift for the abstract. The model for this boar motif was a classical head of Apollo.

17

An Iceni gold coin. The crescent design derives from locks of hair on the forehead of classical coin portraits. Kings' names on the coins include *Aesu*, *Saemu* and *Antedios*, perhaps indicating subkingdoms of the tribe.

can only guess where they might have been.

However, there must have been a centre near Norwich, close to the later Roman town which bore the tribal name, *Venta Icenorum*, 'market of the Iceni', whose ruins still remain at Caistor-by-Norwich. It stands to reason that the Roman town was close to an important native site which preceded it, although as yet no trace of earthwork or crop mark has been observed. Somewhere in the line of bluffs above Caistor, it is likely that there is a pre-Roman settlement awaiting the archaeologist's spade. On the northern coastal plain another concentration of coin and metalwork finds could point to a second subdivision of the Iceni settled by the sea, perhaps at the well-preserved earthwork at Warham St Mary. In the south-west of Norfolk major finds in the Brecklands are also localised, especially in the valley of the Little Ouse where four coin hoards have been found. Even more significantly, a large occupation area (with, as yet, no traces of defence works) has recently been identified near Saham Toney, south-west of Norwich. This place seems to be the most productive Iceni site yet. Not only have there been domestic finds of coins, rings, pins and fine decorated brooches for cloaks and dresses but coin moulds reveal that coins were actually minted there, suggesting a site of considerable importance, if our limited ideas about Iceni culture are not misleading. Fascinating as the prospects are from Saham Toney, our information is as yet dependent on chance finds. Only when the hilltop there is dug will hard answers begin to emerge about the state of Iceni civilisation on the eve of its eclipse.

Because no pre-Roman Iceni centre has yet been identified and excavated archaeologists are still in the dark about the royal family. For instance, when Tacitus speaks of a 'palace' is it a simple anachronism? If there were three different sections of the tribe, were there three kings? What was Prasutagus' relationship to the king 'Antedios' named on the coins who is thought to have ruled around the time of the Roman Conquest? Was Prasutagus a puppet king set up by the Romans to further their interests in opposition to other branches of the royal family, perhaps after Antedios had been deposed or died? But most important of all, who was Boudica? We know she was Prasutagus' wife – but what was the ancestry and royal status which (along with her charismatic personality) enabled her to command such allegiance when the revolt broke out? These are all questions which probably can never be answered, but political in-fighting between pro-Roman and anti-Roman tribes and groups should never be underestimated when dealing with these events. In the meantime only the full excavation of an undoubted Iceni royal centre could give us some answers to questions which we see at present only through Roman eyes.

Detailed study of Iceni coinage has furnished one of two further clues. We know that before the Roman Conquest, they minted their own coins, but in a far more limited way than the rich Belgic tribes of the south-east. The circulation of the coins was extremely restricted and hence probably comparatively few coins were made (so few in fact that no two dies that have yet been found were ever alike). Initially the coinage was in gold, and carried no inscription. It is only in its final stages – just before the revolt – that the coinage bears the tribal name in the form 'Eceni': these pieces were apparently issued during the reigns of Prasutagus and Boudica herself and they were buried in large numbers when Boudica's revolt was suppressed. These later coins which proudly blazon the tribal name were struck only in silver. By the time of the Roman Conquest, and probably a good while before, the Iceni gold supply (bought or traded from elsewhere in Britain) had dried up. More noticeable still, the beautiful Iceni gold metalwork, torques, bracelets and ornate chariot and horse gear, which has been found in a number of East-Anglian hoards dating from the first century BC, seems to have ceased to be manufactured even before the Claudian invasion: possibly the Iceni were being starved of precious metals by their wealthier and more powerful Belgic neighbours.

The limited circulation of Icenian coinage, and its small-scale manufacture, could suggest that their rulers were unfamiliar with the use of coinage as a means of trade and very likely did not understand the principles of finance. This would explain much of what followed. Rather like the British administrators did in the Raj, the Romans let the Iceni retain some privileges and a token independence in return for the

This silver coin of the Iceni, from the period of the revolt, proudly bears the tribal name, a practice followed by no other British people. Some carry the legend *Subprasto* ('Under Prasutagus'?). As yet there is no *Bouda*.

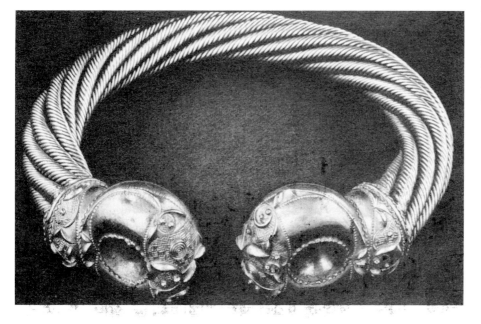

The great electrum torque (neck-ring) found at Snettisham in Norfolk. Is this like the 'large gold bracelet' that Boudica wore round her neck?

payment of tribute, the provision of auxiliary recruits for the Roman army, and the acceptance of 'aid'. 'Aid as imperialism' is not a new concept, and like many Third World countries today the Iceni accepted loans from Roman financiers to help them become, by degrees, 'Romanised'. This probably involved buying Roman luxury products just as it might today include, say, buying a Coca-Cola monopoly. But Prasutagus can hardly have known what he was letting himself in for. The kind of men who were behind the loans in Rome understood all too well the dictates of international finance. The emperor's tutor, Seneca, was one; a philosopher and a poet, a clever, rich man who intended to get richer.

The first Iceni unrest

Having overrun the south-east, the Romans pushed their armed forces towards Wales and into the south-western peninsula. Meanwhile behind the military zone the colonists, tradesmen, developers and entrepreneurs moved in to open up the new province. A new Roman colony at Colchester close to the *oppidum* at Gosbecks was made the capital of the province of Britain. A great trading post was also set up to which the resources of the province could be brought and where the produce of the Roman world could be bought and sold: pottery, glass, fabrics, wine, olives, corn. This place was to become London.

As the armies advanced north and west a military frontier was established running in a line from Lincoln via Gloucester to Exeter. A military road linked by a string of forts – the Fosse Way – enabled forces to be moved from point to point along this line. Perhaps the conquest was originally intended to end at this barrier, much as it had ended on a similar line in Germany. After all, beyond it were only recalcitrant tribes in mountainous regions like Wales which seemed unlikely to yield much profit. But troubles beyond it – including violent resistance by a British leader known to history as Caractacus – gradually pushed the Romans further forward into the Welsh mountains. These troubles also altered the Roman attitude to the tribes behind them.

In AD 50 the Roman governor decided to 'disarm suspects on this (the Roman) side of the rivers Trent and Severn'. Hence it became forbidden under Roman law to carry arms, except hunting weapons. Not only the tribes hostile to Roman rule were included, but even client kingdoms like the Iceni who had no Roman troops occupying their land and who expected the Romans to be on their side. Units were sent in to search out and confiscate all Iceni arms, and especially their great iron swords which were finely welded and decorated by skilled Celtic smiths and were prized as heirlooms and marks of aristocratic status. Uproar fol-

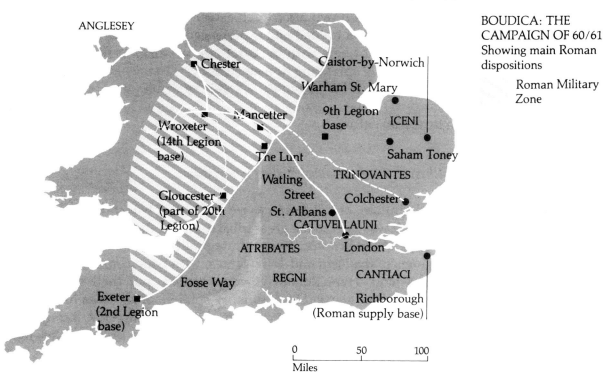

BOUDICA: THE CAMPAIGN OF 60/61
Showing main Roman dispositions

Roman Military Zone

lowed. The Iceni were the first people to rebel and they immediately sought help from their neighbours the Coritani and the Catuvellauni. They attacked one of the Roman auxiliary units sent to them but were then swiftly forced on the defensive in 'an enclosure surrounded by a crude and rustic bank with a narrow entrance' (Tacitus *Annals*). This obviously refers to an Iron Age hillfort. There they were easily overcome. (There are no known hillforts along the southern and south-western border of the Iceni kingdom except Wandlebury near Cambridge, and though excavation in the fifties did not prove this, it is perhaps the likeliest spot for the incident.)

The revolt of 50 was a minor affair. Prasutagus himself retained his position as client king of the Iceni, so it may have been another section of the tribe under another leader who revolted, with Prasutagus remaining, as we suspected, pro-Roman. But the incident is interesting because it shows how quickly the tribe were to react to Roman terror tactics. Sown in Iceni minds was the fear that the Romans might not be their friends for long. The Romans were also alerted, for soon after 50 the governor set up a permanent colony for army veterans at Camulodunum, giving them lands appropriated from the estates of the Trinovantian house.

Establishing a *colonia* in conquered territory was a tried and tested Roman practice. It was a good way of pensioning off old hands who wanted to settle down after their sixteen-year term of service; it provided a reserve of trained and experienced troops in an emergency (an important factor here with the front line 150 miles to the west); it was also a means of spreading Roman civilisation to the natives; a town laid out on the Roman model to show locals what a high standard of living Rome could bring. A model town, then, but the veterans did not prove to be model citizens.

Colchester: 'blatant symbol of alien imperialism'

Camulodunum, or Colchester as we shall call it, was chosen for obvious reasons. It was next to the great tribal capital at the Gosbecks, centre of the 'King of the Britons'. It was strategically placed between the client kingdoms of the Iceni and Trinovantes, with good communications by sea and land. Here Roman veterans settled, put their savings into businesses and married local girls, as soldiers of all times have done. They built little villas in the surrounding countryside, brought in Roman farming methods and ran their estates with British slaves; they constructed small houses like modern Mediterranean town houses and opened shops in Colchester itself, importing the staples of Mediterranean life by road from the warehouses of London, or by sea up the river Colne.

They were not expecting trouble. The turf bank of the legionary fortress built here in 43 was levelled and buildings erected over it, most in timber and wattle but including a stone forum on the site of the present town hall (the site has been the administrative centre of the town ever since), a theatre, and most striking of all, the Temple of Claudius. This was the biggest Roman temple in Britain (105 feet by 80 feet) standing on a plinth in a precinct 400 feet by 500 feet and surrounded by a wall of finely faced stone. The building was decorated with alabaster and red, green and black marble expensively imported from as far away as Italy, Greece, Asia Minor and North Africa. In front of the entrance steps stood a great altar flanked by statues, one of which was a bronze mounted statue of Claudius himself. The temple would have had a college of priests to conduct the services, and it appears that the large income needed to support them came more from local taxes than from gifts from worshippers. No wonder then that this 'blatant symbol of alien rule', as Tacitus calls it, created such resentment among the Britons.

The colonists needed land to grow crops, and this was taken from the natives who lived around Colchester. The same was done with the Catuvellauni at St Albans, though there the colony itself was mainly populated with locals who were encouraged to 'go Roman' and live in the town. Towns were an innovation in British life in the 50s – urban life here was unknown before the Roman conquest – but because they were all destroyed in Boudica's revolt in 60–61, archaeologists have been able to date these early developments securely and give us a fantastically vivid picture of life before the holocaust.

High Street Colchester was the main shopping centre then as now. On the north side, for instance, there was a timber-framed seedsman's warehouse with wattle and daub walls and painted plaster. Further along was a pottery shop stocked with hundreds of Samian bowls – mass-produced household ware – and jars, glasses and lamps (there was a local lamp industry in the town). Amazingly these shops were found to have been on the same footing as the modern shops: property boundaries in this part of Colchester have remained unchanged for 2000 years! On the other side of the street, next to the Red Lion hotel, another pottery shop was found recently which sold decorated bowls for the upper-class end of the market; over seventy of these were found still packaged in the crates in which they were imported from factories in central Gaul. Here too were found quantities of coriander for seasoning food, dill, anise, pine cones, opium poppy, lentils, and figs – not dried but fresh. (Was the Colne valley temperate enough in the first century to grow figs?) The impression all this gives is of a high-class delicatessen for Romans of wealth and good taste. Southwards along Lion Walk, where a mass of timber-framed houses and shops was found, this impression was confirmed in 1974 when a fruit shop was found with plums, olives and a pile of calcined dates in a remarkable state of preservation. These kinds of products, along with wine and fish paste, would have been imported in amphorae, or storage jars, from the Mediterranean; to a shop like this the Roman veterans and their British wives would have sent their slaves to buy all the products which gave the Romans a sense of well-being in a foreign land. The colonial life here, it seems, was a good life.

The beginning of the revolt: Tacitus' story

In AD 60 during the reign of the vicious and unpredictable Emperor Nero, Prasutagus died 'after a life of long and renowned prosperity', says Tacitus. At this point the Iceni were still a client state of the Romans, nominally allies rather than an occupied, conquered race. Prasutagus clearly hoped that he might be able to preserve this precarious independence after his death by a show of loyalty to Nero, and he made the emperor his co-heir with his two daughters. But this only invited the appropriation that followed. After he died Roman agents moved into Iceni country and plundered the royal household; Iceni chiefs were deprived of their hereditary lands and Prasutagus' widow Boudica was flogged and her daughters raped by Roman slaves. The Romans thought they could reduce the Iceni to provincial status and dispense with their traditional royal family by such off-hand and brutal treatment. Seeing the way the wind was blowing, the Roman investors in Rome, men like Seneca, called in their loans. Unbowed, the Iceni decided to revolt, and with them the Trinovantes and other tribes, 'having secretly plotted together to become free again,' adds Tacitus, indicating that the rebellion was to some extent planned in its opening stages. Their leader was Boudica.

Our only accounts of the revolt are Roman, and our only reliable one is Cornelius Tacitus' *Annals*. Tacitus was a highly-educated upper-class Roman, but one with a wide and sympathetic interest in the Celtic and Germanic peoples in the north and west of the empire. Although he was only a boy at the time of the revolt, Tacitus' story has particular value because his father-in-law, Julius Agricola, later a famous governor of Britain, fought in the campaign of 60–61 as a junior officer. It is surely reasonable to think that in later years the young Tacitus must have heard his in-laws talking about these events, and must have read Agricola's memoirs, which are not now extant. Tacitus also commands our respect as a narrator because, although he gives us, inevitably, a one-sided account of Boudica, he was, as he says himself, 'dedicated to writing history without anger or bias', and it is quite clear that he was antipathetic to many aspects of Roman imperialism. Thus, though we cannot be sure he is not simply imputing motives to Boudica for dramatic effect, and without good evidence, time and again he suggests that the Britons had genuine grievances against colonists who in their turn are portrayed as incredibly insensitive to a different culture. In short, it would be impossible to tell this story without Tacitus, and impossible to interpret much of the archaeological material now coming to light.

The 'positive' image from the gem seal found in the burned villa at Foxton: a treasured imperial gift?

The destruction of Colchester

Not surprisingly Colchester was the first object of the rebel army, with its amenities, its well-fed veterans, and its gleaming extravagance, the Temple of Claudius. On the way the Roman settlers out in the 'bush' were the first to be killed. One villa site in the path of the Iceni was at Foxton near Cambridge, and here excavators have discovered evidence of a brutal destruction. The place had been broken into and burned down; shattered lock bolts perhaps tell of the doors being battered down; evidence of fire was everywhere; a beautiful onyx cameo (of a type given by emperors in gratitude for service done) had been prised out of its gold setting and thrown into the cesspit. Of the owners there were few traces, though they will not have had time to escape: there were remains of their last meal which was a bowl of oysters. As in a twentieth-century guerrilla war, such as that in Rhodesia, the isolated settlers on their farms were the first to be murdered.

As the rebel army moved south, rumour spread like wildfire. Tacitus says that in Colchester people were seized with foreboding of some terrible disaster. Shapes like human corpses were left by the ebb tide; delirious women screamed that destruction was at hand; dreadful moans were heard in the senate house, and the theatre echoed with shrieks; a blood-red stain was seen in the sea, and at the estuary a phantom colony was seen in ruins. These signs, says Tacitus, 'were interpreted hopefully by the Britons, and with terror by the settlers'.

The Roman governor Suetonius, however, was too far away to help. He was engaged in attacking the great druidic stronghold on the island of Anglesey when the storm burst. The veterans at Colchester frantically appealed for help to the imperial agent in London, Catus Decianus. But he sent them only two hundred men, poorly armed. The veterans prepared to protect themselves and, without rampart or trench, improvised defences around the precinct of the temple itself.

The end came swiftly. Boudica surrounded Colchester and burned down the town. Most buildings were wooden and the place was swept by a firestorm. In the pottery shop in the High Street stocks were smashed to pieces before it was fired, leaving the modern archaeologist fragments of red Samian burned black. In the glass shop near the forum the heat was so intense that molten glass poured onto the floor and cooled in twisted shapes. A Roman bandsman's gear was stamped on and broken before his house was fired. Traces of human remains, the bones of people who died in the fire, have also been found. Those who escaped – and the Romans had evacuated none of the women and children – fled to the one area that had withstood the fire and the one place where the veterans might hope to hold out against Boudica's hordes: the precinct of the temple itself. There they resisted for two days before the building was taken by storm and all inside it slaughtered. The equestrian statue of Claudius was overturned and its head hacked off and thrown into the river Alde in Suffolk by one of Boudica's men. The temple itself was razed to the ground, but the great vaulted plinth on which it was constructed was virtually indestructible: it is still possible to walk inside it today, deep below the Norman castle of Colchester which was later constructed on the site.

Bronze head of the emperor Claudius, perhaps from the equestrian statue which stood in the temple precinct at Colchester.

In a final outrage the rebels even desecrated the Roman cemetery beyond what is now the west gate of Colchester, mutilating statues and breaking tombstones. Two exceptionally fine examples are now exhibited in Colchester Museum: Longinus, a cavalry officer from the Balkans, is shown proudly riding over the conquered race; his face has

Tombstones from Colchester, Longinus on the left and Facilis on the right. By AD 60 the Romans were already confident enough of peace to lavish money on these public monuments to stability, military pride and religious feeling.

been smashed away by one of Boudica's followers but the Briton cowering below him has been left intact. The tombstone was thrown over and shattered. Marcus Facilis, an Italian centurian, was depicted in his best parade armour:

> Here lies Marcus Favonius Facilis, son of Marcus of the Pollian tribe, centurion of the Twentieth Legion Erected by his freedmen Verecundus and Novicius.

Facilis' tombstone had been broken in half and his haughty nose knocked off.

The revolt spreads

Things now took on a momentum of their own. With their vast supply of fine horses the Iceni aristocracy possessed great speed and mobility. They and their allies, the Trinovantes, moved south, destroying other

26

towns and settlements including Chelmsford (a large Roman site as yet only partially excavated) and the native colony at St Albans where the Britons living a Roman life-style received short shrift from the 'army of liberation'. Wherever archaeologists have been able to examine the levels from the period there seems to have been killing and destruction. But the Britons were not a leaderless mob. When the commander of the nearest Roman legion, the 9th, based at Longthorpe in North Cambridgeshire, rushed his forces south towards Colchester in an attempt to crush the revolt in the bud, he fell into a carefully planned ambush in the wooded country north-west of Colchester. The legionaries (probably about 2000 strong) were wiped out, and only the cavalry were able to escape. Boudica must have laid her plans well to overcome a strong force of battle-hardened regular troops, and doubtless she attacked them in line of march. It was a major triumph, and one to lift Iceni morale sky-high. Suddenly the whole Roman presence in Britain was at stake. The governor, Suetonius Paulinus, was with the main Roman army far away in Wales, and had perhaps only just received news of the seriousness of the revolt. With the 9th gone, Boudica's next prey was defenceless.

London: first-century boom town

London is a Roman creation. It was set up around AD 50 to exploit the wealth of the new province, and the exploiters had crowded in. By 60 its population was numbered in thousands, perhaps more than ten thousand. Here was the office of the procurator, the emperor's agent Decianus. Here too were many merchants, no doubt including people from established provinces like Gaul and Spain. One person then living in Londinium as it was called was Aulus Alfidius Olussa, a Greek from Athens who died aged seventy before the end of the first century and who was buried near Tower Hill.

London seems to have owed its origin not to a fort (there is no evidence for a military site then) nor to an established Iron Age ford. Its attraction seems to have been its location at about the tidal limit of the river at that time. This made it possible for seagoing vessels to sail upstream against the strong current. By 50, with the Fosse Way frontier established and 'a time of unbroken peace' in the offing, south-east England was secure and sufficiently stable for continental merchants and Roman bankers to invest heavily in trade with Britain and to develop a new civil port. By 60 London was an undoubted commercial success. Through it came the many imports and exports of the new province, and according to Tacitus, though London was not dignified with the title of colony, it was 'crowded with traders and [was] a great centre of commerce'.

Recently archaeologists have located the civic centre of this, the earliest London. It lay across where Gracechurch Street is now, near the Bank of England, bounded by Cornhill to the north and Fenchurch Street and Lombard Street to the south, in other words where the later basilica and forum were built. A series of wattle and daub buildings lay along the main east-west street, probably houses and shops, while where the forum later grew up, across Gracechurch Street, there was a large gravel area which was perhaps London's earliest market place. A grain dump found in one of the houses adjoining the main street suggests that some merchants were already setting up lucrative warehouses, for such a store would be for civilian, not army consumption. The town was extensive – debris of this period has been found stretching out to Newgate – and its loss would have been a major blow to the whole Roman effort in Britain; indeed it would very likely cause the imperial policy makers to question the worth of further investment in the province.

Suetonius, though a military man, understood these realities clearly enough, and after destroying the druidic centre in Anglesey, turned his two legions eastwards, he himself riding on ahead day and night down Watling Street (the military road to the frontier) to see whether the Roman investment in Londinium could be saved.

When Suetonius arrived in London his intelligence reports showed him that the situation was worse than he could ever have guessed. The 9th was out of action, Colchester wiped out, and other tribes were joining the Iceni. Survivors will have given him some idea of the size of Boudica's army. London of course had no walls, and, we may presume, after a stiff wine in the procurator's office, Suetonius decided that the town could not be saved. It was now a question not of saving London, but of saving the whole province. 'Unmoved by tears and prayers,' says Tacitus, 'Suetonius gave the signal for departure.' Those who could went with him back into the military zone. Others will have fled over the Thames into the pro-Roman tribal areas of the south. Some tried to hire boats and get back to Gaul – among them was Decianus himself, the emperor's procurator whose rapacity had done so much to inflame feelings before the revolt. Perhaps the Greek Olussa went with him, clutching his moneybags. The rest, the old, the women and children, those who were too attached to the town or simply unwilling to leave their new shops, waited anxiously for the last dawn of the first London.

London destroyed

The archaeological evidence makes the catastrophe that enveloped London in AD 60 dramatically clear. Wherever you dig into the foundations of London you come across a red and black layer of burned ash and soot. Food jars have been found which were thrown into rubbish pits. There is a hoard of money whose owner buried it for safety but never came back to collect it. The familiar burned Samian has been picked up east and west of the Wallbrook. In the marketplace smouldering debris spilled out over the gravel surface of the main street. Gracechurch Street was the centre of a large area of conflagration, but there were major gaps in the area of burning, showing that fires were started separately: this is what is to be expected in a new town where there was plenty of open space and ribbon development. The debris also provides confirmation of Tacitus' picture of a mass evacuation prior to the arrival of Boudica's army. There is a general (though not complete) absence of domestic objects from the portions of burnt buildings that have so far been excavated. Many escaped then, though possessions were certainly left behind in some houses, and these were perhaps those of people who perished, as many certainly did. There were no prisoners, says Tacitus, 'they could not wait to cut throats, hang, burn and crucify . . . Roman and provincial deaths at the places mentioned are estimated at seventy thousand'. This may be an exaggeration, but there is no doubt that many settlers met very cruel deaths. The later writer, Dio Cassius, in his *Roman History*, may just be adding lurid detail to titillate his readers when he describes how rich Roman women were hung up, their breasts cut off and sewn to their mouths, how they were tortured and impaled on sharpened stakes. It may be that such details were invented like some modern atrocity stories – Huns bayoneting babies, Vietnamese Russian-roulette – but it may be, as Tacitus implies, that such rites were done in fulfilment of religious practices demanded by the Druids. Unfortunately we are in the dark as to the true nature of druidic involvement in the war, the degree to which they spurred on Boudica's war of liberation. Whether these details are true or not, the many severed skulls of this period found in the silt of the Wallbrook stream close to the financial heart of Boudican London near Gracechurch Street, may well be the heads of captured Romans and British collaborators beheaded by Boudica's vengeful troops. It is known from illustrations on such monuments as Trajan's column in Rome that Celtic and Germanic tribes decapitated their enemies and displayed their heads: such seems to have been the fate of these Londoners.

So the investment in London went up in smoke. After the firestorm the ashes settled. Boudica had reached her moment of decision. The impetus of the attack had come to a halt. What should she do now? She seems to have had no alternative. She had to follow Suetonius back up Watling Street into the Roman military zone and attempt to deal the decisive blow. Any delay and the Romans would be able to send reinforcements from Gaul to Suetonius' army supply base at Rich-borough in Kent, and attack her from behind. She may also have known that a swift victory might have far-reaching effects. The rebellion had been so savage and destructive that a further loss of regular troops might give the upper hand to those men in Rome who favoured pulling out of Britain altogether. After all, why go to such expense to consoli-date a province whose profits might never be very great? Boudica herself may have known how the disastrous defeat of Varus in Ger-many 50 years before, with the total loss of three legions, had led to the withdrawal of Roman forces there and the establishment of a Rhine frontier.

How much control Boudica had over her forces we shall never know. Did she even know that other risings were taking place from Lincoln-shire down to the south-west? That at Margidunum just north of Not-tingham Romans were being slaughtered? Or that rebels were in arms as far away as Somerset, where archaeologists have only recently associated with Boudica's revolt a terrible massacre of British women and children inside one of the gates of the Iron Age hillfort at South Cadbury? It must have taken great personal force to keep some sort of order in her army, still more to cajole them away from the prospect of more loot and into a situation they must have feared – a pitched battle with Suetonius' legions.

The last battle

Where did the climactic battle of the war take place? Tacitus gives a description of the battlefield, to the effect that Suetonius held a defile with woods behind him and open country in front of him: apparently at a point where wooded hilly country broken with defiles opened out into a flat plain. But Tacitus does not say where this was. Most scholars have assumed that Boudica followed Suetonius up Watling Street, and that somewhere on that road, presumably near to the military frontier, his supply bases and his lines of communication, Suetonius offered battle in the strong defensive position described by Tacitus. There have been many fruitless attempts to be more precise but not long ago Dr Graham Webster suggested a site at the village of Mancetter near Nuneaton, and recently archaeological discoveries are adding colour to his hypothesis.

Mancetter (later called Manduessedum, the 'place of chariots') lies below a wooded line of bluffs cut by pronounced ravines. In front, over the river Anker, a wide plain opens out which is crossed by Watling Street. Along the river the defences of a very large Roman military base have been found, and chance finds have included fragments of Roman armour from legionary and cavalry units, and a hoard of military issue

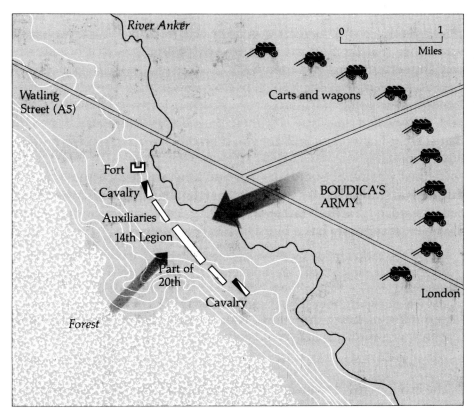

THE BATTLE
BETWEEN BOUDICA
AND SUETONIUS IN
THE POSITION AT
MANCETTER
SUGGESTED BY DR
GRAHAM WEBSTER.

coinage. Finds identify the site with the 14th legion, and we know from Tacitus that the 14th was the backbone of Suetonius' army in the decisive battle with Boudica. Accordingly this camp may have been set up during the period when the Fosse Way frontier was established. After the fall of London, Suetonius therefore fell back on a base he already knew, a rendezvous for the reinforcements he had ordered in from the forts along the Fosse Way, a defensive position where he could stand and fight without being surrounded by Boudica's superior numbers.

If Dr Webster is right, then it was along the Anker that the Romans arrayed their army, with the woods behind them. The legionaries (all the 14th and part of the 20th) were in regular order in the centre, the light armed auxiliaries on their flanks and the cavalry on the wings. The position was very narrow, fronted by ditches and to the left anchored on a fort which has been discovered near the point where Watling Street crosses the Anker. The Roman numbers may have been around 7000 or 8000 legionaries and 4000 auxiliaries and cavalry. In front of them the British on foot and horse seethed over a wide area and kept up a terrific racket to frighten the Romans. So confident were they of victory that they stationed their wives and families in carts to watch the slaughter.

31

Only Iceni nobles can have owned war gear like this bronze shield, which would have been backed in wood and leather. Early first century.

Their numbers cannot be ascertained. Tacitus clearly thought there were over 100,000; Dio gives a quarter of a million. We can say with confidence that the Romans were heavily outnumbered, if immeasurably superior in arms and training.

Tacitus and Dio say that the respective leaders gave speeches to their troops at this point. It is unlikely that Tacitus knew what Boudica had said, but one line rings true, a taunt to the men: 'Win the battle or perish: that is what I, a woman will do; you men can live on in slavery if that's what you want.'

Tacitus' version of Suetonius' speech, however, may actually reproduce some of the general's words at that fateful moment, for it may have been heard by Tacitus' father-in-law, Agricola, and recorded in his memoirs. It certainly has a blunt soldierly air about it:

> Ignore the racket made by these savages. There are more women than men in their ranks. They are not soldiers – they're not even properly equipped. We've beaten them before and when they see our weapons and feel our spirit, they'll crack. Stick together. Throw the javelins, then push forward: knock them down with your shields and finish them off with your swords. Forget about booty. Just win and you'll have the lot.
>
> *Annals* Tacitus

The Britons crowded up on the Roman line before Suetonius gave the order to attack. A volley of several thousand heavy javelins was thrown into them at about forty yards, followed by a second. The casualties must have been terrible from that alone, for few of the Britons can have had any body armour. Then the Romans attacked in tight array, stabbing with their short swords.

There is nothing romantic about ancient battles, and in this one the Britons had no chance, despite their numbers. In fact their numbers made it worse. They were crushed onto each other so they were unable to use their long swords properly. The Roman cavalry now started to move out of the narrow position and work round their enemies' flanks. Soon the packed rear ranks broke. In such battles more people are killed in the flight than in the battle itself, and here the Romans consciously took revenge. Driven against their carts the Britons were slaughtered even when they tried to surrender: men, women, children, and pack animals too. The Romans must have gone mad with blood lust. Tacitus says that 80,000 Britons were killed. The Romans lost 400 dead and a larger number wounded.

Boudica poisoned herself. Dio adds that she was buried secretly with great honour, but where this took place we have no means of knowing. The discovery of her burial place would cause an archaeological sensation, but it is unlikely. To us she must remain an enigma, more alien and less comprehensible than the Romans who hated and destroyed her.

The clear-up

'The place of chariots'. Beneath Mancetter's Anglo-Saxon church and Elizabethan hall lie Suetonius' legionary defences. Was this the site of Boudica's defeat?

For a time the future of the Roman province of Britain hung on a thread. In a few months the revolt had spread from Norfolk to Somerset. Now the Roman military establishment would make sure that it never happened again.

Ten miles from the battlefield a great supply base was set up at a place called the Lunt, near Coventry, as the first stage in the Roman army's campaign of revenge. The most striking feature of the fort there was a *gyrus*, a circular arena with a wooden fence for breaking in horses. It has been suggested that this unique feature could have been part of a collecting point for Iceni horses after the battle. Other buildings included a large granary, stable-blocks and equipment sheds, barracks, foundries where cavalry equipment could be manufactured, and an exceptionally large headquarters block which indicates the presence of a top-ranking officer. The fort was short lived. It was begun around AD 60 because of the rebellion, when the new fort was suddenly constructed very hurriedly. This fort was very extensive indeed, for remains have been uncovered well beyond the 4½-acre site which can be seen reconstructed today. In fact the outer defences of the Boudican period fort have not yet been located, so it may have extended over the

The grim reality of the Roman occupation: reconstructed *gyrus*, or horse ring, at the Lunt; on the skyline are the spires of Coventry.

whole of the Lunt plateau in the loop of the river Sowe, comprising at least 25 acres.

When the immediate military situation in the Midlands was resolved, and the bulk of the Roman forces moved into Iceni territory, the huge first camp was replaced by a more compact $4\frac{1}{2}$-acre fort centring on the *gyrus* and the HQ building. This smaller version was built in the early sixties and abandoned and dismantled around AD 80 by an army demolition squad. A fascinating insight into the mentality of the Roman military hierarchy in Britain was provided by the discovery that the fort had been reoccupied in the late third century at the period when the Saxon Shore forts were being constructed by the Romans against Anglo-Saxon invaders. It seems that when the Roman army decommissioned the fort in AD 80, they maintained ownership of the site. They had learned their lesson from Boudica. Her rebellion had been fanned by native resentment of appropriation of their land for military use. So for nearly 200 years the Lunt (and others in all probability) were kept as open spare sites for forts, ready for any future trouble.

Back into Iceni land

So we can imagine the Lunt plateau in the aftermath of Boudica's revolt

34

as a scene of extraordinary activity: a vast military encampment, the slopes all around covered with stockades for horses and dumps of grain; smithies furiously producing horseshoes, the coming and going of cavalry detachments; a constant stream of Iceni horses being broken in on the arena of the *gyrus*; Roman reinforcements training along the river Sowe, the slopes and the almost vertical face of the escarpment. All this would be prior to Suetonius' drive into Iceni territory. The whole army was kept 'under canvas' (ie, in tents in the field) for the winter in order to finish the war. Two thousand regular troops were transferred from Germany with eight auxiliary infantry battalions and a thousand cavalry: a measure of Roman losses in the campaign. Then Suetonius pushed into Iceni and Trinovantian land, establishing new winter quarters from which he could ravage hostile or wavering tribes with fire and sword. 'But the enemy's worst affliction was famine,' says Tacitus, 'for they had neglected sowing their fields and brought everyone available into the army intending to seize our supplies.'

As the army tightened its grip on the Iceni, a chain of forts was constructed across East Anglia, including ones at Saham Toney, at Warham, at the Gosbecks, and probably at Caistor-by-Norwich. After the fire and sword came a second stage. The Iceni were to be Romanised through and through in order to enjoy the full benefits of Roman civilisation. The new generations who grew up after AD 60 would grow up in a Roman world.

Within a few years of the revolt, one branch of the Iceni was moved from its tribal centre and settled in a new city planned along the lines of the Roman model at Caistor-by-Norwich. It was to be called Venta Icenorum, the market town of the Iceni. It was never a great success, although it was later dignified with a forum, baths and public works. The site laid out after the revolt was small compared with other tribal capitals, but it still proved too big; many plots were never taken up and it remained half empty for a long time before it contracted to the present walled city in the late first century. After the Fall of Rome the city was never reoccupied and its walls still stand today, up to twenty feet high in places, under their earth banks. The lines of its streets were still visible from the air in the days when its great central rectangle was laid out to crops.

And what of the Iceni themselves? They remain an enigma. We know little of them before Boudica and even less after. Almost a generation of men must have been lost in the war and the famine, devastation and slavery that followed their defeat. The royal family and leading men will have been ruthlessly purged. The peasants lived on – perhaps the imposition of Roman rule meant little to them – and after the Fall of Rome we lose sight of them. But it may be that the British-speaking fen dwellers, the itinerant horse dealers and thieves who lived on the fringe of Norfolk society for centuries afterwards were the last of the Iceni. Let the imagination play and it is not difficult to see in the dark Celtic-looking faces you see today in Norwich streets the descendants of those people. As for Boudica herself no personal trace has ever been found. The costly tomb which Dio Cassius says was built for her is an intriguing but remote possibility. Her memorial lies in the pages of the historians of her bitterest enemies.

The glory of the Iron Age. Iceni horse on a gold coin found near Norwich.

CHAPTER 2

KING ARTHUR

Then Arthur fought against them in those days with the kings of the Britons, and it was he who led their battles.

Nennius *History of the Britons*

There is no myth in British history, and few in the world, to match the story of King Arthur: the knights of the Round Table, Guinevere, Lancelot, the quest for the Holy Grail. Since the Middle Ages these tales have exerted their fascination and continue to do so today, particularly in a declining Britain where the myth of a golden age has obvious attractions. But beneath the legend lie the real events of the fifth century; the period of the fall of the Roman Empire. This time remains the darkest, the least documented, in British history. Yet through the shadows modern historians think they have distinguished a remote war leader, a real-life British hero who is said to have died around 500, and whose fame, it is thought, grew from successful battles against the Anglo-Saxon invaders who poured into Britain from northern Europe and Scandinavia after the fall of Rome, the ancestors of today's English. But are the historians right?

In spite of their obscurity the years following 500 were some of the most important in the 2000 years of recorded British history. It was then that the key racial and linguistic alignments of Britain were defined. The Celtic inhabitants of Britain were driven into Cornwall, Wales, Strathclyde and Scotland by the Anglo-Saxon newcomers who settled in the east and south in what was later to be called England. The dispossession of the Celtic people of Britain by the Anglo-Saxon invaders was the subject of a huge literature in the Middle Ages, and in Arthur it had its greatest hero.

The purpose of this chapter is to look at the way in which Roman civilisation in Britain came to an end, and to see what justification there is to link a historical Arthur to these events. Go into any bookshop today and you will find yourself in no doubt that he existed. A mass of Arthurian books is available, from reputable academic works to theories from the lunatic fringe. In them Arthur emerges as everything from cult hero to guerrilla generalissimo, Dark Age Superman to Dark Age Che Guevara. They remind us that every age makes of Arthur what it will. In the

Glastonbury Abbey and the 'Tomb of King Arthur'. There is evidence that there was a Celtic monastery here before the West-Saxon conquest of Somerset, but the Arthurian connection was made only in the later twelfth century.

eighteenth century Gibbon contented himself with noting that 'the severity of the present age is inclined to question the existence of Arthur' and wisely avoided conjecturing a career for him. Macaulay in the early nineteenth century thought him 'no more worthy of belief than Hercules'. It has been the twentieth century which has sought to corroborate the details of the myth and find a historical Arthur. The Victorians perhaps paved the way for this. Books like Tennyson's *Idylls of the King*, which were based on the legend, had a fantastic emotional impact on the late Victorians, with its stress on chivalry, heroism, and nationalism, and its dark strain of sexual jealousy and betrayal. All this appealed to the Victorians' nostalgia for a lost golden age.

But Victorian England was also the era of the birth of scientific archaeology. Remarkable discoveries were made in Greece, Crete, and Turkey by the German, Heinrich Schliemann, which were thought to have proved that the Homeric legends were 'true', that Agamemnon and Achilles had existed and that Troy was sacked by the Greeks just as had been described in Homer's poems. We now know that Schliemann was wrong in most of his conjectures about Troy and Mycenae, but it is perhaps not surprising that British scholars of the early part of this century, brought up in this intellectual milieu, should have been the first to try to reconcile the legend of Arthur with historical fact, to work out a rational account of the Arthurian story and to suggest that behind the tale of Arthur and his knights lay a historical armoured cavalry leader with a brief to drive back the Anglo-Saxon hordes as Roman power in Britain ebbed.

As at Mycenae and Troy, finds of the right period have been pressed into service. Since the Second World War historians have not only gone back to Glastonbury and Cadbury and 'found' Avalon and Camelot, but have built up a detailed history of Arthur's empire and its political ideologies. We shall look at the sources for these conjectures later. Let us simply note now that it is a natural impulse for societies to construct a golden age retrospectively, and for the most part such speculations are no more than that. An example of this was the discovery of 'Arthur's tomb' at Glastonbury. In the mid twelfth century Geoffrey of Monmouth's fanciful book, *History of the Britons*, fired the imagination of the credulous intelligentsia of the time. In 1191, six years after the destruction of their abbey by fire, and with their restoration fund badly needing a boost, the monks of Glastonbury dug secretly in their old cemetery and 'discovered' the remains of a large man buried in a tree trunk. This, they claimed, was King Arthur himself, and they produced a forged inscription to prove it. Eyewitnesses had not mentioned a woman, but it was soon said that Guinevere had also been found. Given the medieval propensity to manufacture relics, no disinterested observer would think this find had any more relation to King Arthur than the subsequent discoveries in the same place of the sword Excalibur and the grave of Joseph of Arimathea. It is interesting to note that the great twelfth-century expert on Glastonbury, William of Malmesbury, who wrote an official history of the monastery just before Geoffrey of Monmouth wrote his book, specifically denies that the burial place of Arthur was known. Nevertheless the 1191 discovery has been accepted as the grave of King Arthur by a number of scholars in recent years.

There is even more doubt about the Arthurian associations with such tourist spots as Tintagel, Amesbury, Winchester and Cadbury. In the main they are the inventions of twelfth-century romantic poets. If we wish to uncover real events behind the stories we must do as William of Malmesbury enjoined us all those years ago: 'Throw out such dubious stuff and gird ourselves for a factual narrative.' The question is, what happened in Britain at the fall of the Roman empire? Bound up with that, there is a second question: did there exist at this time a war leader called Arthur? In much of this chapter we will be examining the historical background to the late fifth century. It is only when we understand the nature of that time that we will be in a position to evaluate the evidence for Arthur's existence.

Portchester in Portsmouth harbour. The Roman curtain walls are complete on all sides. Occupied by the Anglo-Saxon invaders in the sixth century, the fort was a burh with a royal hall in the tenth century.

A world in decline?

Portchester on the south coast of England. This massive Roman fortress, the best preserved in northern Europe, was one of a dozen built around the year 300 to defend Britain against the incursions of Anglo-Saxon invaders. The society it was to protect was already under stress, with class divisions, a decline in trade and depopulation of towns, a falling birthrate, high inflation, the gradual collapse of a money economy, and the growth of great private rural estates.

In 410 came the end of 350 years of Roman colonial rule, a period as long as that in which the Portuguese ruled over Angola, longer than the British supremacy in India. The Romans did not simply abandon England and sail back to Italy. Their armies had been gradually withdrawing in the preceding years, and before that there were several periods when the Britons had elected their own emperors and cut their links with the Roman government on the continent. What happened in 410

40

was a formal severance of responsibility for defence. But Britain had been a Roman province for so long that the Roman influence remained long after the Roman departure. The problem of how long *Romanitas* continued here is one of the cruxes of early English history and archaeology. Historians now recognise that the western provinces of the Roman empire remained a recognisably sub-Roman civilisation for centuries under the barbarian Germanic tribes who took over.

The first few years of the fifth century were critical for the western Roman empire, threatened on all sides by barbarian peoples breaking through the frontiers. One barbarian chief, Alaric, King of the Visigoths, appeared in Italy in 401 and besieged Rome in 408, finally entering it in 410. Other Germanic peoples, the Vandals, Suevi and Burgundians, struck into Gaul in 407. It was to meet this challenge that the Romans were forced to withdraw troops from Britain. The Britons themselves were under increasing threat from Scottish, Pictish and Anglo-Saxon raiders, and with no help forthcoming from Rome, elected their own leaders, one of whom, Constantine, held power from 407 to 411 and led troops into Gaul against the Roman government there. According to the *Gallic Chronicle*, Britain, deprived of fighting men, then suffered a large-scale invasion in 408. 'The provinces of Britain laid waste by the Saxons: in Gaul the barbarians prevailed and Roman power diminished.' What happened next is the subject of argument. The general view is that though their leader Constantine was fighting in Gaul and called himself an emperor, the Britons did not consider that they had ceased to be part of the Roman Empire. In 410 they appealed for help to Emperor Honorius in Rome but he could do nothing except order the local communities to arrange for their own defence. Rome had troubles of its own: in the same year it was sacked by the Visigoth Alaric.

A different perspective can be seen in the works of the late fifth-century Byzantine writer Zosimus, which explains how the Britons were able to resist the Anglo-Saxon invaders successfully. According to Zosimus it was the Saxon ravages (presumably culminating in the 408 attack) which forced the inhabitants of Britain to secede from the Roman Empire in a kind of UDI, and become once again 'another world'. They organised their own defence, took up arms, and 'braving every danger freed their cities from the invading barbarians'.

Some historians have suggested that this revolt went hand in hand with a social revolution, a peasant revolt like the Bacaudae in Gaul, and that the peasantry successfully opposed the Romano-British upper class and defeated the Anglo-Saxons. The appeal to Honorius in Rome would then have been a last plea from the threatened landed class. It has even been proposed that this revolution went hand in hand with a radical religious movement, Pelagianism, a new kind of puritanism

Magnus Maximus, emperor of an independent 'world of Britain' after his revolt in 383 when he was *Dux Britanniarum*. Prototype for many of the later fictitious exploits of Arthur. The reverse of this gold solidus shows two emperors and a figure of Victory and was copied by Alfred the Great 500 years later.

41

A silver bowl from the Water Newton treasure, used by the Christian community.

Loot for Anglo-Saxon invaders. Silver plaques from the Water Newton hoard, buried around 350.

born out of a time of stress. However, it is now thought that this theory is unlikely to be true and that there was no movement for social reform. In fact it is probable that the people who reorganised Britain's defence in the early fifth century were the Romanised urban upper classes, the *curiales*, in the areas where town life still functioned.

Two contemporary sources throw some light on this dark period of British history: a biography of St Germanus and St Patrick's *Confessions*. In 429 St Germanus came to the island as an agent of the Catholic Church in Rome to combat the spread of the heretical Pelagianism, and though there were serious incursions in the south by Saxon and Pictish pirates, according to the biography, organised Roman town life still continued. Local magistrates were still in charge in the cities and there was obviously nothing unusual in a bishop from the continent travelling through the province to correct ecclesiastical observance. By the time of St Germanus' second visit in 447 the island was still holding out against the Saxons, if the author of the saint's biography is to be believed: writing in the 480s (which was precisely the supposed period of the Arthurian wars) he speaks of Britain as essentially Roman in administration and orthodox in worship, and most remarkably, 'a very wealthy island'.

St Patrick

The most interesting source for this period is the *Confessions* of St Patrick. Patrick, the patron saint of the Irish, was in fact a mainland Roman Briton taken into slavery in Ireland at the age of sixteen in one of the raids around 400; one of thousands seized by pirates. His father owned a small villa in the west (perhaps in the region of Carlisle), was a local town councillor, and a church deacon. Escaping from captivity in Ireland the young Patrick took passage on a trading ship to Gaul, which was then being devastated by far-reaching barbarian raids. The key point about Patrick's narrative is that when he returned to Britain in c. 415, five years after the Romans had left Britain, there is no suggestion of anarchy, and when he wrote his account in the middle years of the century the imperial Roman system of local government was intact. The local town councils, for example, were still responsible for raising taxes for the government. It was still a world where professional rhetoricians could earn a living as they could in Rome; a world where a letter writer could address the British dynasts of Strathclyde as 'fellow citizens'. We can therefore assume the continuation of a feeling of identity with Rome in the Romano-British ruling class, the senatorial aristocracy and the local landowners. This is the kind of background we would expect for an historical Arthur.

Vortigern

When did Britain fall? Several sources indicate that the crucial breach took place in a period ten years on either side of 450. The *Gallic Chronicle* says the island fell under Saxon domination in 441 or 442. According to the Anglo-Saxon historian Bede the 'coming of the Saxons' took place in 448 or 449. This last date was derived from the most important source for the fifth century, the British cleric Gildas. Gildas wrote his book, *On the Ruin and Conquest of Britain*, in the 540s and his account is generally interpreted as meaning that in 446, 36 years after they had applied for help to fight the Anglo-Saxon invaders, the British government made an appeal to the Roman consul, Aetius, for military aid against Pictish and Scottish invasions. When this aid was not forthcoming, Anglo-Saxons were introduced as friendly mercenaries, and this was, according to Gildas, the fatal step which led to the collapse of British rule in the east of the island. Most important, it was not self-governing cities or local oligarchies who brought in these troops, but a dictator. According to all later sources, by the 430s a large part of Britain had fallen under the sway of a British leader called Vortigern ('Great King') and according to British and Anglo-Saxon tradition it was he who invited increasingly large numbers of Anglo-Saxon mercenaries from Germany and Denmark to fight for him. What little we know of Vortigern shows that for a time he had something approaching absolute power. He was even able to arrange the migration of a whole people, the Votadini under their leader Cunedda, who were forced to leave Lothian and made to settle in North Wales, in order to resist Irish incursions.

Like many dictatorships, the new order of Vortigern was strong, unscrupulous and efficient. Although Gildas was writing in the 540s he must have spoken to men who remembered Vortigern's rule. He says that this was a time of prosperity and that the people were successful against the attacks from the Picts and Scots. This view, though, may only reflect the experience of the ruling party, because, as in many periods of decolonisation, there were many rival factions. These came to a head in civil warfare which coincided with two shattering blows. In 443 the whole Roman world was swept by a plague, the severity of which has been compared with the Black Death, and which must have hit Britain around 446. At the same time the Anglo-Saxon mercenaries settled by Vortigern in Kent, led by Hengist and Horsa, revolted.

The Saxon Revolt

Until recently historians believed that the Romans had been employing Germanic mercenaries in Britain for over fifty years before they departed in 410, and that many of the mercenaries had settled around the cities, were used to Roman life in towns, and had perhaps married Romano-British women. This familiarity with the Roman towns, it was argued, facilitated the changeover to Anglo-Saxon rule in the eastern parts of Britain. Recently, however, the archaeological evidence for this picture, namely the date of Anglo-Saxon military cemeteries which had been assigned to the late fourth century, has been seriously challenged. At present it seems best to follow the traditional scenario for the coming of the Anglo-Saxons as outlined by Gildas and Bede. The wars which precipitated the fall of Britain began as a struggle between various Romano-British parties, some or all of whom may have hired Anglo-Saxon mercenaries. Our sources for instance suggest that Vortigern had opponents who had purely Roman names; one, Ambrosius Aurelianus, is said by Gildas to have been born into a family who had been emperors in Britain; another opponent, Vitalinos, is recorded fighting a battle against Ambrosius. The break-up of Britain in the fifth century, then, reminds us of twentieth-century liberation wars fought, for example, in former Portuguese or Belgian colonies in Africa, with several opposed factions fighting each other, with perhaps Vortigern's 'British Patriotic Front' fighting against Ambrosius' Roman party which opposed his nationalist dictatorship. Both sides may have employed Anglo-Saxon mercenaries.

In the middle of this internecine strife, Britain was further disabled by far-reaching Germanic raids described by Gildas in graphic terms. When supplies and money for payment ran out, Vortigern's federates devastated with fire 'all the neighbouring cities and lands . . . until it burnt nearly the whole surface of the island, and licked the western Ocean with its red and savage tongue'. Some Britons were enslaved by the Anglo-Saxons, others fled overseas, others retreated to forests, off-shore islands, and most of all 'to the high hills, steep and fortified', the old Iron Age hillforts. This was not an organised campaign of conquest, but a violent raid, for Gildas describes the Anglo-Saxon mercenary armies retiring to the lands they had been given by Vortigern in the east, presumably Kent and East Anglia. Gildas' impression of continuous, destructive raids may be exaggerated. Rather, the atmosphere may have been like a Dark Age gold rush of impoverished immigrants from the then 'third world', the underdeveloped lands of the Germanic north, into the rich agricultural provinces of the Western Empire. These new 'barbarian' settlers – though initially invited – found themselves militarily strong and politically and socially unabsorbable. Despite Gildas' dramatic tale of devastation, they may not have been the only, or even the chief threat to internal security in late fifth-century Britain. But for thirty years between the 460s and the 490s they provided the ideal enemy in a prolonged war organised by the surviving senatorial aristocracy of Roman Britain. Nothing provides a better stimulus to preserving one's identity as a ruling class than an external foe, especially one comprising 'uncivilised' immigrants. According to later traditions about this 'patriotic war', the army leader at the climax of the struggle was Arthur.

Gildas, however, is our only reliable source for these events. With Vortigern dead, the British organised resistance against the invaders. Under the leadership of Ambrosius they fought a number of successful battles culminating in a great victory in the 490s, at a place called Badon Hill. This battle, says Gildas, gave forty years of peace to Britain, though, as he wrote in the 530s or 540s, 'not even at the present day are the cities of our country inhabited as formerly; deserted and dismantled they lie neglected until now, because although wars with foreigners have ceased, domestic wars continue'. Gildas does not name the British leader at Badon; as we shall see, it is considerably later traditions which insist that he was Arthur.

Wroxeter: 'This is how it ends: not with a bang but a whimper'

Archaeologists have been able to corroborate Gildas' picture. Although the Roman cities were not deserted everywhere, some were abandoned at this time, or their populations shrank dramatically. In Cirencester, for example, the second city of Roman Britain, archaeologists have established that civic life continued into the 440s; the defences were repaired, flood prevention work carried out at one of the gates, and the piazza of the forum kept clean. But soon after that time, whether caused by the great plague or by the Saxon revolt, unburied bodies were found in the streets and the town seems to have contracted to a few wooden huts inside the amphitheatre.

The most vivid picture we yet possess of declining late Roman city life comes from Wroxeter near Shrewsbury. Unlike most Roman towns, Wroxeter did not become a modern city; it still lies under farmland, and is now being painstakingly uncovered. The present excavation is around the basilica of the baths complex, formerly a great brick hall the size of a cathedral nave. This centrepiece of Roman civic pride fell into disuse around 350, and was demolished to be succeeded by shanties.

To the great surprise of the excavators, however, a later phase has been discovered which shows that the area was rebuilt. The basilica area was levelled, covered with thousands of tons of carefully laid rubble, and on this base a large number of timber buildings were erected including a massive wooden hall laid on beams, 125 feet long and 52 feet wide with a narrow extension 80 feet long. This hall, with its porticoed façade, wings and steps, was the central structure of a complex of

Wroxeter. *Right* The great basilica before it fell into disuse.
Below The hall built during the Arthurian period on the levelled site.

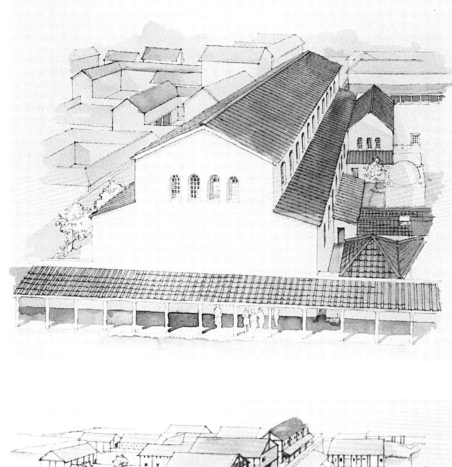

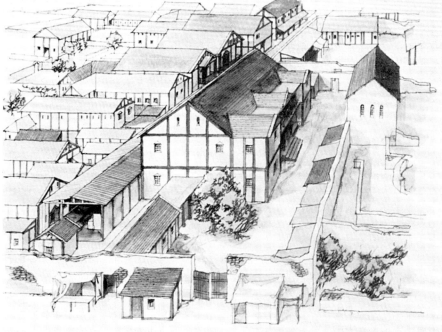

related timber buildings. South of it were rows of timber booths separated by a finely sifted gravel street roofed like a pedestrian precinct. At the upper end of the street was a series of large wooden buildings with classical façades, 'perhaps the last classically inspired buildings in Britain until Wren and the eighteenth-century revival', as the excavator has called them.

Who can have been the initiator of this drastic reorganisation of a whole city centre? It needed wealth, a high degree of organisation, and strong motivation. It was certainly not the work of demoralised peasant villagers, nor was it effected by Irish or Anglo-Saxon invaders. It has the hallmarks of Roman public works, only constructed with timber: we must surely be looking here at a complex of religious or public buildings or the private domain of some great man.

The end of this phase, the last occupation of the main area of the city, is equally intriguing. These halls were not sacked or hurriedly abandoned. They were deliberately dismantled and all useful materials taken away. When? The excavators are not sure, though a date towards the end of the fifth century is the present thinking. Why? This may be easier. Wroxeter is a large town, 200 acres with two miles of walls, and thus difficult to defend without a large fighting force. The likelihood is

The 'Old Work': surviving masonry of the Wroxeter basilica. For the illiterate Anglo-Saxon immigrants it was easy to imagine such ruins as the work of a race of giants: 'wondrous is this wall-stone; broken by fate, the cities have decayed, the work of giants is crumbling'.

47

that the city was abandoned for a more defensible site. And if the princes of Powys had Wroxeter as their main centre up till around 500, could the city have been the base of Vortigern, who appears in the genealogies of Powys? Or could it possibly have been Arthur's base? We shall probably never know, but this massive injection of energy, capital and manpower into what was evidently a declining town suggests the

The façaded buildings at Wroxeter: town houses of an Arthurian military aristocracy, or of a mercantile class who still kept open the old trade routes with the Mediterranean?

influence of one of the powerful leaders struggling for control in sub-Roman Britain, a man who wished to restore something of the grandeur of Rome, albeit in timber.

'Trusting their lives to the hills . . . precipitous and fortified'

As the cities declined, many of the warlords went back to the hills, renovating the Celtic Iron Age hillforts which had been abandoned when the Romans first conquered Britain. These citadels were easier to defend than long and badly maintained city walls. They suggest an atmosphere of retreat and fear, such as Gildas describes ('terrified by the wolfish villains'). Stand inside them and images are evoked of refugee compounds, robber barons, warlords surrounded by their armed followings, private armies. This is the background modern historians have seen as Arthur's, in the period when Anglo-Saxon mercenaries settled in Kent, Sussex, East Anglia and the Thames valley and spread their incursions deeper into southern and western Britain.

South Cadbury, one of the most atmospheric sites in Britain. Occupied from the fifth century BC this massive Iron Age hillfort was the scene of a massacre in Boudica's revolt; it was refortified in the Arthurian period; Ethelred the Unready made it an emergency burh and mint. After that its enclosure was given over to the plough.

A late local tradition connected Arthur with one of these hillforts, South Cadbury in Somerset, 'that is Camelotte', and when the Camelot Research Committee dug there between 1966 and 1972, they caused a sensation. On top of the fort they found the 18-acre area had been refortified with a drystone wall, inside which had been timber buildings including the feasting hall of a Dark Age warlord. Elements of the refortification strongly recalled Roman military architecture; imported pottery from the Mediterranean gave a hint of aristocratic luxury and showed the buildings were occupied in the last quarter of the fifth century – precisely the time at which Arthur is supposed to have flourished.

Although the name Cadbury-Camelot has stuck, the excavators did not, in fact, find Camelot, for that name is the invention of a French poet who wrote in the twelfth century and is therefore of no value to the historian save as a symbol. Nor was anything turned up to connect the place specifically with King Arthur. What the dig did prove was that in the later fifth century (c. 470–500) someone was powerful enough to wall this hillfort, erect buildings and build gates; someone whose retine was large enough to need such an extensive site; someone who built in a hybrid Roman-British style.

At the time it was thought Cadbury was exceptional and must have been the fortress of a particularly great leader. Now archaeologists know it was not unique, for many other Iron Age hillforts were refortified at this time in the south-west and elsewhere. Indeed such reoccupation seems to have been the rule rather than the exception: over a dozen instances have been found in Somerset alone, and forty in the south-west as a whole. Many others await investigation, such as the fort hidden under woods at Amesbury in Wiltshire, a particularly interesting early Christian site which etymologists connect with Ambrosius Aurelianus and which was taken from the Britons by the West-Saxon kings relatively early in Anglo-Saxon times.

The significance of these hillforts is not yet clear. For instance, do they represent centralised control of a dictator like Vortigern, a generalissimo like Ambrosius, or are they local defences as Gildas implies? Tempting as it is to associate such impressive works with tyrants and their military élites, we cannot be certain that the men who rebuilt them commanded more than local allegiance; we do not even know whether such men were rulers at all (the forts could have been organised by confederacies of local peasants, farmers or aristocrats). But dating at a number of sites now seems to link them with the specific situation of the

THE WARS OF THE ARTHURIAN PERIOD

○ Sites of Anglo-Saxon cemeteries so far discovered to show the progress of Saxon settlement by the late fifth century (c. 500)

x Anglo-Saxon settlements, c. 500

■ Reoccupied Iron Age hillforts, c. 400—600 (a preliminary distribution based on research by P. Fowler)

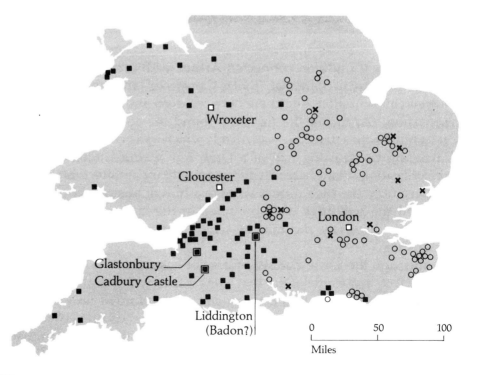

war with the Anglo-Saxons in the period *c.* 470–500, which is exactly the period when Arthur is thought to have lived. Evidence from one site examined in detail, Cadbury-Congresbury in Somerset, shows that it was reoccupied in the mid to late fifth century, but within half a century the timber and stone ramparts had begun to collapse and the ditch had filled up with silt and stones almost to the top. Only then was the imported pottery arriving at the site: a hint that the temporary crisis had passed, the new phase defences were no longer needed, and imported goods were now coming in: calm after the storm?

The siege of Badon Hill

The storm in question was the series of battles between the Britons and the Anglo-Saxons mentioned by Gildas which took place in the last quarter of the fifth century. The war culminated in the siege of Badon Hill – *Mons Badonicus* – which took place perhaps a little before 500. According to Gildas, who wrote his account 43 years after the battle, this was the 'last great victory of the fatherland'. As we have seen he tells how, nearly a century after the Roman departure, Romano-British armies led by Ambrosius Aurelianus beat back the Anglo-Saxons and won a peace which lasted up to the time that Gildas was writing. His story is confirmed by archaeology: the British recovery after Badon is recognised in the lack of sixth-century Anglo-Saxon pottery in such areas as Sussex, Essex and Hertfordshire which have all yielded fifth-century material; similarly, judging by modern finds of their grave goods, the Anglo-Saxon expansion in the Upper Thames ceased for fifty years after Badon. Badon is surrounded by controversy. Gildas names no leader of the Britons for this battle, nor do we know the leader of the Saxons, though modern writers conjecture a joint force from Kent, Sussex and Wessex under the South Saxon Aelle, who Bede and the *Anglo-Saxon Chronicle* say was overking of the settlers at this time.

The story would be clearer if we knew where Badon Hill was. Gildas implies that the battle was in the south-west and the fact that it was a siege of a hill – a *mons* – strongly suggests that this was another reoccupied hillfort. Several sixth-century battles took place at hillforts: Old Sarum and Barbury Castle in Wiltshire, Dyrham Camp in Gloucestershire. We do not even know whether the Britons were the defenders or the besiegers at Badon. There are several possibilities for the battle site, but the best would seem to be Liddington Castle, a prominent Iron Age hillfort near Swindon in Wiltshire. Next to it is a village called Badbury which philologists say could have come from a Celtic *Badon*. It lies in a central position between the main Anglo-Saxon settlements as they stood in the year 500, the Romano-British areas controlled by the cities

Liddington Castle: the view towards the Cotswolds and the rich villa society centring on Cirencester fifteen miles away. Below are the Great Ridgeway, Ermine Street, and the M4.

of Gloucester, Cirencester and Bath and the zone of reoccupied Iron Age forts which stretches through Gloucestershire, Wiltshire and Somerset. On a good day Liddington can be seen from Cirencester, fifteen miles away, its scarped western side standing out clearly: a separate, isolated hill. Most important, Liddington marks one of the great Dark Age road junctions, at the intersection of Ermine Street, another Roman road going due south, and the Great Ridgeway, which cuts across central England and which runs right underneath the ramparts of the castle. In the early medieval period these roads were still in use, and therefore Liddington was a key site. Also, a recent excavation on the fort has revealed reoccupation and refortification, and pottery which was imported at the time the battle took place. It seems likely that this was the site of the battle which saved Romano-British life in the Cotswolds and the south-west for fifty years, but our knowledge may be increased and it would be unwise to build too much on a conjectural identification.

There is no disputing the historicity of Badon. Gildas places it securely at this time. But what justification is there for accepting the accounts of Arthur's leadership at the battle?

The twelfth battle was on Badon Hill where 960 men fell in one day at a single onset of Arthur; and no one killed them but he alone, and in all the battles he came out victorious.

That quotation appears in one of the most famous passages in British historiography, the tale of the twelve battles of Arthur and his leadership at Badon, and it is found in Nennius' *History of the Britons*.

We must now examine the sources of the Arthurian myth, sources which many historians believe to contain a hard core of truth which proves the existence of Arthur. There are two key texts: the *Annals of Wales*, and Nennius' *History of the Britons*, and both are thought to contain authentic survivals from fifth- and sixth-century history. On these two books the evidence for a historical Arthur rests, and because they are so important we must look at them as they appear in the composite Welsh historical manuscript, Harleian 3859 in the British Library. The book is a miscellaneous collection which includes the *Annals of Wales* and the *History of the Britons*. Though now in the same book, these are two quite distinct items. The book was written in Britain in the early 1100s, that is 600 years after the events it describes.

The annals and history are very different in origin. The material in the annals dates from long before the 1100s. The last entry, dated 954, is followed by the family trees of the South Welsh kings of the tenth century, so it is likely that our text is at one or more removes from a document compiled soon after 954. The content of the annals, however, goes back to the mid fifth century. There are two famous entries, one relating Arthur's death:

> (490–516). Battle of Badon in which Arthur carried the cross of our Lord Jesus Christ on his shoulders for three days and nights and the Britons were victorious.

> (c. 511–537). The fight at Camlann in which Arthur and Medraut were killed.

However, these annals were only kept as a contemporary record from round the year 800, and the spelling of the names in the earlier sections indicates that they were originally written only in the eighth or ninth century. This warns the historian that the annals may be unreliable as evidence for reconstructing fifth-century history; they are not a contemporary record. The monk who wrote the Badon annal did not receive the news from a messenger hotfoot from Arthur's campaign HQ: it is a later scholar's reconstruction, and that means we have no way of knowing what was originally written down here. Moreover, most of the entries in this section of the annals are short and laconic in the extreme, which suggests that there is a *prima facie* case for viewing as late additions the apparently mythic details of the 'three days and

The *Annals of Wales*: the key folio in the Harleian MS. In the right-hand column is the entry starting *Bellu(m) Badonis*, and at the bottom *Gueith Ca(m)lann*, the death of Arthur.

nights' and the reference to the cross. The eminent Arthurian scholar, Thomas Jones, considered that originally the annal read simply: 'Battle of Badon in which the Britons were victorious.' We will discuss the significance of the annal referring to the death of Arthur later.

Nennius: 'I made a heap of all I could find'

We can see why the legendary details should have been added to the account of Badon, some time after 800, by turning to Nennius' *History of the Britons*. This contains the most famous piece of Arthuriana of all, but as a source the history is even less reliable than the *Annals of Wales*. Written around 830, that is over 300 years after Arthur's supposed death, the history survives in manuscripts written in the tenth century and later. By the ninth century Arthur had become a folk hero, and Nennius credits him with many miraculous deeds. There is no evidence that Nennius had a reliable source for the events of the fifth century. For instance he gives us the famous list of the twelve battles of Arthur, a list of strange and obscure names and, at first sight, curiously circumstantial detail.

> Then Arthur fought against them (that is, the Anglo-Saxons) in those days with the kings of the Britons, but he himself was the leader of battles. The first battle was at the mouth of the river Glein. The second, third, fourth and fifth on another river called Dubglas in the district of Linnuis. The sixth battle on the river Bassas. The seventh battle was in the Caledonian forest, that is, Cat Coit Celidon. The eighth battle was in Fort Guinnion in which Arthur carried the image of St Mary, forever virgin, on his shoulders and that day the pagans were turned to flight and a great slaughter was made on them through the virtue of our Lord Jesus Christ and through the virtue his mother St Mary the Virgin. The ninth battle took place in the City of the Legion. The tenth battle he fought on the shore of the river which is called Tribruit. The eleventh battle took place on the mountain called Agned. The twelfth battle was on Badon Hill, in which nine hundred and sixty men fell in one day from one attack by Arthur, and no one killed (or overthrew) them but himself alone. And in all the battles he was the victor.

The list has been understood by some as a straight record of fifth-century wars. On inspection this proves not to be the case. It is generally agreed that the list has been taken from a Welsh battle poem of a kind fairly common in early Welsh literature. These poems have a tendency to ascribe to their heroes battles which they never fought in order to enhance their glory, and most scholars agree that even if Arthur did exist, he cannot have fought in all the battles that Nennius refers to. In two of them he certainly did not, and as we have seen there is no good evidence that he fought at Badon Hill.

Another objection is that although Gildas wrote in living memory of the battle, and although he mentions Ambrosius as the leader of the British resistance, he does not mention Arthur, or any leader, at Badon. Most suspicious of all are Nennius' romantic details, the figure of 960 men (probably a Welsh poetic construction, 'three three-hundreds and three score') and the assertion that 'no one killed them but he alone'. This is not an account which can be squared either with history or with common sense, and it seems most likely that Nennius gave the glory of Badon to Arthur because the leader at that battle was unknown. But if the *Annals of Wales* and the *History of the Britons* cannot be accepted as primary sources for the fifth century, do they offer us any clues as to where the story originated? For instance, where do the names in the battle list come from?

The men of the north

Whoever fought these battles, their names and the other early poetic references to Arthur (*c.* 900) surprisingly do not take us to the south-west or to Wales, but to Cumbria, southern Scotland, and the ancient kingdom of Rheged around the Solway. It would be fruitless even to attempt to identify most of the battle names, but one, Cat Coit Celidon, the battle of the Caledonian forest, is unequivocally northern and is usually taken to refer to the wooded country north of Carlisle. This could suggest that the poet's milieu, and the background to the Arthur story might have been in this area. Other names bear this out. For instance the battleground named as Mount Agned in the British Museum manuscript has a second name, Bregomion or Breguoin, in a Vatican version which philologists have identified with Bremenium, the Roman fort at High Rochester in the Cheviots. A battle was indeed fought there (as we know from other sources) by Urien of Rheged in the later sixth century. The site is on the Roman road called Dere Street which runs south from Edinburgh, an ideal place for a clash between the warring tribes of southern Scotland, on the borders of the British tribes of the Votadini and of Rheged. Its gates still standing today to the height of a man, its artillery platforms overgrown, this windswept fort was abandoned by the Romans in the later fourth century. Urien's battle there was known in northern poetry in the Dark Ages, but it was not fought by Arthur. It happened fifty years after his time when the Anglo-Saxons were penetrating the Cheviots. In the last quarter of the fifth century, the period which we associate with Arthur, they were not in this region.

'The first battle was at the mouth of the river Glein.' There is a river Glen in Northumberland, and here an Anglo-Saxon royal hall has been discovered with its associated buildings, including a fort-like enclosure taken over from the British predecessors on the site. Could this famous place, later chief residence of the Northumbrian royal family, have been Nennius' Glein? It is not impossible that an early battle was fought here at a major Celtic site conquered by the Anglo-Saxons. But, again, a late fifth-century battle with the Anglo-Saxons is out of the question. They were not here until the mid sixth century.

Other speculations can be made about northern battles in the list, but cannot be proved. In the end, as with all the fictions in Nennius' list, a case can be made to support almost any identification, but all evaporate on close inspection. All we can say is that they are not the battles of a fifth-century leader fighting the Anglo-Saxons. A gloomy conclusion, perhaps, but there does seem a case for thinking that the battles which form the background to the Arthur story were part of the internecine warfare of the northern British border tribes.

What, then, lies at the root of the stories? Could there even have been an early leader in the north-west whose local fame spread wide? If there were indeed battles in this region which were transformed into the list of battles by a later poet, in what social and political context did they take place?

The main town of the border region in Roman times was Carlisle, and local redevelopment is now giving archaeologists the chance to explore a five-acre site within the old city. A late developer among Roman towns, Carlisle was probably raised to the status of one of Britain's five provincial capitals in 369, and in the nineteenth century plentiful evidence was recovered to indicate that it had a rich urban life in the late Roman period. Columns, sculpture, coins, stone buildings and temples, and numerous inscriptions can be seen in Carlisle Museum. Its walls enclosed 70 acres, and urban life continued well after 400. After the Romans left Britain, Roman buildings were substantially rebuilt in timber, roads were maintained, and the aqueduct remained in use as late as 685. In the twelfth century William of Malmesbury mentioned an arched building which was still standing in his day and which had on it an inscription to Mars and Victory. Some answers to the problem of continuity between late Roman Britain and early Anglo-Saxon England may turn up here during the next few years. Already there are tantalising clues. The *Life of St Cuthbert* by Bede describes a settled Christian community there in the seventh century with a convent as well as a diocesan church. Had they been there before the advent of the Anglo-Saxons? A church which might have been built before the fifth century is the now demolished early church of St Alban, the British proto-martyr. The Anglo-Saxon church of St Cuthbert (eighth–tenth century) was built into an already existing Roman building. In 685 the citizens had enough respect for the Roman past to conduct the Anglo-Saxon monk Cuthbert 'round the city walls to see a remarkable Roman fountain that was built into them'.

The town of Carlisle serves to remind us that the Roman Empire did not fall in one moment in history, and that a kind of Roman life may have lasted two centuries longer here than it did in, for example, Cirencester, or a century longer than at Wroxeter. In this border region British rulers in the Dark Ages claimed Roman descent through their genealogies. Perhaps they were Romano-British landed aristocrats, originally delegated power by the last official Roman governments, like some Third World rulers today who rise from obscurity and set up dynasties, monarchies, even 'empires' with the blessing of departing colonial powers. Could the background to the Arthur story – or at least, the milieu in which the story arose – be these petty chiefdoms, former town councillors of the north, who made their squalid timber Camelots in the temples and ruins of Roman Carlisle? One last piece of evidence may point that way.

'The last dim weird battle of the west'

I have left till the end the entry quoted earlier from the *Annals of Wales*, which refers to Arthur's death in a battle not mentioned by Nennius. This is the most intriguing of all pieces of Arthuriana, and the most difficult to interpret.

(c. 511). 'The fight at Camlann in which Arthur and Medraut were killed.' Here are the great figures of the story. Medraut-Mordred is traditionally the traitor, though in this brief statement we cannot tell whether he is Arthur's friend or foe. Unlike the Badon annal the style is curt, more in line with the rest of the compilation. It uses a different word for 'battle', the Celtic *gueith* instead of the Latin *bellum*. We must remember that the language shows that it was written a good deal later than the fifth century: like the Badon annal this was not written down in its present form until 800–1100. Were the names added then? Or could the entry derive from an early record and therefore give us a definite testimony for Arthur's existence?

As it happens, one of the Roman forts on Hadrian's Wall bore a name, *Camboglanna*, which philologists think could be represented in a late form in the annals' Camlann. Until recently this fort was identified with that of Birdoswald which stands over a great sweep of the river Irthing east of Carlisle. Now, however, scholarly opinion tends to support a new identification with the fort at Castlesteads which is close to Birdoswald, and which is also situated on a sharp curve of the Irthing, as is implied in the name *Camboglanna*, meaning 'crooked glen'. The site is certainly an appropriate one for an epic finale. We should not dismiss the possibility

that a battle at Camlann took place in the Dark Ages: it is mentioned in the annals and it became far better known than Badon. Indeed it became a byword for a tragic, irretrievable disaster. Could this be the one genuine Arthurian reference? The site of the 'last dim weird battle of the west', as Tennyson put it? Is it possible that Arthur existed as a chieftain and warleader in the Solway region, not fighting heroic warfare against the Anglo-Saxon invaders, but engaged in a desperate dogfight between rival British dynasties, battling it out in the sub-Roman twilight? The idea has a certain appeal. Arthur as a kind of anti-hero, an interpretation which suits later twentieth-century taste, and is as typical of our preoccupations as Tennyson's were of his. Did the deaths of two obscure leaders of unknown tribes give birth to the whole story, give birth to one of the greatest figures in the literature of the world? The supernatural magus of folklore? It is possible. Yet, reluctantly we must conclude that there is no definite evidence that Arthur ever existed.

Like Schliemann's discoveries at Troy and Mycenae the modern search for King Arthur has stimulated exciting finds and theories which are changing our view of the end of the Roman world in Britain. But no

The 'crooked glen' of the river Irthing near Birdoswald: scene of Arthur's death in the *Annals of Wales*?

59

more than with the siege of Troy is there convincing evidence that King Arthur's wars actually took place.

After the Fall of Rome Celtic Britain sank into its Dark Age. Then, faced with the rising aggressive power of the Anglo-Saxon imperialists – Offa, Alfred, Athelstan – the British needed a hero. It didn't matter whether he had ever existed in the flesh; the hope of his return was enough. As Malory put it in *Morte Darthur* a thousand years on:

> Yet some men say King Arthur is not dead but had by the will of our Lord Jesus Christ into another place: and men say he shall come again and win the holy cross. I will not say it shall be so: but many men say that there is written on his tomb this verse: 'Here lies Arthur: once and future king.'

The reader, however, might prefer to keep in mind the advice of John Ford's newspaper editor in *The Man Who Shot Liberty Valance*: 'When the fact becomes a legend, print the legend.'

CHAPTER 3

THE SUTTON HOO MAN

Upon the headland the Geats erected a broad high tumulus plainly visible to distant seamen . . . within the barrow they placed collars, brooches and all the trappings which they had plundered from the treasure hoard. They buried the gold and left that princely treasure to the keeping of the earth, where yet it remains. . . .

Beowulf

In the summer of 1939 while German armies massed against Poland and the stormclouds of war darkened Europe, the greatest British archaeological discovery was made in an oval mound in a barrow cemetery on the edge of an escarpment overlooking the river Deben near the Suffolk coast. In the sandy soil the impression of a wooden ship ninety feet long was revealed, bearing the treasures and war gear of a noble warrior, probably a king of the Dark Ages. The richness and craftsmanship of the artefacts forced a revision of our view of the early Anglo-Saxons as a primitive culture. But the act of revision is fraught with difficulties. Central among them, strangely enough, is the fact that the experts cannot agree whether there was ever a body in the grave. If there was, who was he? If not, what is the significance of the apparently royal regalia, and why such a lavish cenotaph? To answer these questions we have to explore the historical and social background of the Sutton Hoo Man.

In the last chapter we left the Anglo-Saxon invaders settling in East Anglia, Lincolnshire, Kent and the Thames valley, fighting at Badon and acknowledging a senior king among themselves, Aelle of Sussex. We did not ask questions about their social and political organisation; whether for instance the immigrants who came over the North Sea were close-knit tribes who already had a tradition of rulership under hereditary kings, or whether they were merely a 'convenient stream of flotsam' as one famous scholar put it; whether they were ruled by kings drawn from a nobility of blood or by warleaders who proved their fitness to rule by their prowess in battle. These are important considerations which affect our view of the origin of the Anglo-Saxon kingdoms, and which we must briefly examine before we can turn to the Sutton Hoo Man himself.

'Fear the Saxon pirates': a fourth- or fifth-century prow from the ship of an English invader.

The East Angles

With Sutton Hoo we move from the confused events of the late fifth century to a period where the modern historian has at least a framework to build on. Soon after the year 500 a number of small Anglo-Saxon kingdoms had come into being in the south and east of Britain. Among these were the East Angles, and because the Sutton Hoo burial was found in East-Anglian territory, historians were quick to suggest that here was the grave of an early king of that region. The first question then is, what was the East-Anglian royal dynasty?

In a manuscript in the British Museum, now catalogued as Cotton Vespasian B VI, the genealogies of the Anglo-Saxon royal families are preserved. They were written down in the Midlands around the year 800. The founder of the East-Anglian dynasty in Britain is called Wuffa, and his descendants were the Wuffingas (possibly 'the Wolf-people'). As we shall see later in this chapter their ancestors probably came from Sweden. According to this source Wuffa and the men who gave their names to the other early royal families, the Oiscingas in Kent and the Iclingas in Mercia, lived in the sixth century. In fact Wuffa would have reigned around 575, which conforms with the thirteenth-century historian Roger of Wendover's statement that Wuffa ruled 571–578. (In another work Wuffa's father Wehha is said to have been the first of the East Angles who ruled in Britain, and this may be true, though Wuffa seems to have been viewed as the founder of the dynasty.) The West Saxons, too, traced their ancestry back to a king in the 500s. These facts are very significant. They suggest that although kings like Offa and Alfred the Great (see the next two chapters) claimed that their families had been royal even before they came to Britain, in fact the early Anglo-Saxon kingdoms, in areas which had settlements from the early 400s, were ruled by men whose real pedigrees probably do not go back that far at all. The earlier names given in the genealogies, such as Offa's claim that Woden was an ancestor, the reference to Adam in Cerdic's genealogy and Caesar in Wuffa's are obviously symbolic rather than biological. So the seventh-century English kingdoms were ruled by the descendants of the illiterate *condottieri* who had seized their chances in the fifth and sixth centuries. It is, let us say, as if Major 'Mad Mike' Hoare had founded his own dynasty in the Congo in the early sixties.

However, there were probably many different types of kings among the first English leaders, and it is not impossible that some powerful and important warrior came across from Europe with his followers and carved himself a kingdom, a man who already belonged to some ancient royal line. Like Wehha and Wuffa he may have been a late immigrant too, in the mid 500s, for the Byzantine writer Procopius records such movements from northern Europe into Britain at precisely this time. The reader must keep that possibility in mind, for we shall see signs at

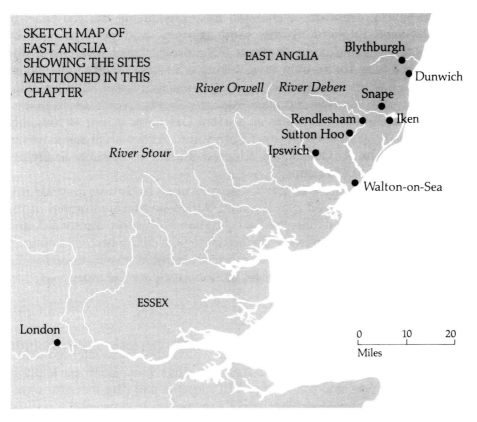

SKETCH MAP OF
EAST ANGLIA
SHOWING THE SITES
MENTIONED IN THIS
CHAPTER

EAST ANGLIA

Blythburgh

Dunwich

River Orwell   *River Deben*   Snape

Rendlesham   Iken

Sutton Hoo

River Stour   Ipswich

Walton-on-Sea

ESSEX

London

0   10   20

Miles

Sutton Hoo linking that burial with Sweden, where the Wuffingas may have originated, a connection which is not explicable if the Wuffingas were merely common soldiers.

The Bretwaldas

If, as the Anglo-Saxon invasions progressed, such men did indeed come over with fairly large tribal units, then this might be a clue to the origins of the overlordship among the Anglo-Saxon kingdoms. Writing in 731 the Anglo-Saxon historian Bede says that prior to the eighth century several Anglo-Saxon kings held a supremacy over all the other Anglo-Saxon kingdoms. The Latin word he uses to express this is *imperium*, which is often used to mean rule over more than one realm. Bede lists the kings who held this hegemony: Aelle of Sussex (*c.* 490), Ceawlin of the West Saxons (*c.* 590), Aethelberht of Kent (*c.* 600), and Raedwald of the East Angles (617–*c.* 624), followed by the Northumbrians Edwin, Oswald and Oswy. Around the year 890 a West-Saxon writer repeats this list and gives an English name for the kings who had this supremacy: *bretwalda* or *brytenwealda*. The second form of this word was probably the earlier, but there are problems in interpreting it since, like many other Germanic words brought from the continent by our

63

Anglo-Saxon forebears, it changed meaning during the 500 years of Anglo-Saxon England. By the tenth century, and perhaps even by Bede's time, it had come to mean 'Britain-ruler', but in origin it was probably a term for an over-king, a king who rules other kings: 'wide-ruler'. As the term also existed in Anglo-Saxon's sister language, Old High German, during the Dark Ages as an expression of empire, it seems that the word signifies an ancient Germanic notion of kingship which the English brought over with them. As we shall see it was in Britain that the Anglo-Saxons adopted Roman ceremonial to dignify their concepts of kingship.

The bretwaldaship had particular relevance to Sutton Hoo for it is now generally believed that the man buried or commemorated in the ship was none other than the East-Anglian bretwalda, Raedwald, and that among the treasures are the actual regalia of the bretwaldaship. If so, the burial would have even more sensational implications for the study of our early history. But let us not anticipate the story.

'A Princely Treasure'

'On the king's breast lay a heap of jewels': a magnificent gold buckle, or, as has been suggested recently, a reliquary (it is hollow). It could be hung from the belt, perhaps.

Sutton Hoo is a dramatic place. In this windswept backwater of Suffolk local traditions about the East-Anglian kings have been particularly tenacious. It was said that Henry VIII's agents had dug there for treasure, and that John Dee, Elizabeth I's magician, had opened a mound there in a journey along the Suffolk coast. Archaeologists have found remains of the Elizabethan diggers' snacks and one of their tools. Near there, around the year 1690, it was said that a gold crown had been dug up weighing 60 ounces, only to be sold and melted down.

But on 23 August 1939 when a group of archaeologists concluded their dig they had uncovered things which had only hitherto existed in the world of myth and stories of *Beowulf* and the sagas. The achievements of eighth-century Anglo-Saxon civilisation were well known, but here suddenly was a window on a world before that, the barbaric splendour of the era before Christianity and a Latin culture had taken root in England.

The finds were, briefly: an impression of the ship itself, long and elegant, which could be rowed or sailed, its wood disintegrated but all the rows of rivets still in place. In its centre where there had been a wooden chamber were a helmet, a sword with gold and garnet fittings, a whetstone, a stand, a rod, spears, a battle-axe, a shield with bird and dragon figures, drinking horns mounted in silver, a set of ten shallow silver bowls with cross patterns, a large fluted classical bowl, three bronze hanging bowls, a pair of silver spoons, a lyre which had been taken to pieces before burial, a great silver bowl bearing the stamp of the Emperor Anastasius, nineteen pieces of beautiful jewellery set with garnets including a gold buckle weighing nearly one pound and a huge

The ghost of the Sutton Hoo ship as it appeared in August 1939. 'A royal vessel with curved prow', as the *Beowulf* poet said: 'They set down their dear king amidships close by the mast. A mass of treasure was brought there from distant lands.'

purse in which there were forty Merovingian coins from the continent.

One problem was immediately apparent: there were no obvious signs of a body. Others intruded only later: for instance parts of the helmet were well preserved, but parts seemed not to be there at all. Had the helmet been smashed before it was committed to the barrow? Had the man been killed in battle?

Of course the first question asked by the archaeologists was: is this a king's burial? It seemed impossible to doubt that Sutton Hoo was royal in the sense that it reflected a royal court, the top layer of Anglo-Saxon society. If the treasures were not actually personal to a king, they could at least be legitimately regarded as 'tribal treasures' kept by the king, *cyning*, 'guardian of the kin'. More than that, most scholars have found it difficult to believe that such a large and valuable treasure can have belonged to anyone but a king in the seventh century. But it should be remembered that though the desire to credit the Sutton Hoo Man with kingship is a natural one, the implication of the term 'king' is not fully understood when used in the context of this early period. We are not yet sure who could be a king, or how many one kingdom might have. The West Saxons, for instance, had five or six 'kings' reigning together at this very period; kings could co-rule; sons could be called kings, raised to the kingship in their father's lifetime; in short we do not know how kingship or succession was viewed in early seventh-century East Anglia.

The coins give us an approximate date for the burial: the latest were minted not earlier than *c.* 620 and not later than *c.* 640. If we are right in

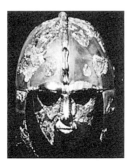

'Above their helmets glittered boar-crests of tempered gold': the reconstructed helmet. From the side it is easy to see its dependence on Roman war-gear.

thinking that the Sutton Hoo Man is an East Anglian king the candidates for the burial would be Bretwalda Raedwald (died *c.* 624), King Eorpwald (died 627), Kings Sigebert and Ecgric (died 636 or 637). But there are other possibilities, such as Ricberht, the pagan who killed King Eorpwald and reigned after him; or Bretwalda Raedwald's son Raegenhere who was killed in battle in 617.

Another possibility is that the burial might have been for the father of a king. Eni, younger brother of Raedwald and father of four East-Anglian kings, may well have died within the limits fixed by the coins, for he would have been born in the later sixth century and thus been an old man by *c.* 630. It cannot be denied that the father of kings whose life spanned the greatest period of East-Anglian history might have received conspicuous honours at the hands of his surviving royal sons. Simply listing the possibilities shows us how difficult it is to pinpoint one man when no personal marks survive.

Was there a body?

In order to establish whether or not there was a body in the ship, scientific analysis of the soil in the region of the burial deposit has been conducted by the British Museum laboratories over many years with the thoroughness of a murder inquiry. The evidence is based on chemical traces which cannot be interpreted with certainty. The conclusion that the Museum team came to in 1975 was that a body had indeed lain in the region of the boat where the sword and jewellery were found.

However, this has been disputed. First, as the excavators knew, the position of the artefacts found in the grave did not indicate that there had been a body lying there. Second, and more serious, top forensic experts from Guy's Hospital, London, who have since examined the evidence impartially found no trace of human remains, either cremated or inhumed, in the boat. In addition the absence of personal objects, such as finger rings, pendants, pins, fragments of cloth, buckles or gold thread, such as might have survived from shoes or clothing, coupled with the lack of a convincing arrangement of the objects that were found, suggested that no body was ever in the grave.

It is agreed that the acid sand in which the ship lay could have eliminated all traces of a body, including teeth, and the extensive chemical tests carried out did reveal a high phosphate content in the ground near the sword in particular, though this last is probably attributable to the remains of ivory items including a chess set.

Top medical opinion is that the cenotaph—a sepulchral monument made for a person who has been buried elsewhere—is the likeliest solution of the Sutton Hoo mystery because of (1) the absence of any trace of a body, (2) the absence of personal items from dress or intimate objects or decoration such as would be likely on the person, (3) the disposition of the grave goods. The forensic report concludes: 'After careful perusal of all the available papers relating to the burial it is our joint view that there is no evidence to support the contention that a human body was ever buried in this ship.'

However in 1979 a re-examination of the excavators' notes for the dig revealed that a complete set of iron coffin fittings were discovered in 1939 only to be missed out of all subsequent discussions of the Sutton Hoo problem. The position of these pieces of metal clearly formed the rectangular outline of a wooden coffin into which the grave goods surrounding the 'body' area neatly fit. This dramatic discovery suggests that we have here after all a normal type of burial for a seventh-century Anglo-Saxon noble. The purist may still argue that the presence of a coffin is no guarantee of a body, but as we know a skeleton can disappear without trace, it is best to accept that there was indeed a body in the Sutton Hoo ship, and we shall assume this from now on.

The so-called 'sceptre', a huge decorated whetstone. Total height 2 feet 9½ inches.

Whose body was it?

The question of whose body it was, and whether it was a king's, depends then more than anything on the interpretation of two objects found in the grave: a long iron stand with a spike at the bottom, and a giant whetstone or stone bar. These have been identified as a standard and a sceptre, and thus as symbols not merely of rank but of office. Indeed the British Museum's publication goes so far as to suggest that the whetstone is nothing less than the sceptre of the Bretwalda Raedwald himself. We must now examine them.

The 'sceptre' is two feet long minus its bronze fitting. It is believed that it was originally designed to be held seated on the knee, and was topped by a small bronze stag; if this last detail is correct it is significant because stags may have been associated with royalty: in the poem *Beowulf*, Hrothgar's hall is called Heorot, 'hart' (perhaps because stags' heads were displayed over the door?). Essentially the 'sceptre' is a whetstone, such as have been found in a number of Swedish graves of this period, but this one is bigger, more elaborate and unused. A giant whetstone seems a natural enough symbol for the power of kings, many of whose poetic by-names centre on war, swords and whetting, and in that context one eminent archaeologist called it 'monstrous . . . a unique savage thing; and inexplicable except perhaps as a symbol proper to the king himself, of the divinity and mystery which surrounded the smith and his tools in the northern world'.

However, whether the whetstone really is specifically royal, or formally symbolic of anything, has yet to be proved. Its nearest links seem

The faces on the whetstone. Ancestral spirits of the Wuffingas?

The iron stand, five and a half feet high: scalp rack, torch or royal standard?

to be with the cults of Thor and, above all, of Woden. One of the early Norse myths tells of how Woden (Odin) disguised himself as a craftsman with a wonderful whetstone. In this case it seems we should abandon any idea of the whetstone being the bretwalda's sceptre.

But could it have been a dynastic heirloom? One ingenious theory suggests that the eight faces on the sceptre are the ancestors of the Wuffingas, and we may add that the genealogies show eight mythical ancestors before the historical figures of Wehha and Wuffa who ruled in Britain. A dynastic symbol of the Wuffingas? If so, another find in the grave falls into place. Near the whetstone traces of a rod were found, a thin gold strip with a garnet and filigree decoration topped by a ring and a gold cut-out of an animal, probably a wolf. Now, the gold purse too depicts wolves. Do we have here a conscious pun on the dynastic name on the part of the craftsman, Wulf = Wuffingas, 'sons of the Wolf'? And could the rod have been a royal talisman? At least here we can show a parallel: in 1656 a rod was discovered in an indubitably royal tomb of the seventh century at St Germain-des-Prés and from later pictures it is certain that rods were part of Anglo-Saxon royal regalia.

The second of the significant objects found in the grave, the iron stand, is about five feet tall with a horizontal openwork grid at the top. It has been seen as everything from a sort of portable torch or flambeau, its head wrapped with burning tow, to a rack on which to hang enemy scalps. But historians have been most attracted to the idea that it was a standard. They point to a fascinating passage in Bede's *History* which describes the Northumbrian king, Edwin, who at a later date, followed Raedwald as bretwalda, using standards as a demonstration of his power:

> So great was his majesty in his realm that not only were banners carried before him in battle but even in time of peace as he rode about among his cities, estates and kingdoms with his thegns, he always used to be preceded by a standard bearer. Further when he walked anywhere along the roads there used to be carried before him the type of standard which the Romans call *tufa* and the English call a *thuf*.

In general this famous passage shows a conscious respect for the Roman tradition on the part of the Anglo-Saxon kings and a desire to emulate them, to confer legitimacy or prestige on their rule by imitating Roman imperial styles. (We shall see this tendency as it develops through the later English kings.) In this connection it is pertinent to remember that the East-Anglian royal clan, the Wuffingas, may have shared in this conscious claim to inherit something of the authority of Rome in Britain since their pedigree incorporated the name Caesar after Woden. A more succinct expression of the divergent pulls in the Anglo-Saxon tradition could scarcely be found. Unfortunately the Sutton Hoo 'standard' with its iron grille and metal cage does not really look like a *vexillum*, a *signum*, or a *tufa* (the Latin words Bede uses to distinguish the Roman standards), nor is it perhaps tall enough to be such. In any case Bede does not connect these specifically with the office of bretwalda, and we must conclude that as yet we have no evidence to link either the 'standard' or the 'sceptre' with the office of bretwalda.

The kingdom of the East Angles

So far in our search for the Sutton Hoo Man we have found evidence of great artistic skill, ambiguous regalia, but no clear evidence for a king, though some for royalty. What proof have we to connect the grave with the East-Anglian royal family at all?

The grave does not exist in isolation, even at the site itself where there are at least sixteen other mounds, some as yet unopened. Let us now consider what we know about the social background of the kingdom in which the burial took place.

As soon as the burial was discovered, attention focused on the small neighbouring parish of Rendlesham, four miles further up the Deben from Sutton. The reason was that Rendlesham had long been known to have associations with the East-Anglian kings. Bede mentions that Swithelm, king of the East Saxons, was baptised by Bishop Cedd of East Anglia 'in the royal village called Rendlesham, that is, the residence of Rendil. King Aethelwald of East Anglia, the brother of King Anna the previous king of the East Angles was his sponsor'. This passage shows us that in Aethelwald's reign (655–664) the place was a royal residence of the East-Anglian kings, that there was probably a church there, and that it had some importance since the reception of a foreign king and the solemnisation of his baptism took place here. This clue leads us to others.

Over the river from Rendlesham is Ufford, a name which derives from the Anglo-Saxon name Uffa or Wuffa. Is it a coincidence that the name of the founder of the dynasty is so close to the royal residence? Similarly the name of another village close to Sutton, Kingston, is one of many in England which indicates an Anglo-Saxon royal estate, and in this case we can prove its antiquity, for a charter survives recording the gift of Kingston and Melton (two miles downstream from Rendlesham) to Ely Abbey by the West-Saxon King Edgar in the tenth century. It is a fair supposition that these estates were ancient East-Anglian royal lands which passed into the hands of the West-Saxon kings of England after the Viking wars.

Most remarkable of all (and here perhaps we enter the world of folk myth) there is a note about Rendlesham in the 1722 edition of Camden's *Britannia*:

It is said that in digging here about thirty years since there was found an ancient crown weighing about sixty ounces, which was thought to have belonged to Redwald, or some other king of the East Angles. But it was sold and melted down.

The story has inspired much spurious antiquarianism (and an M. R. James ghost story), and has generally been rejected on the grounds that crowns were not worn in Anglo-Saxon England in the seventh century, but this may not be true. When the tomb of the Merovingian Childeric II (who died in 675) was found at St Germain-des-Prés in 1656, those present saw 'a great gold trapping in the form of a crown round the head of the king'. It was clearly some sort of diadem and similar to those worn by the Romans. This would conform with our understanding of the admiration the Anglo-Saxons had for Rome. That said, until we find out more about the exact location of the dig, we have to reject this intriguing story as any help in piecing together the Sutton Hoo story, though it certainly adds to its mysterious aura.

Raedwald's royal hall?

The royal hall of the Wuffingas at Rendlesham, the existence of which is implied in Bede's *History*, would have been like the contemporary hall of Edwin at Yeavering in Northumberland which has been excavated with great success. The hall at Yeavering was around ninety feet long, and built in timber like some of the later medieval tithe barns which survive today. Its interior may have been decorated like Heorot in the poem *Beowulf*, with tapestries depicting scenes of the ancient heroes of Scandinavia. There would also have been ancillary buildings including, perhaps, a wooden temple converted to Christian use. At Yeavering there was in addition a remarkable timber structure like a segment of an amphitheatre with a hole for a totem at the centre, clearly a moot where gatherings could be addressed, and a large fort or corral for livestock adapted from its Celtic predecessor on the same site.

Unfortunately neither fieldwalking nor air photography has yet disclosed any sign of such structures at Rendlesham. Painstaking local research has, however, narrowed down the location of the first Anglo-Saxon church referred to by Bede. The site of the present Church of St Gregory is a possibility, but more likely still is an isolated two-acre strip of glebe land half a mile north-east of the church. Here a sizeable Anglo-Saxon cremation cemetery was discovered in 1837, and is possibly the burial place of the staff of the royal village. If we are right in supposing that this is close to the early religious centre at Rendlesham, then the pagan temple and the wooden church which succeeded it could both lie nearby. The early Christian missionaries concentrated

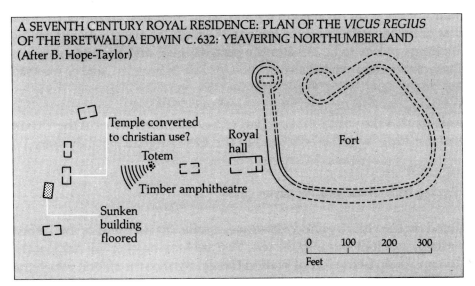

A SEVENTH CENTURY ROYAL RESIDENCE: PLAN OF THE *VICUS REGIUS* OF THE BRETWALDA EDWIN C.632: YEAVERING NORTHUMBERLAND
(After B. Hope-Taylor)

Temple converted to christian use?

Totem

Timber amphitheatre

Sunken building floored

Royal hall

Fort

0   100   200   300
Feet

Below Yeavering, Northumberland. The telltale crop mark which revealed the site of the royal palace of Edwin. The fort or corral is visible in the upper part of the photograph.

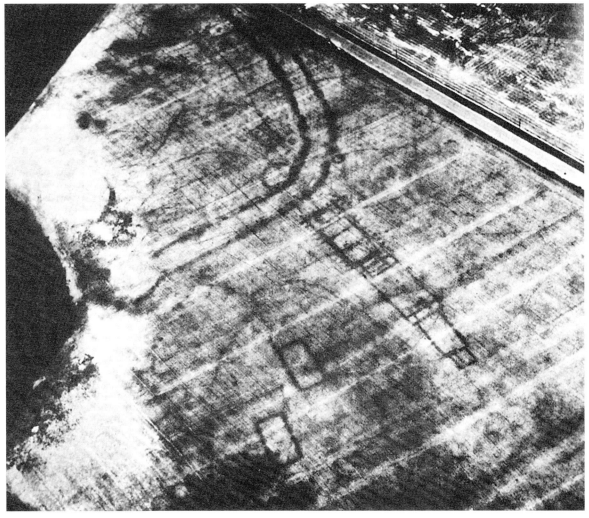

their attention on royal courts; kings were their first converts, and the first churches were built for the use of kings. So we would expect the Wuffinga palace to be close to the early church, and the pagan shrine. This relationship existed also at Old Uppsala in Sweden, and as we shall see there may be a family connection between Uppsala and the Wuffingas of Rendlesham and Sutton Hoo. Taken all in all, these factors suggest that the south-eastern part of Suffolk, the valleys of the Deben and the Alde, was the heartland of the East-Anglian royal dynasty.

'Serving both Christ and the pagan gods'

Stand on the cliffs by Old Felixstowe, a mile or two south of the Deben estuary, and look out into the sea. You are looking over the ruins of the Roman Saxon Shore fort of Walton Castle. By 1800 the cliff on which the fort stood had been eroded by the sea and now only fragments of masonry can be seen during exceptionally low tides. All we have to show us what the place was like is a series of sketches made in the seventeenth century showing a rectangular fort with drum towers at the corners. Here in the 630s the first East-Anglian bishopric was founded with the support of the Wuffinga kings. Like other Saxon Shore forts which were taken over by the Church, such as Burgh Castle, Bradwell, Portchester, and Reculver, it evidently passed into the hands of Anglo-Saxon royal leaders early on in the migration period. When the kings adopted Christianity it could be given to the Church as a secure place to build a bishopric. The proximity of Walton to the sites in the Deben valley again points to the importance of this small area to the East-Anglian dynasty.

But if the royal family had become Christian by the 630s, would a king have been commemorated in unconsecrated ground in a pagan barrow field? When did the family start burying their kings in Christian churches? Does the Sutton Hoo boat grave in fact have any specifically pagan or Christian features about it?

The barrow field is not a Christian graveyard. Nor is ship burial a Christian mode of interment. There is nothing ritually pagan or Christian about it, indeed nothing formally religious at all. The two silver spoons have been interpreted as christening spoons carrying the names *Saulos* and *Paulos* in Greek letters, and could thus refer to Saint Paul's conversion and subsequent change of name; but unfortunately it is not certain that they do not both read *Paulos* in which case the theory collapses. In any case it would be difficult to be sure that such items were there because of their Christian significance and not because of their value as exotic silver bullion. This possibility is made more likely by the presence of the rich Byzantine bowls in the grave. Some bear cross motifs, but we cannot therefore assume that their owner was Christian: the bowls are just the sort of treasure we might expect a barbarian chief to gain through gift, exchange, trade or pillage. The fact that the artefacts do not conclusively prove that the grave is a Christian one may be significant. Could the Sutton Hoo Man have been buried before Christianity was thoroughly accepted by the East-Anglian royal house? Bede gives a description of the reign of King Raedwald (599–624) which supports this idea, as it was a period where adherence to Christianity was superficial and wavering.

Raedwald had been converted in Kent but his attitude was ambivalent and opportunist. On his return to East Anglia he apostatised and eventually seemed to be serving both Christ and the gods whom he had previously served; in the same temple he had one altar for the Christian sacrifice and another smaller altar on which to offer victims to devils. Raedwald was not alone. King Eorpwald was killed by and succeeded by a pagan, King Ricberht (ruled 627–628). Another successor, Ecgric, who does not appear in the genealogies, is not known to have been Christian, and was killed in a battle (636 or 637). A pagan burial which had been influenced by Christianity is not inconceivable in this atmosphere. But it seems unlikely that there are any overt Christian signs at Sutton Hoo. The grave certainly seems pagan, or at least resolutely old-fashioned in a way that draws on the pagan roots of Anglo-Saxon England.

Commerce: kings and merchants

The grave might be pagan but other items in it indicate that the people who lived in these pagan times travelled far more extensively than we imagined. Byzantine plate, Merovingian coins, an Egyptian Coptic bowl, imported glass: all these hint at a lively mercantile life. The extraordinary range of rich pieces in the grave can now be seen to have been foreshadowed by earlier isolated finds of Anglo-Saxon antiquities in the Deben valley area: imported blue glass vessels, a gold *cloisonné* disc brooch, a Coptic bronze bowl of Egyptian origin found at Wickham Market which is a little north of Rendlesham. It would seem, then, that the Deben valley in the sixth and seventh centuries was an area open to trade imports and foreign culture coming into Suffolk from the southeast. Archaeologists are following up those clues and looking at the origins of Ipswich and wondering whether the unexpected number of early settlement finds there might indicate that the town owes its origin as a port to the patronage of the Wuffinga kings of the seventh century.

In the later seventh and eighth centuries the Dutch coast opposite East Anglia was the centre of a thriving trade, with towns such as

Dorestad on the Rhine being particularly large entrepôts between Britain and Europe. We know that foreign merchants were already in England in the seventh century, because Bede mentions a Dutchman (or Frisian) in London in 679. Bede also says that in 731, when he was writing, London was 'a market for many people who come by land and sea'. The merits of special trading places which are easily accessible by boat are obvious, but archaeologists now suspect that many of these places owe their origin to royal patronage; the kings wished to control wealth coming in. (Charters dating from the early eighth century prove that royal tolls controlled coastal markets, and they may have existed earlier.) There is increasing evidence that there were a number of coastal riverside trading posts in Anglo-Saxon England, some laid out at royal command, all with a merchant class who, though insignificant by royal standards, dealt in luxury goods and used them themselves. Many of these trading stations were called *wics*, and this name may indicate how old some of our towns are. London appears as *Lundenwic* in a seventh-century law code; the predecessor of Southampton was *Hamwih*; York's name was *Eoforwic*. Others are still *wics* today: Fordwich on the Sarre in Kent, with its impressive early Anglo-Saxon cemeteries, and Ipswich itself. (The word *wic* was borrowed by the Germans from the Latin *vicus*, and obviously here means a trading emporium. As a '*wic* reeve' looked after royal tolls in London in the seventh century, it may have acquired this meaning early on, and we may presume other *wics* were also under royal control.)

The archaeological excavations at Ipswich have not had the publicity of other Anglo-Saxon town digs, but we now know that this was an impressive urban site with a large number of early burials on a 30-acre site showing imported glass, pottery and amphorae, and the extensive production of the Middle-Anglian pottery known as Ipswich Ware (*c.* 650–850). Less than five miles away from Sutton Hoo, does Ipswich have the same relation to the royal sites in the Deben valley as mercantile Southampton is known to have had to the royal and ecclesiastical centre of the West Saxons at Winchester? If so, then as early as the seventh century the town may have been set up by the Wuffingas as a port for traders to sell their wares in the East-Anglian kingdom under royal supervision. In other words, Ipswich may have been one of the chief sources of the Sutton Hoo Man's income.

The Swedish connection

There is one foreign connection which takes us further. Almost as soon as the details of the Sutton Hoo excavation were known and a reconstruction of the helmet published, Swedish archaeologists announced that the helmet, sword and shield had been made in Sweden. (The helmet, with its remarkable tinned plates illustrated with scenes from legend, may be considerably older than the burial.) As we have seen, the Sutton Hoo finds indicate a royal or aristocratic boat burial and this type of burial was common in Sweden during the Anglo-Saxon period. We know from documents and poems that expensive decorated swords and armour were sometimes kept for generations as heirlooms. (The Avar sword owned by King Offa was a treasured possession in the West-Saxon royal house over two hundred years later.) Could these artefacts be Swedish family heirlooms, revered as ancient possessions of the royal house? By the time of the burial (c. 620–640), the Wuffinga dynasty had been established for four generations in East Anglia and one of their leaders had risen to become bretwalda, a status which may have made them all the more conscious of their ancient Swedish origin. Close parallels between war gear from Uppland, Sweden, and the Sutton Hoo helmet and shield (the latter are now thought to be from English Anglo-Saxon workshops), the similarity of the Sutton Hoo gravefield and the royal mounds at Old Uppsala, have suggested to many that if the Wuffingas came to England from Sweden, they were an offshoot of the royal house of Uppsala, the Scylfings.

Who was he?

It is tempting to agree with the British Museum team's conclusion that the man commemorated here was Bretwalda Raedwald, and he does remain perhaps the strongest candidate even though we must probably discount the idea that the grave goods are a bretwalda's regalia. The arguments for the 'sceptre' and 'standard' are far from conclusive. What we can say is that the burial is most likely a kind of memorial to a dead king. If it is a cenotaph and not strictly a burial, it may be a memorial to a king who had resigned his power, or a memorial to a king killed in battle or possibly a pagan king buried in a church. But most likely there was a body, and we can presume that he was East Anglian and a Wuffinga, and that he was commemorated in the old Swedish way by burying him in a ship with his war gear and other costly objects associated with him. There is nothing formally religious about it, pagan or Christian. It is a barbaric manifestation of Anglo-Saxon wealth and power from a time before Christianity had been fully assimilated. But in a 'political' sense it is conservative: even in those days the ceremony would perhaps have been considered magnificently old-fashioned.

*   *   *

Sutton Hoo

There are at least seventeen mounds at Sutton Hoo and many have not been examined. Several are likely to have been ship burials: the telltale signs are clearly visible – an indentation along the length of the mounds in the centre which marks the collapse of the wooden chamber over the centre of the ship. Indeed this collapsed appearance may be the salvation of future archaeologists, for it gives the mounds the appearance of having been robbed, and maybe discouraged Henry VIII's men, John Dee and other tomb robbers. It seems unlikely that the burial field was used by the East-Anglian royal family after the mid seventh century, although later inhumations have been found there including a severed head which gave a carbon dating in the mid eighth century. If, as seems likely, Rendlesham continued to be a royal residence up until the time that the last of the East-Anglian kings was killed by the Vikings and the royal line ceased, it is probable that the family church was somewhere near the site of the present Church of St Gregory. The pagan grave field at Sutton was left with its ghosts until the sixteenth century when they were disturbed by the excavations of Henry VIII and John Dee. They were then left until 1939, when Basil Brown re-examined them.

But there is one curious legend which we might add to the Sutton Hoo story. According to an eleventh-century historian of Bury St Edmunds, who based his information on Suffolk tradition, in the dark days of the Viking invasions when the old kingdom of the East Angles finally collapsed, the martyred King Edmund, last of the line of the Wuffingas, was first buried near his royal residence, at Sutton, before he was moved to his final resting place at Bury St Edmunds in the 930s. Is it really conceivable that the East Angles would have temporarily interred their king in the church closest to their ancestral graves? It is tempting to believe this, but I personally think it unlikely. Certainly though, we will only know the answers to the origin of the dynasty when the palace and church at Rendlesham are located, and when all the mounds at Sutton are excavated. Until then the truth behind the enigma of the Sutton Hoo Man will elude us.

A detail from the purse: man between wolves. A pun on the 'wolf-people'? Possibly – but the theme recurs in Dark Age art in Ireland and throughout Scandinavia.

CHAPTER 4

OFFA

In modern times in Mercia there ruled a mighty king called Offa, who struck all the kings and regions around him with terror. He it was who ordered the great dyke to be constructed between Wales and Mercia, stretching from sea to sea.

Bishop Asser *On the Deeds of King Alfred*

One spring day around the year 787, Welshmen riding the cattle-rustling trails into Anglo-Saxon England came back with astonishing stories. Thousands of Anglo-Saxon levies had moved into the border country with horses and carts carrying rations, tents, rope, nails and weapons. But this time, unlike the mounted expeditions of so many previous years, they had not come to burn crops, seize goods and wield weapons of war: this year they had come to use tools – spades, axes, adzes and hammers. For they had been ordered to create a huge bank and ditch along the whole frontier – 25 feet deep, 60 feet across – from the Irish Sea to the Bristol Channel. Like modern motorway constructors they were to cut a swathe through the green countryside.

The English penny was created in the seventh century, and, from the eighth, becomes one of our most important sources for Anglo-Saxon government. Offa's coins are among the finest.

In some places Anglo-Saxon villages were being left on the Welsh side, the powerful local magnates helpless before the overlord who had willed the deed. The first work gangs burned off brushwood and grass, cutting down trees and clearing obstacles. Great beacons were lit on the hills to align the longer sections and massive wooden posts hammered in for the shorter ones. Oxen commandeered from local farms dragged heavy ploughs across the blackened earth to make a line for the marker ditches. Then the main gangs set up their camps, most of them farmers doing their military service.

Doubtless like infantrymen of all times they grumbled and cursed and sang songs while they sweated. A Welshman who knew some Anglo-Saxon might have found out from them that this particular length was the job of his English neighbours, the people known as the Magon-saetan who lived in what is now Shropshire. The men doing other sections might have come from far away and would have had quite different dialects: East Angles, Kentishmen, Peak dwellers from what is now Derbyshire. There would have been specialists too: smiths from Gloucester, quarrymen and masons from Northamptonshire. At one

'Roman genius and energy': Offa's Dyke near Edenhope Hill, Shropshire.

sector our Welsh observer might have seen a mounted party ride up past the lines of diggers and the dumps and stakes and stones, up to a vantage point to watch progress. Among them was the man who had set all this in motion and who supervised each stage with an expert eye; a man to whom all showed deference or fear; an old man but still in full powers: Offa, 'King of the Mercians and of the whole fatherland of the English'.

The foregoing scene is imaginary, but much of its detail comes from recent archaeological examinations of Offa's Dyke itself. Curiously, there is no proof that Offa built the dyke from Offa's contemporaries: we have to wait till Bishop Asser, writing a hundred years later, tells us that 'it was Offa who ordered the great dyke to be constructed between Wales and Mercia, stretching from sea to sea'. The dyke still divides the two nations – it is still something of a disgrace for a true Welshman to live on the wrong side – and no one who has walked the Offa's Dyke Path could fail to be impressed by a structure which still runs along a large part of the 150-mile Welsh frontier and still stands twenty feet high in places.

To follow it over Edenhope Hill or through the heights of the Clun Forest cannot but invite questions. What was it for? How was it built?

Who was the king that, in the so-called Dark Ages, had the power and vision to make it? One historian has compared the labour involved to the building of the Great Pyramid, and Britain's leading motorway contractors threw up their hands in despair when asked to cost it today. Strangely enough, there has never been agreement among historians about what the dyke was for, what it looked like when it was first built, or even about its exact course. Offa too remains something of an enigma. He is held to be a key figure in the story of the unification of England. Yet there is no modern biography of him, and none from the eighth century either. The sources for his reign are diffuse, fragmentary, and heavily dependent on later traditions which the historian often considers unreliable. In the last few years, however, some fascinating archaeological discoveries have begun to throw new light on his story.

Mercian origins

Until the Viking invasions of the 860s and 870s, England was divided into several kingdoms, of which Offa's Mercia was one. These kingdoms crystallised gradually out of the various settlements of the Anglo-Saxon races in Britain after the fall of Rome. Racially diverse though these kingdoms were, there was a tradition from early on of rule by an overlord, a 'bretwalda' (a word originally meaning 'wide-ruler' but which came by Offa's time to mean 'Britain-ruler'). The bretwalda was a king to whom other kings were subject; they paid him tribute, attended his court, obtained his permission for their grants of land in their own territory, and fought under his leadership in war. This overlordship was held by kings of Sussex, Wessex, Kent and East Anglia for short periods between the late fifth and the early seventh century, and as we have seen in the previous chapter, it has been argued that the greatest of all Anglo-Saxon archaeological discoveries, the Sutton Hoo ship treasure, is the burial of the East-Anglian bretwalda, Raedwald.

Three successive Northumbrian kings were overlords in the seventh century, fighting bitter wars with the Mercians on their southern border, and at times they took tribute from all the kings south of the Humber. In the 660s and 670s the Mercian Wulfhere held similar power, and for most of the eighth century Mercia was supreme over all the lands south of the Humber under its kings Aethelbald and Offa; they more than any of the others paved the way for the future unification of the English.

Mercian origins are obscure. Like the other English peoples they were illiterate pagans when they came to Britain. The arts of writing came only with their conversion to Christianity after 655, so the foundation of their kingdom around the Upper Trent, which may only have happened in the 580s, was recorded generations later. Offa in fact claimed that his family had emigrated to Britain from Angeln in Schleswig, now on the German-Danish border, and that his ancestors had been kings there. In particular Offa seems to have regarded as a kinsman his namesake the legendary Offa of Angeln, who, the poets said,

> whilst still a youth gained the greatest of kingdoms . . . no one of the same age achieved greater deeds of valour in battle: with his single sword he fixed the boundary against the Myrgings at Fifledor.

It is unlikely that the two Offas really were related, but the fact that the historical king bore the legendary name *and* built a great boundary has led some scholars to think that he was consciously imitating Offa of Angeln, whose legends he might have known from childhood. The claim that the Mercians had been kings before they ever came to Britain certainly gave Offa a more impressive pedigree than other English kings, and was used to justify his overlordship at the height of his empire. But it may be something Offa or his propagandists invented. Why, we shall see.

Offa seizes the throne

Offa came to the throne through that most successful kind of *coup d'état*, the one which is transformed in later records into a legitimate takeover of power. He seems to have gone to a great deal of effort to conceal from posterity the fact that it was a *coup d'état*, and were it not for some sources appearing over-anxious to justify his claim, we would never have been able to recover even a partial truth.

His story begins with the killing of King Aethelbald in 757. At his death Aethelbald had been 'Rex Britanniae', bretwalda, ruler of all England south of the Humber. Although he was an old man he was still violent and over-fond of women when he was murdered at night by his bodyguard at Seckington near Tamworth. We do not know who instigated the act. Aethelbald's heir, Beornred, succeeded him, but civil war broke out and his kinsman, Offa, seized the throne. Thirteenth-century historians writing at the abbey of St Albans, a stronghold of pro-Offa feeling, said that the people had risen against Beornred because of his unjust and tyrannical rule, and that they expelled him under the leadership of Offa, whom they unanimously elected king. This account may be no more than a later interpretation of events. A marginal note in a Mercian manuscript of the early ninth century gives us the official line which Offa wanted the world to believe: Beornred was a 'tyrannus', a usurper, and Offa overcame him in battle and took the kingdom.

Offa's claim to be king was as great-great-grandson of Eawa, brother of the Mercian King Penda. Beornred's relation to the royal line is unknown, although he was clearly viewed as Aethelbald's heir, and Offa's view of him as a usurper accounts for his omission from the surviving list of Mercian kings, although he reigned for at least a few months. The list of kings was obviously tampered with by Offa. The fact that Beornred survived in exile (and probably had children) made Offa's stress on his usurpation politically necessary, even after he was burned to death in Northumbria twelve years later.

So Offa came to the throne after the murder of one king and the deposition of another. The whole affair smacks of modern power politics. But that should not surprise us. Most accessions were contested in the Dark Ages, and the succession of the eldest son was by no means guaranteed. In fact almost any ablebodied kinsman stood a chance if he was tough enough, and Offa was certainly to prove that.

The civil war in Mercia between Beornred and Offa must have made news everywhere, so eminent had been the Mercian position in Britain before Aethelbald's assassination. In Northumbria the news was received along with the defeated contender. The kings who had bowed to Aethelbald and paid him tribute would not do the same for Offa. Who was he in any case? A distant kinsman of Penda's brother. Political power advanced and receded quickly in the Dark Ages and was dependent on the personal charisma of the man who wielded it. In the first years of Offa's reign there is no sign that the neighbouring kings who had submitted to Aethelbald brought him gifts or asked his permission to grant land. To many in Mercia in the 750s it must have seemed that for all Aethelbald's violent and lascivious behaviour, he had protected the poor, kept the peace – and been a bretwalda.

The tribes of Mercia – the ancient peoples of the Midlands

By the winter of 757 Offa found himself relatively secure in Mercia, and we can imagine him spending Christmas in the royal hall at Tamworth with his young wife Cynethryth and the Mercian bishops and chiefs who had backed his seizure of power. The kingdom he had gained probably comprised only the heartland of Mercia, roughly bounded by the Thames, the Fens, the Don and the Trent to the north-east (Lindsey still had its own kings), the Mersey to the north-west, and the Wye and the hills of Powys to the west. We should not think of the Mercians as one people, or even one race. They were the dominant tribe among about thirty peoples who lived in central England, some of which rejoiced in primitive and now completely obscure names: the Unecung-ga, the Noxgaga, the Hendrica. All these had their own

81

ealdormen and their own tribal centre at this time, and some of the large ones still had their own kings, but all were to lose their independence to Offa. Even though many of these local names were used as late as the tenth and eleventh centuries, Offa's reign signifies the end of this primitive system of local government which had lasted nearly two hundred years, and the creation of a unified kingdom in middle England.

In his day the landscape of central England was given shape and order by the small Mercian tribes. Some of them numbered several thousand households, like the Hwicce in the Severn valley whose name survives in Wychwood in Oxfordshire, 'the wood of the Hwicce'. Some numbered only a few hundred households like the Gifle in the Ivel valley in Hertfordshire, or the Hicce who gave their name to Hitchin. A West-Saxon traveller or merchant coming up from the south would say that he entered Mercia as soon as he crossed the Thames at Kempsford or Cricklade south of Cirencester, but to a Mercian he was entering the land of the Hwicce: Mercia proper was the land around the upper Trent. The North Mercians, numbering 7000 households, had a centre at 'Northworthy' (now Derby) and their main divisions underlie the later counties of Derbyshire and Nottinghamshire. The South Mercians, made up of 5000 households, lived west of the upper Trent, and their main tribes were the Pencersaetan, whose royal centre was Penkridge, and the Tomsaetan in the Tame valley. The territory of the Tomsaetan stretched from the church at Breedon-on-the-Hill to King's Norton south-west of Birmingham, a distance of over thirty miles. This was the heartland of the Mercian empire, with the royal church at Repton, the bishopric at Lichfield and the main residence at Tamworth. The Tomsaetan were administered by their own ealdorman, and the council of the elders of the Tomsaetan met well into the ninth century. It may be that they were regarded as the royal tribe, and certainly the Mercian kings spent more time there than anywhere else.

The names of all the Mercian tribes are given in an intriguing document called the *Tribal Hidage*. It is a tribute list, drawn up to aid the Mercian king's ministers in exacting taxes from the provinces and regions of the Mercian empire, and it may have been compiled for Offa, though the obscurity of many of the names in it suggests that it is earlier still. Perhaps it was the work of Wulfhere, the first Mercian bretwalda. But the system of government it represents functioned in Offa's time; indeed the Mercian kingdom reached its apogee under Offa. To get a feel of the way these early peoples shaped the landscape, and to perceive the physical continuity between their world and ours, look, for instance, at the fields between Radway and Kineton in Warwickshire. Here it is possible to stand on the boundary between the Mercians and the Stoppingas (one of the small groups who made up the Hwicce) near

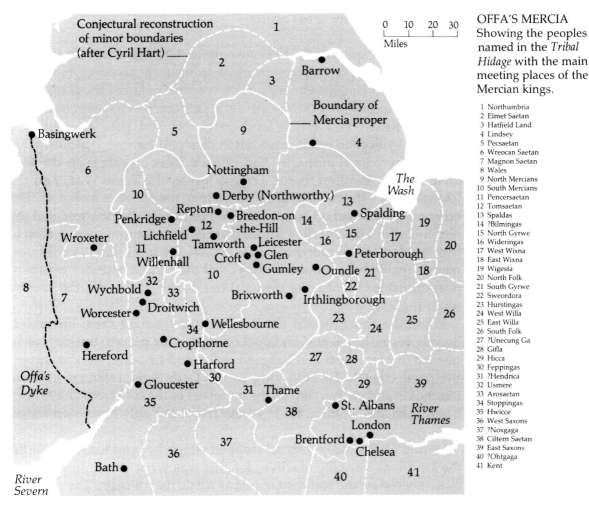

Conjectural reconstruction
of minor boundaries
(after Cyril Hart) ——

1

0 10 20 30
Miles

OFFA'S MERCIA
Showing the peoples
named in the *Tribal
Hidage* with the main
meeting places of the
Mercian kings.

2

3

Barrow

Boundary of
—— Mercia proper

● Basingwerk

5   9   4

6

Nottingham
●

10   ● Derby (Northworthy)   13   *The
Wash*

Repton●   ●   ● Spalding
Penkridge●   ●Breedon-on   14   19
            12   -the-Hill
Lichfield●   15   17   20
Wroxeter   Tamworth ●Leicester   16
11   Croft ●●Glen
Willenhall   ● Gumley ●Oundle 21   18
            32   10   22
8   Wychbold ●   33   ●   ●
7   ●Droitwich   Brixworth● Irthlingborough
Worcester●   23   25   26
                                   24
            34 ●Wellesbourne
         ●Cropthorne
Hereford●
*Offa's   ● Harford
Dyke*   30
         ●Gloucester   27   28
35   31 Thame   29   39
            38
                  ● St. Albans   *River
                  London   Thames*
      37   Brentford●●
            36   Chelsea
   Bath●
*River   40   41
Severn*

1 Northumbria
2 Elmet Saetan
3 Hatfield Land
4 Lindsey
5 Pecsaetan
6 Wreocan Saetan
7 Magnon Saetan
8 Wales
9 North Mercians
10 South Mercians
11 Pencersaetan
12 Tomsaetan
13 Spaldas
14 ?Bilmingas
15 North Gyrwe
16 Wideringas
17 West Wixna
18 East Wixna
19 Wigesta
20 North Folk
21 South Gyrwe
22 Sweordora
23 Hurstingas
24 West Willa
25 East Willa
26 South Folk
27 ?Unecung Ga
28 Gifla
29 Hicca
30 Feppingas
31 ?Hendrica
32 Usmere
33 Arosaetan
34 Stoppingas
35 Hwicce
36 West Saxons
37 ?Noxgaga
38 Ciltern Saetan
39 East Saxons
40 ?Ohtgaga
41 Kent

the once royal village of Wellesbourne. The creation of the modern shires in the tenth century ignored this ancient division, but it still marks the diocesan boundary between the bishoprics of Worcester and Coventry (then called Lichfield), showing that when the Mercian kings in the seventh century accepted Christianity and divided their land into dioceses, the dioceses were formed on the old tribal territories. The still existing hedgerow near Radway was an old boundary even in Offa's time. Such configurations defined his kingdom. When he and his court stayed 'in the region of the Stoppingas' he will have been entertained in the royal hall of those people at Wellesbourne (which remained a residence as late as 862); he will have collected his taxes or food rent from his reeve in Kineton ('King's tun') and may even have ridden the bounds to confirm any grant of land there '. . . from the marl pit to the milldam and on to the oak copse'. A king in the Dark Ages knew his landscape intimately. It was *his* patrimony.

The court on the move: a bad winter

There was no capital of the Mercian empire. Offa was itinerant and only ruled by moving from place to place, constantly showing himself to friends and cowing his enemies. He stayed on his farms and estates and on those of his leading landowners and monasteries, taking taxes, food and hospitality, and giving land, privileges and gifts in return. He travelled by Roman roads often left in disrepair for four hundred years except where local authority had remade them. Apart from the four great roads – Watling Street, Ermine Street, the Fosse Way, and the Icknield Way – the concept of a well-defined road system had gone. The economy was based on highly localised centres of distribution, and the terminology of the charters shows that communications were geared to this: roads to local markets, roads which the local militia could use, roads suitable for a mounted army, and then the wonderful wealth of peasant names identifying the local tracks, the 'foul way', the 'stubby way', the 'clay way'.

When the court moved about, Offa and his chief men, his prefect Brorda, his bishops, and his court officials, rode horses, but carts were needed to carry tents and baggage, relics and treasure, the contents of the royal chapel. To be a king in the Dark Ages required physical toughness and energy, but all the members of the court must have been hardy men and women, for in winter travel can only have been miserable.

During Christmas 763 travel stopped altogether and for four months the king was virtually inactive, for this was what the eighth century remembered as 'the bad winter' just as we do that of 1947. 'The snow lay thick over the whole country, frozen from the start of winter through to the middle of spring,' wrote a monk in Northumbria; 'trees and crops were killed off, and even the fish died' (Symeon of Durham *History of the Kings*). Even in our era of high mechanisation and electronic communication, we know what chaos can still result from a really bad winter, and even in modern states crops can fail. In 763 it was disastrous. 'Bread shortage,' says an Irish annalist. On the continent there was the same bleak tale. And as always in those days a hard winter brought fires in towns built of wood in closely packed tenements. The Northumbrian annalist notes that London, Winchester, York and other towns burned down that winter. Faced with disasters like this a king was powerless to act. Without telephone or telegraph, his letters delivered by hand, he could not rule in these conditions. All he could do was to keep to his hall and his nearby estates, use up the supplies of food laid in for winter, and hope the royal poets had a good fund of stories to recite at table. The only consolation was that the Welsh were hardly going to raid in this weather.

Christmas in the royal hall

Christmas was usually spent at Tamworth. This is certainly true of the later Mercian kings, and probably of Offa too. On Boxing Day 781, for instance, we find him there making grants of land to Worcester Cathedral, the official business being transacted before the meal. (In earlier times, and perhaps as late as Offa's day, these grants were accompanied by an archaic ritual in which the king joined hands with the queen and the bishop, and placed a turf from the land on a gospel book.) In the king's chamber that day were Queen Cynethryth, bishops Eadberht of Leicester, Hygeberht of Lichfield and Hathored of Worcester, and the Mercian chiefs Brorda, Berhtwald and Eadbald. There would also have been thegns, royal officials, and abbots from nearby Mercian monasteries. Altogether twenty or thirty people sat at table for the feast, supervised by Offa's steward and served by royal staff who lived and worked at the residence and its attached farms. These servants would be there all year round, and when Offa came to stay his assessors went on ahead to check that stocks were plentiful, bread baked, animals ready for slaughter and that the beer was brewing. (With no hops to act as preservative, beer went off quickly, and only hardened drinkers preferred it stale.) The feast on Boxing Day 781 was a grand occasion but there were times when Offa was there only with his bodyguard and his chief court officers, for it was an expensive matter to feed the bishops and ealdormen and their retinues. The list of food and drink needed for one night's upkeep for the king and his court in the early eighth century gives an idea of how much was consumed: 10 jars of honey, 300 loaves, 12 casks of Welsh ale, 30 of clear ale, 2 old oxen, 10 geese, 20 hens, 10 cheeses, a cask full of butter, 5 salmon, 100 eels, and 20 pounds weight of fodder (*Laws of Ine*). It can be imagined how efficient the food rent system had to be, to feed the court as it moved about, to make sure that food from surrounding estates arrived at the royal centres, and the kings rarely gave land to their churches or to their followers without imposing the obligation of providing the king's *feorm*, his food rent. When Offa gave an estate at Westbury-on-Trym in Gloucestershire to the church at Worcester, he released it from the now customary dues of military service, but he insisted on keeping his ancient taxes, 'two big casks of pure ale, a cask of mild ale, a cask of Welsh ale, seven oxen and six wethers, forty cheeses . . .' and so on. Food and accommodation were major concerns of Dark Age kings, and much administrative expertise went into making the system work smoothly.

Tamworth today has been gutted by modern developments, although it has a fine Norman Castle, and it is difficult to picture it as it was in the eighth century except when you stand down on the flood plain of the Tame and the Anker and look westwards. Here the southern edge of the citadel was protected by water, marsh and reeds, and the road south-west crossed by a causeway. The northern side of the town was and is heavily wooded. In Offa's day it would have seemed as if the settlement was in a great clearing in the forests between the Tame and the Trent.

We know a great deal more about Offa's Tamworth than we did only a decade ago. It had been a royal seat, and was maybe the main seat, as early as the late seventh century. It was then known as Tomtun, 'the settlement by the Tame'. At that time there may have been no more than a small wooden hall and chamber with a wooden chapel and a corral. Sometime in the mid eighth century a defensive ditch with stakes in the inner face of the bank and possibly a palisade were dug to enclose the site, so forming what the Mercians called a *worthig*, and from then on it was known as Tomeworthig, 'the enclosure by the Tame'. The charters show that from 781 the Mercian kings regularly kept the festivals of Christmas and Easter at Tamworth. From the ninth century there was a permanent treasury here for the receipt of royal dues and it may be that royal archives were also kept here, as charters written elsewhere were occasionally brought to Tamworth for royal approval at Christmas.

Offa's watermill

In 1971 a sensational discovery was made in connection with Offa's Boxing Day feast in 781. In the south-east corner of the defences at

The Tamworth watermill as uncovered by excavators: the wooden floor of the wheel house. The mill is to be preserved and reconstructed in Tamworth.

Tamworth archaeologists found the intact timbers of a two-storey Anglo-Saxon watermill. Four radiocarbon dates place the structure in the mid eighth century. It was of the horizontal-wheel type, which you can see in Crete today, and was chiefly remarkable for its high-quality craftsmanship, with glass and lead in the windows, a main bearing of high-quality steel, and lava querns imported from the Rhineland which may be the 'dark stones' referred to in a letter from Charlemagne to Offa on the subject of trade with England. Because there is as yet a lack of evidence with which to compare the Tamworth mill, it is difficult for the archaeologist to be sure whether he is looking at something which served a royal establishment, a farm, or some sort of urban nucleus, but the quality of the finds and their discovery within a known royal centre argue that the mill served the king. Here then, the flour would have been ground to make hundreds of loaves for the court at Christmas 781.

Offa's palace

Historians have always taken the presence of such gatherings to mean that Offa had a 'palace' in Tamworth, and they are probably right, though it is as well to remember that of the two grants issued there in 781, only a tenth-century copy speaks of a palace, the other referring simply to a 'royal seat'. Nevertheless several sources mention Offa's royal hall, and we are surely entitled to think that there was one here, and a splendid one at that. But where was it? Finds of reused Roman building material in the south-east corner of the town, and then the discovery of the mill in the same area, directed archaeologists' attention there. But recently it has been suggested that the great building stood in the raised open space in the town centre by the church. As the ground is now the graveyard it cannot be excavated, and in any case it is unlikely that eighth-century layers would have survived in such deeply disturbed soil. But the kind of building envisaged gives us a new perspective on Offa's forceful style of kingship.

It is thought that the top of the hill inside Tamworth was artificially built up to form a massive rectangular platform on which the royal hall was constructed. There are no English parallels for such a platform, but the structures at Gamle Uppsala in Sweden would be similar, and the general proportions of such a work could be inferred from a platform at Uppsala (160 feet long) and a comparable seventh-century hall at Yeavering (80 feet long) or the ninth-century hall at Cheddar (110 feet). It is even suggested that provision was made for drainage of the platform, which would be an engineering achievement of the kind we might expect from the man who built the dyke.

What did Offa's royal hall look like? A later writer who may have had an earlier source says that 'for its magnificence it was the wonder and marvel of the age', which seems to imply not merely great size, but also exceptional decoration. We know that contemporary continental palaces were painted with frescoes showing the deeds of heroes, Roman and Frankish, and the ninth-century palace in Winchester evidently also had some figured wall paintings. It is perhaps going too far to imagine that Offa had his hall decorated with the deeds of Constantine, Theodosius, and Offa of Angeln, but we can certainly picture it as an aisled hall a hundred feet or so long with a central hearth, porch and royal chamber, and it may have been hung with tapestries wrought in gold and silver thread, such as we find described in literary sources. Whether the hall was of stone or wood, or both, we cannot say, but the poet who wrote the great eighth-century epic poem *Beowulf* may have described it if, as many scholars think, he composed his poem for Offa's court: 'Lofty and high gabled . . . strongly braced inside and out . . . its high roof gilded, its mead benches decked in gold.'

So we can imagine Tamworth in Offa's time enclosed by its circuit of ditches, the royal hall on its platform with a royal chamber, a chapel, and one or two outbuildings of a reasonably dignified character. We would expect workshops for royal craftsmen, especially for a smith or metalworker. There would be sheds for animals, barns for storing hay, a couple of larger farms with plots for cultivation and pasturage for cattle, all within the defences. By the river was the mill, and on the southern side of the town the land flooded during winter up until this century, so in the eighth century in the wet season that whole side of the citadel must have been protected by a great expanse of water, and approachable only by causeway. Our plan of Offa's royal seat shows for the first time all the evidence which exists. To the modern eye it may appear more like something seen on a news bulletin from a Third World country, but in the eighth century in Britain all roads led here.

Summer residences

In the heyday of his Mercian empire Offa spent the early part of the year in Mercia, and then moved down towards London and Kent, holding great autumn synods at his farms and churches in the Thames valley, at Brentford for instance, or Chelsea. Here questions of church observance, ecclesiastical policy and royal ideology were determined by the king and his bishops. If Offa was not campaigning in the west against the Welsh, then on his way south he could enjoy the royal pursuits of hunting and hawking in the forests and hills of Leicestershire where he had many estates. Some estates, like Croft Hill, remained meeting places for centuries. Others are forgotten: Great Glen which preserves

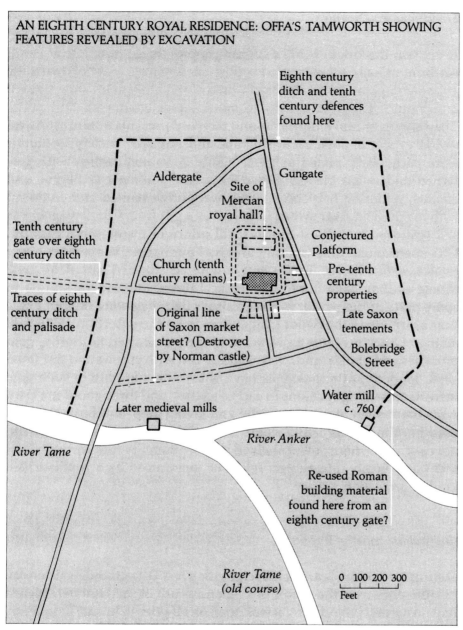

AN EIGHTH CENTURY ROYAL RESIDENCE: OFFA'S TAMWORTH SHOWING FEATURES REVEALED BY EXCAVATION

one piece of sculpture from the church Offa knew; Gumley, a favourite residence on its wooded knoll fronting the Welland valley, a 'famous place' where Aethelbald held court in 749 and Offa in 772 and 779. Further south in Northamptonshire we find Offa staying at Irthlingborough on the Nene. Some of these sites were perhaps no more than hunting lodges where the bishops and nobles slept in tents, but some were undoubtedly full royal establishments with a wooden hall and ancillary buildings.

Tribute and kingly gifts

Every year the kings of Offa's subject peoples would meet him at one of his farms or halls, an appointed spot on his itinerary, and, following the ancient tradition of Anglo-Saxon (and Celtic) kingship, they offered him tribute. This was usually in money, precious metals and cattle. They also gave him kingly gifts and received presents in return. As we would expect in such an aristocratic and militarist society, weapons were particularly prized as gifts: highly decorated swords with patterned and inlaid blades, gilded hilts and pommels of filigree and enamel, glittering heirlooms which were often named and endowed with magic. The Avar sword Offa had as a gift from Charlemagne was still treasured by a West-Saxon royal prince in the eleventh century. Offa spent much time hunting and had permanent keepers on many estates, so fine horses, hawks and hounds also formed part of the royal tribute as they have done since biblical times, and indeed still do in some parts of the world: in King Faisal's day they were offered every year as tribute to the Saudi king at Riyadh by the desert princelings of Arabia. Other presents to Mercian kings include saddle cloths, gold brooches and fibulas, and even a feather bed with pillows and fine linen slips. Modern anthropologists have shown how important such gifts were in cementing relations in early societies, and throughout the Dark Ages the system of paying tribute and giving gifts (and hostages) was used in ruling wider lands where real political power in our terms did not exist, and where power shelved into 'segmentary rule' through local men, and finally into subject relations guaranteed by a sophisticated kind of protection money.

A ninth-century sword found recently at Gilling West in Yorkshire. The hilt has five silver bands and the pommel is set with patterned silver panels.

'Bretwalda': 'ruler of Britain'

During the middle years of his reign, the 770s, Offa gradually extended his influence over the whole of England south of the Humber. Mercia had no natural boundaries; it was open on all sides to hostile kingdoms, and it was a long and continuous struggle for a Mercian king to keep his kingdom intact. He had to try to create natural boundaries, which in practice meant subduing all the other peoples to his rule. That in the long run was Offa's aim.

In 771 the campaigning season opened with the mounted army of the Mercian aristocracy riding over the Thames and into Sussex where they overcame in warfare the 'Haestingas', the men of West Sussex. The move may have been to consolidate Offa's influence in Kent. Offa's eyes were on Kent throughout his reign, the oldest, most settled and most civilised kingdom in England. With its close continental contacts, Kent was also the most 'modern': here the obscure Kentish kings of Offa's day were the first to mint the pennies which became the staple of English currency for 700 years and which stayed with us until the coin reform of 1971. The churches of Canterbury, where the conversion mission of Gregory the Great first took root, had the finest libraries, and produced the most sophisticated books and art. It was perhaps a case of a backward people coveting the benefits of a more civilised life style.

Offa appears in Kent as early as 764, attesting a charter with the archbishop and a local king. During the next years several grants of land there carry Offa's confirmation, but this does not mean that Kent was incorporated into the Mercian kingdom. However, in 775 Offa took an army into Kent, presumably to effect just that, and a hard battle was fought at Otford near Sevenoaks. Our sources, such as the *Anglo-Saxon Chronicle*, do not name the victor, but their silence is tantamount to an admission that Offa failed. For the next ten years the kings of Kent minted coins and issued land grants without reference to Offa. Doubtless propagandists back in Mercia claimed a victory for him saluting him in the royal hall as a 'battle-winner', a 'plunder-lord', a 'bracelet-giver'. That function of a king was important to his chiefs and warriors, the landowning class who, in exchange for gifts and privileges, formed his mounted host and his shield wall in war. In the Dark Ages kings needed to fight often in order to give land, booty, treasure and slaves to such men: that was their rightful expectation from the *heretoga*, the leader of the war host.

Whatever happened at Otford did not stop Offa. In 778 he launched another mounted expedition, this time deep into Wales, devastating the land and seizing loot: cattle, slaves, raw materials, precious metals. The next year, after the spring assembly of the Mercian ealdormen and their contingents from all the regions, Offa moved south and attacked Cynewulf of Wessex. The two kings fought at Benson, an ancient West-Saxon royal village on the north bank of the Thames near Abingdon, and Offa carried the day. The victory at Benson was followed by the annexation of a great tract of what is now Berkshire to Mercia, in whose hands it remained for fifty years. At St Albans it was later claimed that Offa also defeated the Northumbrians in war, but there is no trace of this in their annals or in Offa's charters. Nevertheless Offa was now the most powerful king in Britain, and could with justification call himself a bretwalda.

In the mid eighties, by which time Offa had already lived and reigned far longer than anyone in that age could expect, the most memorable phase in his life unfolds. He begins to appear not merely as a barbarian warleader, but as a statesman with a European perspective. If any single event contributed to this, it was Offa's taking direct control of Kent in 785, either through internal dissension or by invasion. The opening up

Kentish sophistication. An initial from a copy of Bede's *History* done at Canterbury in Offa's time.

of contacts with Kent seems to have brought a flood of civilised influences into Mercia – some of them continental – and the last ten years of the reign see a positive explosion of Mercian power, prestige and cultural achievement.

The fly in the ointment was Archbishop Jaenberht of Canterbury. He and Offa did not see eye to eye. The archbishop was a Kenting born and bred. He was educated in the 'family' of the church of St Augustine in Canterbury, was a former abbot there, and as far as we can tell he hated the shrewd and uncompromising Mercian. Offa could not tolerate the spiritual headship of England lying with a province which viewed him as an enemy. In 786 Offa invited the Pope's legates over to report on the Church in Britain, and to cement his own standing with the Pope. The legates were charmed and impressed, and the next year in an 'acrimonious synod' Offa announced that a new archbishopric would be created for Mercia, at Lichfield, depriving Archbishop Jaenberht of part of his jurisdiction – all with the blessing of the Pope. Archbishop Jaenberht was left speechless: no protest is recorded, though his reaction can well be imagined.

Offa's thirtieth jubilee and the anointing of his son and heir

Despite the fineness of the cutting, it is unlikely that we have here a portrait of Offa. The style of Ibba's coin in particular suggests a Roman model.

Offa's wider plan now came to fruition. In 787 with great ceremony his new archbishop consecrated his son Ecgfrith king in Offa's own lifetime – such was Offa's burning desire to keep the throne in his own line. It was the first recorded consecration in England, and was perhaps inspired by Charlemagne's sending his sons Pippin and Louis to Rome for papal unction in 781. Only the Church of Rome could confer legitimacy on a Christian king in the West, and Offa had recognised this early on in claiming divine protection for his accession.

The ceremony of 787 seems to have been accompanied by a commemorative issue of coins to mark this most significant year in Offa's life. Initially Offa had done little to change the coinage minted in Canterbury, but now there came a dramatic change. Offa's bust appeared on the coins, and the quality of the workmanship makes continental coins look crude in comparison. In fact their quality is such that scholars have thought an actual portrait of the king is intended. Looking at the coins, it is the technical and artistic brilliance which first catches the eye, then the realism and variety of the portraits. Sometimes Offa is shown with elaborately dressed hair arranged in curls, cut to give hints of light and shade. On others he is diademed and draped like a Roman emperor. He is also shown wearing rich jewels; he has either an ornament on a fine chain round his neck, or a triple branching spray, contrasting strongly with the drab garb of most later kings. In the eighth century many church commentators criticised aristocrats for wearing too extravagant a dress and too many ornaments. One of Offa's correspondents, Alcuin, an English scholar living in France, has a few barbed remarks to make in one letter about current fashions in Britain. 'Some silly fool will think up with a new fangled idea, and the next minute the whole nation is trying to copy it.' We cannot say whether Offa himself liked such ostentation and coveted gems and adornments, or whether these are the touches of the die cutter, but that Offa masterminded this 'imperial' issue there seems no doubt.

Most fascinating of all, Offa at this time had coins struck in the name of his queen, Cynethryth, mother of the young heir, portraying her bust with name and title. This is the only instance in the whole of Anglo-Saxon coinage of a coin being issued in the name of a consort. Cynethryth was praised as a most compassionate woman by Alcuin, but we should be wary of thinking the coin issue a demonstration of affection. Such public gestures were infrequent in Dark Age rulers, and despite Cynethryth's sinister role in later legends, she was no Evita. In fact Offa was probably simply imitating the classical Roman custom of putting the empress's portrait on the coinage. Mothers of kings, though, had great status in Anglo-Saxon society, and the coins certainly showed the integrity of Offa's line to the other rulers of Britain.

We do not know where the consecration ceremonies of 787 took place, or the details of the consecration. Was there, for instance, a full ritual anointing or merely a laying on of hands? It is likely that Offa himself took part, and in raising his son to joint kingship he may have ritually renewed his own rule, or celebrated his accession to a wider domain. It was, after all, his thirtieth jubilee. Not only the great men of Mercia would have been there, but Offa's subject kings, and ambassadors from Charlemagne and the Pope will have seen the heir Ecgfrith displayed in royal regalia on the balcony of a great Mercian church, from where the people could see him and join in the acclamation. Offa knew better than most how unstable power was, but surely at this moment, with his son consecrated, he permitted himself a feeling of pride. The line which extended from Offa of Angeln was assured.

Brixworth – Offa's royal church?

It is easy to imagine these events, when one visits Brixworth in Northamptonshire which has the finest Anglo-Saxon church of the period in all England. This great building is still substantially intact. Its aisles or side chapels have gone, and the main west doorway with its balcony above was replaced in the tenth century by the tower and stair turret we see today. Otherwise this is still a major church dating from the high

Brixworth, a fine eighth-century Mercian royal church, now stripped of its side aisles. The ring-crypt is below ground, around the end apse at the right-hand side of the photograph.

noon of the Mercian empire. It may even be Offa's church, for it has some unique features. Outside the walls of the east end is a remarkable ring-crypt, a covered circular corridor below ground level, intended to facilitate the circulation of pilgrims round a relic shrine. Like others of the period it is modelled after the ring-crypt built by Pope Gregory the Great at St Peter's in Rome in around 600. At Brixworth we know there was a special veneration for Boniface, the Devon saint martyred in Germany in 754, and the probability is that Brixworth possessed a relic of Boniface and that the present church was built in the late eighth century to house it. We also know that the place was later a royal residence. Taken together these facts suggest that Brixworth was a Mercian royal church, and that the likeliest patron was the great builder Offa himself.

'A great dyke from sea to sea'

In the late 780s Offa took the decision for which he is best remembered: to build the dyke along the Welsh frontier. There had been such dykes before in England, but Offa's surpassed all these earlier works in scope.

94

Why did he do it?

Up till now, historians have believed that the dyke was a frontier marker, an agreed boundary between peoples with wide gaps to allow passage on the tradeways from Wales. This view was upheld despite the Welsh chronicles' record of continuous warfare with Offa, from a battle at Hereford in 760 to one at Rhuddlan in 796. Recent archaeological discoveries have now upturned this interpretation.

We know now that the dyke was not a mere boundary, but a fortified barrier. It was a sharply scarped bank, 25 feet from the bottom of the ditch to the top of the bank, surmounted by a wooden palisade and in some places by a stone breastwork the remains of which were found in the ditch. There may even have been towers. The dyke was also continuous; in the so-called 'gaps' or 'gateways', where there seemed to be no trace of the earthwork, excavations revealed Offa's ditch below the present surface. Soldiers, traders and travellers will therefore have passed into Wales through structures which have yet to be identified, fortifications on the dyke, or sally gates.

From the construction techniques, archaeologists have also been able to deduce that the dyke was not built by one great gang, but by many different groups who each dug a few miles. We might connect this with the *Tribal Hidage*, which lists the peoples who owed Offa military service. Their service could simply have been commuted to work on the dyke, which would then have been built by subject labour, including the men of Wessex, Kent and East Anglia.

Although earlier scholars did not believe that the dyke could have been garrisoned, it is obvious that the labour of manning it would be far less than that of building it in the first place (and it could have been built in one summer). Patrols would have been perfectly adequate if they were linked to the beacon system which was used in Anglo-Saxon times and which survived through the Armada right up to Elizabeth II's jubilee. The sight lines on some of the central sections of the dyke are nearly twenty miles in either direction, and the beacons could swiftly bring news of a Welsh raid to the assembly points for the local levies. Within hours, hundreds of armed warriors could converge on any trouble spot. Throughout the eighth century the heartland of Mercia had lain open to Welsh incursions. Only fifty years before Offa there had been violent attacks right across to the Fens. Now there was a secure defence.

The most surprising new discovery about the dyke is that it does not run where we thought it did. Three test digs on its presumed northern sector have revealed that there is no evidence that the last twenty miles of the dyke ran through northern Flintshire from Treuddyn to the Irish Sea near Prestatyn. Place-name evidence is unequivocal that a parallel earthwork known as Wat's Dyke had up to the last century always been called Offa's Dyke in a major section stretching fifteen miles from the river Alun near Treuddyn up to the river Dee at Basingwerk (a known Mercian fortress). As there is no longer any reason to believe that Offa's Dyke extended to the Irish Sea, we must now assume that it originally ran near due north to the Dee. In the 890s Bishop Asser said the dyke ran 'from sea to sea'. but he did not specify its terminations. The later medieval version of the Welsh annals states that in 787

> In the summer the Welsh devastated the territory of Offa, and then Offa caused a dyke to be made between him and Wales, to enable him more easily to withstand the attack and that is called *glawd Offa* from that time to this day, and it extends from one sea to the other, from the south near Bristol to the north above Flint between the monastery of Basingwerk and Coleshill.
>
> *Brut y Tywysogion*

The line of Offa's Dyke from the Wye to Treuddyn and then along the northern stretch of 'Wat's Dyke' to Basingwerk fits this description exactly.

'Roman genius'

To us the vision and confidence which lies behind such a work perhaps smacks of the ideology of the 1000-year Reich. But the man behind it was a military genius with exceptional engineering skill who has rightly been credited with 'Roman genius and energy'. That verdict has proved all the more true now we know that the models for the dyke were not the great boundary ditches of the continental Anglo-Saxons, but Roman frontier works. Offa need not have seen for himself the Roman northern walls. One of the books we know he possessed (and which was surely read to him) was Bede's *History*, where he could find out how to make just such a work, 'constructed with sods cut from the earth and raised high above ground level, fronted by the ditch from which the sods were cut, and surmounted by a strong palisade of logs. Severus built a rampart and ditch of this type from sea to sea, and fortified it with a series of towers'.

'The good King Offa'

As they grow older, dictators often become more religious, especially in societies where every act on earth has significance in the ideal hierarchy. In eighth-century Europe the whole structure of society was felt to be mirrored in heaven, and kings like Offa saw themselves in the same

relation to God, the supreme overlord, as their subject kings were to them. They never tired of pressing home the analogy. They gave gifts to God and his saints, founded churches, gave alms to the poor, made pilgrimages to Rome, and even kept vigils in holy shrines much as peasants do in some parts of southern Europe today.

Offa was no different. But of all the king's gifts to churches only one can be identified today. We know from a note in a thirteenth-century St Albans manuscript that Offa gave a Gospel book to the church at Worcester. As it happens a fragment of a late eighth-century Gospel book can still be seen in the Cathedral Library in Worcester. This has been there for nearly nine hundred years, and was probably written at Canterbury, where Offa had his best-quality books made. It is not impossible that we have here part of the beautiful book which Offa presented to Worcester, and hence the only surviving artefact which can be associated with him personally. There is no reason to think that Offa himself was literate – few Dark Age kings were – but he understood the symbolic and practical value of the book. 'I am delighted that you are so keen on encouraging reading,' Alcuin wrote to him, 'so that the light

Offa as benefactor. This thirteenth-century drawing shows him building his stone church at St Albans. Though anachronistic in all its detail, the picture reminds us that a Dark Age king might often 'plan himself the structure of the buildings and measure out the foundations with his own hands'.

97

of wisdom, now extinct in so many places may shine in your kingdom. You are the glory of Britain, the trumpet of the gospel, our sword and shield against the enemy.' The enemy of course was paganism, and Alcuin's greatest fear was that the avaricious and worldly Mercian kings, for all their qualities, might allow the Church to fall to 'secular priority'.

The murder of Aethelberht

In 792 Offa sent ambassadors to Rome to cement his alliance with the papacy. But soon afterwards there occurred an incident which shows how tenuous was the Church's hold on Dark Age kings. The *Anglo-Saxon Chronicle* says simply that Offa ordered Aethelberht, king of the East Angles, to be beheaded. By the tenth century the cult of St Aethelberht was well established at Hereford, where he was buried, and later chronicles were in no doubt that Aethelberht had been innocent and Offa's role in the affair 'most treacherous'. By the twelfth century romantic legends were in circulation which told a story of passion and intrigue in which the young East Anglian king was in love with Offa's daughter and murdered by Offa's wicked wife. In these legends the place of execution is said to be Sutton, near Hereford.

'Stained with blood'

It is possible to untangle some of the truth behind the Aethelberht story through the coins. Initially Aethelberht minted coins in his East Anglian kingdom which bore the name of the overlord Offa. Then, some time before his death, we find coins issued in his own name, implying that the king had rejected Mercian overlordship and asserted the independence of his kingdom. How he came to be at Sutton is difficult to say, but his execution undoubtedly shows how Offa felt he could deal with his subject kings. They would be deposed or even killed if they caused him trouble. On this theme Alcuin wrote home to one of Offa's ministers, Osbert, in 797, following the deaths of Offa and his son within months of each other:

> Thinking of our long friendship, I wanted to write to remind you of my feelings and tell you how I am, for we are unlikely now to have the pleasure of meeting and talking confidentially . . . I do not believe the noble youth died through his own sins: it was the vengeance of the father's blood that fell on the son. For you know as well as I how much blood the father shed to secure the kingdom for his son. It proved the undoing not the making of his kingdom.
>
> Alcuin *Letters*

David harping. A painting created at Canterbury under Offa's overlordship. Like Charlemagne Offa would have felt that David was a 'mirror for princes', 'a warrior king who held his neighbouring peoples in check with his powerful hand'. As Alcuin reminded both Charlemagne and Offa, David also 'diligently worked at correcting the people' in their moral life.

In another letter Alcuin had spoken of Offa's 'fine character and modest way of life . . . devotion to the Christian religion and seriousness of demeanour'. The figure of the dictator as a puritanical strongman is one we recognise today; in the eighth century the Church often asked the impossible of essentially simple men.

Events like these perhaps give us a clue to Offa's 'personality', if we may, anachronistically, use such a modern term. His stress on his own royal ancestry; his single-mindedness in securing the throne for his son, going so far as to have him anointed in his own lifetime; his supervision of a written genealogy to justify his claim (a blatant piece of what we would call propaganda); above all his ruthless liquidation of rivals: all this suggests a gifted but aggressive and touchy man, not unlike some

Third World dictators today. His heavy emphasis on an overtly moral private life cannot disguise the fact that like most successful Dark Age kings (and a reign that lasted 39 years was success in itself), Offa was also uncompromising, cruel and avaricious. All these traits were ascribed to him in the letters of Alcuin, a man who knew Offa well enough: 'Never forget Offa's fine character, his modest way of life, his concern to reform the life of a Christian people,' he wrote, 'but do not follow him in his cruel and greedy acts.' However we should remember that an eighth-century man (even a thoughtful churchman like Alcuin) did not find such a personality incompatible with that of a great Christian king.

The last years

Offa maintained his supremacy until his death. And he did so by personal charisma and energy even though he was now about sixty. At Whitsun 795 he held a great court in London in the role of overlord. Formerly controlled by the kings of Kent, London's port tolls were now a source of revenue for Mercia, and Offa had a palace and a private church within the walls of the Roman fort in Cripplegate from where he could supervise the 'mart of many nations who come by land and sea' (Bede, *History*, writing in 731).

That summer Offa sent an army into Wales and devastated Dyfed. He retired to Tamworth for Christmas, and in the New Year received ambassadors from Charlemagne who came bearing gifts and letters. Some time before the two kings had quarrelled over Charlemagne's request that Offa's daughter, Aelflaed, should marry Charlemagne's son, Charles. Offa had refused unless his heir, Ecgfrith, married Charlemagne's daughter, Bertha. Charlemagne had immediately broken off relations with him and closed Frankish ports to English traders. Yet the tone of the letters was friendly: 'to his dear brother Offa, good wishes . . . It is in the interests of everyone that the bond of holy love and the laws of friendship formed in the unity of peace between kings should be sincerely preserved . . . . We recognise in you not only a strong protector of your country but a devoted defender of the Faith'. Charlemagne once more offered full protection for English merchants abroad, and, 'with regard to the dark stones which you asked us to send, have a messenger come to choose which kind you want. . . . . We will gladly order them to be given and help with transport. And as you have told us the size of the stones you require, so our people have a request to make about the length of their cloaks, namely that you should have them made like those we used to get in the past.' With the letter there were presents: church vestments and rich cloths for each of the bishops in England,

and gifts for Offa himself, silks, a belt and a Hunnish sword, booty from Charlemagne's seizure of the Avar ring in Hungary. Charlemagne's letter ends: 'May Almighty God preserve you, dear brother, in long life and prosperity to protect his holy church.' As Offa listened to the letter being read out in the royal hall at Tamworth, and reflected on the silks and the Avar sword, he must have appreciated the gesture greatly. He was an elder statesman now – both men were getting on – and there is nothing an old tyrant likes better than to gain respectability in the world.

Offa's death

On 29 July Offa died at Offley in Hertfordshire, on one of the estates he had given to St Albans. His Mercian retainers and chief men – Brorda his prefect and chief court officer, one of the old guard on whom Offa had always relied – were by his bedside. The changeover of power was rapid, the way prepared. Ecgfrith was acclaimed king. But events moved fast. On 17 November Ecgfrith died. The East Angles and Kentishmen immediately rose in revolt and the new Mercian king, Cenwulf, a distant cousin of Offa, put down the rising in Kent with revolting brutality, ravaging as far as Romney Marsh and leading their 'king', Eadberht Praen, a renegade monk, in chains back to Mercia where Cenwulf cut off Eadberht's hands and put out his eyes.

Though it was only in the 820s that the Mercian kings' role as overlords finally collapsed, their hegemony never really recovered. If anything, the violent resistance engendered by the long period under Offa's iron hand paved the way for the rise of the West Saxons.

The Mercian legacy

In conclusion, what are we to make of Offa's kingship, and his role in the development of eighth-century England? His was still a Germanic society, of course, in law, in speech, in social order and the forms of kingship. But we cannot ignore the great intellectual impact of the Roman legacy in the development of Anglo-Saxon civilisation. For the so-called barbarians of the seventh and eighth centuries, the Roman empire cast the same sort of afterglow as the British Empire did in post-colonial Africa, and their kings were as susceptible to its style as Amin was to the Sandhurst tradition, or Bokassa to Napoleonic ceremonial. Vigorous and violent, naive yet cunning, they legitimised their rule with the trappings of empire.

The ruins of Rome stood around them in tangible form, of course. But it went deeper than that. The Northumbrian bretwalda, Edwin, unsophisticated but immensely proud, as Bede portrays him, made the point of having the insignia of Roman office carried aloft before him in public. He was baptised by a Roman missionary in the Roman city of York, and for all we know held court in the still standing Roman HQ building there. Such men were setting themselves up as civilised heirs of Rome. And prodded by the missionary zeal of the Catholic Church, they learned fast. By the time we get to Offa, a man of far greater power, prestige and sophistication than his predecessors, the Roman legacy had generated a new style. We can see it in the palace with the stone church inside the Roman fort in London; in the 'wonder and marvel of the age' at Tamworth; in the Roman-style basilica at Brixworth; in the dyke with its palisades, ditches and wall walks; in the beautiful coins representing Offa as a new Theodosius.

'Offa, King of the fatherland of the English'

Offa began his reign an illiterate barbarian, whose accession can have cast few reverberations over the Channel. Not long before his death four decades later, the grizzled old dictator was an honoured visitor at the papal court in Rome, a figure of European stature. It is ironic that for all the ruthlessness with which he secured his kingdom, his only son died childless so soon after him. But of his achievements there is no doubt. He left his successors a strong unified kingdom in central England where there had been a mass of disparate tribes. And he left too the concept of a kingdom of all the English. It was to be the West Saxons, Alfred and Athelstan, who would turn that concept into fact.

Offa's burial

Offa's career is as yet an imperfect jigsaw puzzle. There is even uncertainty over his burial place. We do not know where the Mercian kings of the pagan period (that is, before 654) were buried, as none of their tombs has ever been discovered. A site near the later bishopric of Lichfield is likely, and one at Offlow in Staffordshire is a possibility. Some of the early Christian kings of Mercia, like Ceolred in 716, were buried in the church of Lichfield itself. In the eighth and ninth centuries Repton in Derbyshire was favoured. There the murdered Aethelbald was buried in 757, in a free-standing mausoleum which still survives to roof height, incorporated into the present church. The later king Wiglaf and his grandson Wystan also lay here, and in the crypt the recesses which held the royal caskets can still be seen with a vaulted roof and twisted columns imitating those in old St Peter's in the Vatican. Around the church at Repton the remains of ninth-century Mercian nobles have been found in elaborate iron-bound coffins, the kind of men who formed Offa's entourage. But at neither Lichfield nor Repton, nor any of the other places (like Offchurch in Warwickshire) which claim him, is there good evidence that they are the place of Offa's burial. I therefore prefer to follow the opinion of the monks of St Albans, who had good cause to remember, for to their chagrin they failed to secure the body of their great benefactor. They said that Offa was entombed at Bedford in a small chapel which by the thirteenth century had been swept away by the river Great Ouse. Why Bedford was chosen is a mystery.

In Wessex, Kent and East Anglia it is unlikely that Offa was mourned, for he had incurred much hatred. But standing by the Great Ouse at Bedford we may perhaps imagine the mounted warriors who formed Offa's retinue riding round his coffin, and in the old Germanic tradition, 'singing of his heroic deeds, praising his manhood and weeping for him'. The words they sang might have been ones formerly declaimed before the king in his royal hall:

Fortham Offa waes geofum ond guthum, garcene man wide geweorthod; wisdome heold ethel sinne.

Best of men the wide world over, Offa was a great warrior who ruled his kingdom wisely and was famous for his victories and his generosity.

Beowulf

A unique gold coin showing Offa, minted in Kent *c.* 790. The model is once again a Roman coin.

CHAPTER 5

ALFRED THE GREAT

One day a certain peasant woman, wife of a cowherd, was making loaves, and the king (Alfred) was sitting by the fire tending his bow and arrows and other weapons. But when the poor woman saw that the loaves she had put over the fire were burning she ran up and took them off, scolding the invincible king and saying, 'Look there man, you can see the loaves are burning and you've not turned them, though I'm sure you'd be the first to eat them nicely done!' The miserable woman little thought that this was King Alfred who had fought so many wars against the pagans and won so many victories.

Annals of St Neots

At Winchester: the apotheosis of 'England's darling'. We have perhaps yet to find the real Alfred.

Few legends are as enduring as that of Alfred and the cakes. Along with Robert Bruce and the spider, Elizabeth and the Armada, the Battle of Britain and the Few, it is a legend of resilience in adversity, of an indomitable spirit that succeeds when all around seems destined to fall. In fact the cakes story is no more than a legend, as it first appears in the *Annals of St Neots*, which date from the early twelfth century.

The tale is rather similar to the story of Bruce and the spider: its point is the humiliating straits to which the great man had been reduced at the nadir of his fortune, in this case after his defeat by the Danes in 878. But though this is only a folk story, the image of the fugitive king sheltering in a peasant's hovel has consciously or unconsciously influenced almost all later writers. What, then, are the facts behind Alfred's decisive war with the Vikings? Who began the Alfred myth? Does he alone among English monarchs really deserve to be called 'the Great'?

'What of the great trouble he had with his own people, who would voluntarily submit to little or no labour for the common needs of the kingdom?'

Nobody in British history has had as good a press as Alfred the Great. He is 'the wise king', 'England's darling', the 'Truthteller'. A story told against him in the *Abingdon Chronicle* seems to be the only one of its kind. The chronicler clearly did not like Alfred; he was a 'Judas . . . piling bad deeds on top of each other'. And why? Because the king 'violently alienated estates from the monastery'. (Whether there was

The burning of the cakes was one of many folk stories about the king which had arisen by the twelfth century. All were interpreted as exemplary moral tales by the Victorians who saw Alfred as one of themselves, a liberal educator and philanthropist.

any community still at Abingdon by his time we cannot say – the site may have been deserted – but William of Malmesbury confirms that the king took the lands and their revenues to his own use.) The story is interesting because it reminds us that although the Church wrote the accounts we have of Alfred and the other Anglo-Saxon kings, and saw them from a largely ecclesiastical point of view, the kings themselves did not necessarily share this perspective. Religious as such men were, they were not, in fact, ruled by their bishops as much as their biographers claimed. It is true that later kings like Edgar, and perhaps Athelstan, relied very heavily on certain bishops who had risen through the royal chapel as Mass priests or secretaries, men they knew intimately. But equally stories like the expropriation of the Abingdon estates are also told of Edward the Elder and Athelstan. Like Alfred, they were prepared to act against the Church if prompted by the exigencies of defence.

At a time when obligations often had to be cajoled out of a recalcitrant populace and surly magnates, kings frequently had to rely on their own resources in land, money and men, to prosecute their wars. Indeed it was partly due to the careful husbanding of the family possessions that Alfred and his father, son and grandsons were able, in the end, to combat the Viking menace so effectively. The kind of pressures which kings faced in the Viking era were sometimes only dimly understood by hagiographers like Bishop Asser.

'The hateful plague of Europe': the Vikings – heroes or villains?

Success or failure for a king in the ninth century was measured by how he dealt with the Vikings. In the last few years the image of the Vikings has undergone drastic revision. From seeing them as destroyers, the climate of opinion has shifted to emphasising their role as craftsmen, explorers and traders; from the bane that the monkish chroniclers write about, raping and pillaging, they have become a creative catalyst in European civilisation. A view which has also gained wide currency is that the numbers of Viking armies were not great, a few hundreds at the most.

However, these revisions are now proving difficult to sustain when seen against the evidence found in the contemporary annals of western Europe as a whole, that is of Ireland, Anglo-Saxon England and Francia. The annals state that some Viking armies were large, numbering thousands of men and sometimes hundreds of ships. They paralysed and overran wealthy and long-established kingdoms. They defeated the 'national' armies of kingdoms like the Franks and the West Saxons. They virtually destroyed learning in England. They were numerous enough to transform the racial and linguistic characteristics of places like Yorkshire, Lincolnshire, Cumbria and Normandy. To deny this and to concentrate on the cultural achievements of this vigorous but barbaric race is to deny the achievements of Alfred the Great and his son and grandson who were among the most effective kings to rule in England.

'My august master . . . commands you to share with him your ancient treasures, and your hereditary wealth, and to reign in future under him'

The first Viking raids, in the 790s, were merely for plunder, but the later Danish armies of the ninth century were out for more lasting gain. In the middle years of the ninth century England was still divided among the four great independent Anglo-Saxon kingdoms: Mercia, Northumbria, East Anglia and Wessex. By 878 only Wessex remained.

The Viking descent on England then was a *blitzkrieg* of a permanent kind. After it there would be no return to the old ways, only change and accommodation. With their traditional ways of raising armies and methods of fighting the old kingdoms found it impossible to resist the Vikings with their longships and their fast mobile armies. One by one they suffered military defeat. And for the kings themselves a terrible fate was reserved which has only recently been elucidated from dark hints in our sources. When in 867 the ancient kingdom of Northumbria ended in flames as York burned down, their king Aelle suffered the 'blood eagle'. This was a Viking rite in which the victim was offered to Odin; the ribs and lungs were cut from the living man and spread like eagle's wings.

The Danes then set up a puppet king in Northumbria north of the Tyne, a man who would pay them tribute and cause them no trouble. In 869 the blood eagle was performed on Edmund, king of the East Angles, the last successor of the Wuffingas of Sutton Hoo. In 874 Burgred, king of Mercia, heir to Offa and the great Mercian kings, abdicated and fled to Rome. Once again a puppet, Ceolwulf, was installed to maintain the *status quo*. Soon after these events large-scale, permanent Danish settlements began to appear in Northumbria, East Anglia, and in Mercia north of Watling Street. To educated men in Wessex it must have seemed that the very survival of Anglo-Saxon civilisation was now in the balance. In this grim atmosphere Alfred found himself king almost by default.

Alfred and the West-Saxon royal family

Alfred was born at Wantage in Berkshire in 849 and died in 899. The world he was brought into was hard and dangerous, and while he was still a child events had moved to make it more so. In 851 the Danes had changed their hit-and-run tactics and spent the winter in England for the first time, in Thanet. The nature of the Viking threat was thus changing even as Alfred grew to boyhood. Alfred's father, Aethelwulf, was king of the West Saxons. There were four older brothers, so in the normal run of things Alfred could hardly have expected to become king. But it was not an era in which kings could expect to live long, and in fact all five of Aethelwulf's sons reigned after him.

The family was a close one. Aethelwulf had pursued a carefully managed policy of looking after the family resources, keeping intact the estates on which they relied for revenue. He also seems to have arranged something similar with the succession, providing for the brothers to succeed each other rather than risk leaving the kingdom in the hands of the under-age children of the eldest. This caused problems for later West-Saxon kings, confronted with claims by the descendants of Alfred's elder brothers; but Alfred was the beneficiary, and his father's foresight may in the end have saved him.

All young noblemen in Anglo-Saxon England were brought up in the saddle, hunting and hawking, and in the martial arts. But Alfred seems to have been more influenced by his father's religious and contemplative bent. In a time of peace he might have been the young son destined for the church whom we meet in so many Dark Age families.

At the tender age of four he was sent to Rome by his father for an audience with the Pope. His poetic sensibility (and perhaps something of his competitive obstinacy?) is revealed in a delightful story about the king's boyhood which he later told to his biographer Bishop Asser. His mother had promised a beautifully illuminated book of Saxon poems to whichever of her sons would first learn it by heart. Although the youngest, Alfred went to a teacher who repeated the book out loud until Alfred had memorised it, and so he won the prize. A determined young boy.

Alfred remained illiterate in Anglo-Saxon until his teens, and in Latin until his mature years. The main span of his life was to be occupied with war. In his twentieth year, now married (to a Mercian noblewoman called Ealhswith), second in command and possibly the designated heir to his brother King Aethelred, Alfred underwent the first great test of his 'dangerous but brilliant apprenticeship'.

Ashdown: the prelude

In the winter of 870 after their successes in Northumbria and East Anglia, the Danish armies began their attack on Wessex. In the next few months nine battles were fought. On 8 January after inflicting a heavy defeat on the West Saxons the Danish forces marched from their new base at Reading up the Great Ridgeway, the prehistoric route which cuts across England into the heart of Wessex. There on the top of the Berkshire Downs the Ridgeway passes by the ramparts of an Iron Age hillfort which commands wide vistas into Wessex. Under it, centuries earlier, a white horse had been cut through the turf into the chalk; it was a familiar landmark, near the junction of old roads. Here on Ashdown, as it was called, the Vikings found the ridgeway blocked by the West-Saxon army under King Aethelred and his young brother Alfred. The actual site of the battle may have been on the lower land to the west of the Uffington horse where a Domesday hundred was called *Nachededorne*, 'at the naked thorn', a prominent tree at the meeting of local tracks (Bishop Asser, who was shown over the battlefield by Alfred himself, says the fiercest fighting took place around 'a single thorn tree'). The battle was won by Alfred's hotheaded impetus, charg-

ing uphill 'like a wild boar' while his brother was still at prayer. The Danes fled till nightfall leaving one of their kings and five leaders dead 'and the whole breadth of Ashdown covered with bodies'.

Ashdown. Looking over the White Horse at Uffington towards Compton Beauchamp and Watchfield in Berkshire.

The victory on Ashdown proved illusory. Within months the English had lost the upper hand. Defeated in further battles, King Aethelred died. The West-Saxon councillors, as Alfred's father had foreseen, had no choice in this extremity but to pass over the king's young sons to the one man who had proved his arm in battle. At twenty-one years of age Alfred became king. His biographer, the Welsh bishop Asser of Sherborne, who knew him well in his later years, portrays him as an oversensitive, highly-strung young man, strongminded and inventive, but something of a hypochondriac, constantly suffering from some sort of nervous illness. (One modern scholar has inferred that it could have been venereal disease – not an impossible idea in view of the libidinous behaviour of Dark Age royal families.) He was in some ways an unlikely king, then, though trained in the kingly pursuits of hunting, hawking and fighting.

His start was not auspicious. Massively reinforced the Danes beat him at Wilton in the heart of Wessex. Weakened by so many engagements, he offered to buy them off. (Ethelred the Unready was by no means the first to pay 'Danegeld'.) They accepted his money and turned

ALFRED'S WESSEX
Burhs of the *Burghal Hidage*.

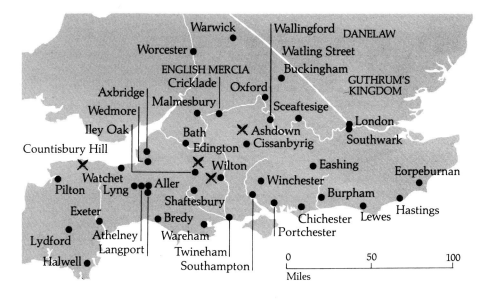

to easier pickings in Mercia. But both the Vikings and Alfred knew they would be back.

In 874 Mercia fell to the invaders, and in the following year the Danish army divided, part of it going to Northumbria, where 'they shared out the land . . . and proceeded to plough and support themselves'. The rest, under three kings, Guthrum, Oscetel and Anwend, went from Repton in Mercia to Cambridge where they remained for a year. The move to Cambridge was the opening gambit in the Danish attempt to defeat and dismember Wessex once and for all. When the campaigning season of 876 opened, Guthrum rode from Cambridge into Wessex and slipped past Alfred's army into Wareham in Dorset. There Alfred made a truce with them, only to see them steal away under cover of night to Exeter where they established themselves within the Roman walls of the old city. Alfred doggedly rode after them with the West-Saxon mounted force, and again they made him promises and gave him hostages. However, when the harvest came this time, rather than fight a major battle they agreed to move out of Wessex into Mercia, and in August 877 they rode up to Gloucester, where there was a Mercian royal hall and church. There they built booths for winter quarters. In the meantime Alfred disbanded his army and prepared to celebrate Christmas. The climax of this game of cat and mouse was at hand.

The crisis – Chippenham

Christmas passed and then Guthrum made his move. In a lightning strike he rode south from Gloucester over the snowy Wiltshire countryside and seized Chippenham which was in West-Saxon territory. Chippenham was to serve as the Viking base for the next four months, and it was well chosen. According to Bishop Asser it was a royal residence. Here in 853 Alfred's father, Aethelwulf, had given his daughter, Aethelswith, to Burgred, king of Mercia. We also know from Alfred's will that Chippenham was a royal estate, and it was probably a hunting lodge, for the royal forests of Melksham and Barden were nearby. The site of the town itself was in a strong position, protected by the Avon on three sides and by a ditch and palisade on the fourth, blocking off the promontory: an ideal Viking base.

The timing of Guthrum's advance gives us another clue to the dramatic events of 878. He came 'after Twelfth Night', according to the *Anglo-Saxon Chronicle*, and it may be that Alfred had spent the festival at Chippenham and that the Danes were trying to take him alive. There is nothing unlikely in this: attacking on major Christian feast days was a common stratagem of Viking armies. More important, and less conjectural, Guthrum made Chippenham his base for the ensuing campaign, and as it is reasonable to think that he and his chiefs were shrewd men of war, we can assume they would not have left Gloucester in the middle of winter for a centre which lacked supplies. They must have known that provisions for their army would be available, and it may be that Alfred's royal assessors had provided Chippenham with provisions because there was to be a royal visit around Twelfth Night. So Guthrum may well have discovered a food store with salted meat, eels, bread, honey and unhopped beer.

The whole operation was typical of Viking warfare. To maintain an army in winter they needed to plunder the country round about and when supplies ran out it was necessary to move to a new base in an undevastated area where the inhabitants could be forced to provide more food, fodder, horses and, if possible, protection money. This was what Viking armies had done countless times before in Britain and Europe, and in the middle of the winter Alfred had no standing army to oppose them. Sitting in the royal hall at Chippenham (which was perhaps in the centre of the town west of the church where late Saxon timber buildings have been found) Guthrum had reason to be pleased. He had a secure base with good lines of communication from whence he could probe deeper into Wessex, devastating, extorting and frightening the inhabitants into submission. It would surely only be a matter of time before he captured Alfred and the West-Saxon king too suffered the rites of the blood eagle.

As soon as their base was consolidated, the Danes moved south along the Fosse Way and 'rode over' and occupied the land of Wessex, in a wide mounted raid which probably struck down as far as the south coast. Recently scholars have proposed that when the Vikings occupied

Wessex they actually started to settle there, but Guthrum would never have done this while Alfred was still in the field. Nevertheless their depredations were enough to force many of the West Saxons to submit to the invaders, according to Alfred's official account in the *Anglo-Saxon Chronicle*, and this must refer to men in positions of leadership, not just the peasantry.

We can follow the trail of destruction. In Hampshire people 'fled across the water', perhaps to the Isle of Wight, although a tenth-century writer thought they escaped to France. In Wiltshire one ealdorman, the king's top local official, 'deserted his king and country' (the words are from a contemporary charter) and fled abroad with his wife. Of Dorset though we hear nothing, nor is the militia of that shire mentioned as participating in the final battle. Were the chief men in Dorset among those who submitted? Could it possibly be that at this time the Danes approached other members of the West-Saxon royal family with a view to setting up a puppet regime after Alfred's death, just as they had in Northumbria, Mercia and East Anglia? In fact Dorset was the stemland of Alfred's brother's son Aethelwold, who was to ally with the Danes as soon as Alfred died. In 878, with the king on the brink of destruction, power politics may have cut through the bonds of kinship and race.

But Finest Hours always tend to be exaggerated in the memory, and though there is no denying Alfred's distress, we know he was not as alone as his account in the *Anglo-Saxon Chronicle* implies. Forces from Somerset were still available to him, for the annalist Aethelweard, a royal kinsman writing a century on, says that Aethelnoth, ealdorman of Somerset, also maintained himself in wooded country with a small force. At this time the West Saxons were reduced to hit-and-run attacks on the Danes, and seizing provisions from wherever they could. Their situation was certainly desperate. If Alfred had given up and fled overseas like Burgred of Mercia then not only England but the whole English-speaking world would not exist today. But after six weeks of roughing it in the swamp came the turning point. Alfred and Aethelnoth were able to construct 'something of a fort' at a place deservedly hallowed in the British story, Athelney.

The country round Athelney was ideal for guerrilla warfare. According to Bishop Asser it was surrounded by reeds and thickets, and abounded with wildlife and marsh birds; punts were the only reliable way of getting about, for the whole area changed from swamp to lagoon according to the rainfall and the tides, so unless you knew the tracks, you could not approach it by sea or land. And Alfred knew it well. He must have hunted, fished and hawked there in his youth, and also as king whenever he stayed at his palace at Cheddar. (As its name means 'island of the princes', Athelney may have been one of the royal estates specifically set aside for the use of the royal athelings, the young princes.) Even today floods can make this part of West Somerset inaccessible. In 878 it was almost impenetrable. From this place was launched the salvation of Wessex and of England.

'Something of a fort'

No trace survives of the fort built by Alfred during Easter 878, and the land is now drained. The low hill, now surmounted by a monument, has been flattened by the building of Alfred's church and the later monastery. We must imagine a comparatively small construction, a couple of hundred feet across, ditched and palisaded with perhaps twenty feet from the bottom of the ditch to the top of the defences. Inside there would have been rough timber and wattle huts with room for extra tents, a refuge for a small force, a hundred men or two hundred at most. This would have been the base for the nucleus of royal support, that is, the royal family, the king's thegns, and the royal bodyguard. As the chronicler Aethelweard wrote, Alfred 'did not cease from daily forays against the barbarians with the help of the men of Somerset only. He had at that time no other reinforcement except the servants who had royal maintenance'. In other words the king was shorn of his wider

'And afterwards at Easter (23 March) King Alfred with a small force made a fort at Athelney.' Alfred's later church was on the site of the present monument, so perhaps it is most likely that the burh of 878 was on the low hill to the right.

support. A king who had only a few acres of marshes as his domain was almost a contradiction in terms. How could he be the 'sustainer of his warriors', 'rewarder of soldiers', 'ring giver to men', when he had nothing? (Patriotism was not a widely appreciated concept in 878) though it existed in the minds of some, not least Alfred himself.

The counterattack

Another event may have had a more decisive influence than we now realise on the fortunes of Wessex that spring which was coincident with the construction of the emergency burh at Athelney. A second Viking army comprising 23 ships and 1200 fighting men had wintered in south Wales, and when Guthrum moved into Wessex, this force sailed across to the Devon coast, apparently part of a planned pincer movement to trap Alfred. But at Countisbury Hill this force was engaged by the men of Devon under ealdorman Odda, and their leader, Ubba, was killed along with 800 men. According to the chronicler Aethelweard, who may have been descended from Odda, the Danes actually won the battle, but their losses meant they could play no further part in the campaign. The way was cleared for Alfred's action against Guthrum.

It is a great pity we know nothing of the underground organisation which Alfred used to assemble an army big enough to attack Guthrum, but such a movement undoubtedly existed. The *Anglo-Saxon Chronicle* tells us that the king was able to make contact with his supporters in Wiltshire and Hampshire and to arrange a rendezvous. At this point Guthrum had retired with his army to the north of Salisbury Plain, and when Alfred knew this he sent out messages to the local leaders to gather their forces and meet him. The time was the seventh week after Easter, says the chronicler, which suggests that the day appointed for the rendezvous was Whit Sunday, 11 May. The meeting place was known as Egbert's Stone; it has not yet been located though we know it lay close to the junction of the boundaries of Wiltshire, Hampshire and Dorset near Penselwood. There the men of Wiltshire, Somerset and part of Hampshire met the king and, the chronicler says (perhaps echoing Alfred's own report), 'they were overjoyed to see him'.

The next day, Monday 12 May if our guess is right, they moved camps to Iley Oak near Warminster where an earthwork shielded by woods offered protection for the army. By now the West-Saxon scouts must have had definite news of Guthrum's position. That night Alfred and his men prepared themselves for battle, perhaps, as was the custom of the time, fasting, praying and swearing on the sacrament to help each other – a necessary precaution when collaboration with the Vikings had become commonplace. Before the break of dawn they mounted and

Opposite The Battle of Edington: one of the decisive events of British history.
Above Alfred's view as he descended onto the royal village (where the present priory church stands?).
Below Guthrum's view up onto the crest of the 'waste down'.

pushed on over the Wylye and up the old white track that leads up the steep chalk edge onto Salisbury Plain:

> then the band of bold men was quickly made ready, men brave in battle . . . warriors marched out, bore banners of victory . . . heroes beneath their helmets at the break of dawn; the shields rang, resounded loudly.

Judith

The Battle of Edington

Guthrum was camped about seven miles from Iley Oak – by a strange coincidence close to another White Horse carved in the turf centuries before, as at Ashdown. The site had not been chosen by chance. It was an important royal estate, probably with a ditched enclosure and hall; it was owned by King Alfred himself, land which years later he gave in his will to his wife. He must have hunted there, and will have known all the tracks, especially the one which comes across the plain to the Iron Age camp at Bratton with its wide view of the well-wooded land of north Wiltshire stretching as far as Chippenham. At the first glimmer of dawn they rode over the top and down the ridge which had given its name to the royal vill below, Edington (*Ethandun*, 'waste down').

There, in the words of Bishop Asser,

> he attacked the whole pagan army fighting ferociously in dense order, and by divine will eventually won the victory, made great slaughter among them, and pursued them to their fortress (Chippenham). Everything left outside the fortress, men, horses and cattle, he seized, killing the men, and camped outside the gates. After fourteen days the pagans were brought to the extreme depths of despair by hunger, cold and fear, and they sought peace.

Although he had defeated the Danes and driven them from Wessex, Alfred knew that they were to remain in the rest of England for good. Despite the bitterness of the war he had fought, his response was therefore to make a pact of reconciliation with Guthrum and enter into friendship with him. This remarkable twist to events brought strong criticism from some hard-line foreign churchmen of the time, but its long-term benefits for Wessex and England were incalculable.

Three weeks later Guthrum came with thirty of his most important men to Aller, 'the marshy island' near Athelney, where Alfred became his godfather and received him from the font. Aller was the closest church to Athelney and as there was not a church at Athelney in 878, it may have been here that Alfred had prayed for victory in his darkest hour, during the spring of that year.

The baptismal ceremonies were completed the following week at

Wedmore, a royal church and hunting estate near Cheddar. Here Guthrum and his chiefs stayed for twelve days and were honoured by Alfred with feasting and gifts. For all Alfred's conventional piety, he and the Vikings understood each other. He was what they expected a king to be: a hard man, ruthless, a battle-winner, a king with luck, and yet generous both to his men and to those enemies who acknowledged him. He was not at all like the meek Christlike figure of Victorian popular histories. He would, for instance, hang his prisoners at the slightest provocation. No one respected a weak king in the Dark Ages.

Alfred's dramatic reversal of fortune – from the hide-out at Athelney to success at Edington – is so extreme that some modern writers have refused to take Alfred seriously, especially as our knowledge of what happened is based on the *Anglo-Saxon Chronicle* account which he sponsored. They have seen his report as an effective piece of dynastic propaganda.

To an extent there is something to be said for this. In the years after Edington, Alfred's subjects would have to take on very heavy burdens in terms of taxation and personal service; building a fleet, a whole system of fortified burhs, a mounted expeditionary force and a general levy which mobilised in two shifts. The thegnly class who provided the core of support for the king were required to be geared to war, rather like the men and women who protect the modern state of Israel. However, the people needed to be informed that, in spite of the defeat of all the Anglo-Saxon kingdoms except Wessex, things could and would get better. The *Anglo-Saxon Chronicle* account of the victory encouraged this attitude, and by being circulated to churches throughout the kingdom could convince as many as could be reached that Edington was a decisive victory; they would be assured that they had a future under the royal house of Wessex. Part of Alfred's purpose may have been to exaggerate his distress during the dark days of Athelney, in order to create an 'Alfred myth', as it were, but distress there certainly was, and Edington is not the only battle in the Dark Ages which abruptly and unexpectedly reversed the drift of a whole campaign.

In 1693 this jewel was found near Athelney. It depicts Sight, one of the Five Senses, and reads 'Alfred ordered me to be made'. It is perhaps the head of a decorated book marker.

The Danelaw

Later that year as they had promised at Aller, the remains of the Viking army left Chippenham and Wessex for good. They moved back into the area they had devastated in 877 to winter in the old Roman town of Cirencester, where they stayed for the next year. In 879 they went to East Anglia (from where they had begun their attack on Wessex), shared out the land and settled there as farmers.

In 886 Alfred formally recognised their presence in northern and eastern England in a treaty with Guthrum which sealed the partition of Anglo-Saxon England into areas where English and Danish law ran. We might compare it to the modern partition of Palestine, and its first thirty years (and more) were just as acrimonious. Alfred's treaty says that the boundary between the English and the Viking zones went 'up the Thames (to London) and up the river Lea, along the Lea to its source and then in a straight line to Bedford, then up the Ouse to Watling Street'. To the north and east of Watling Street the political influence of Danish settlers and Danish army organisation predominated. Here Scandinavian law was enacted, and hence this part of England became known as the Danelaw.

The Danes were a mercantile people, and as early as the 880s they planted towns in the East Midlands where they could buy and sell their produce and import goods. Some of these became the wealthiest centres in England after London and York. The 'Five Boroughs' in particular (that is, Lincoln, Stamford, Derby, Nottingham and Leicester) became a kind of Viking republic, ruled by their own 'army' councils, with their own lawmen and merchant class.

The Danish settlement of the east and north of England created a social revolution which permanently affected language and custom. Its marks are still with us today: in the Danish place-names of Lincolnshire and Yorkshire; in the surviving Danish words in farming dialect in the Lincolnshire wolds and the hills of north-west Yorkshire. In time the descendants of these settlers would become part of the Anglo-Danish nation ruled by Alfred's grandson. But for Alfred this new, vital but violent element in English history was to preoccupy him for the rest of his life. In 878, with the salvation of Wessex behind him, and already at 29 years of age a hard-bitten and successful king, Alfred could for the first time look to the future.

'What of the cities and towns he restored, and the others which he built where none had been before?'

It is one thing to win a war, another matter entirely to use the peace constructively. There had been great warleaders before Alfred's day. What distinguishes him from any other Anglo-Saxon king was the combination of his military ability with an originality of mind, a breadth of vision. In the same way that Charlemagne had done on the continent, Alfred added a new dimension to English kingship. His conception of royal authority, developed by his powerful and gifted successors Edward and Athelstan, made acceptable to most people the extension of the tribal kingdom of Wessex into the kingdom of England, with territorial limits roughly the same as they are today. Where Offa's

Restoring cities: a tenth-century picture of a stone stronghold. Alfred's burhs were usually of wood and earth, though he built halls in stone.

empire foundered on brutality to the regions, Alfred seems to have been the first king who identified himself with the English irrespective of local affiliations. In short, it is what Alfred achieved *after* his victory which raises him to the ranks of greatness.

Alfred's first revolution lay in the planning of towns, and our knowledge of what he did has been the single greatest contribution made by archaeology to our understanding of Anglo-Saxon history in the last two decades. There had been fortified centres in Wessex before Alfred, and in building small burhs like Athelney in West Somerset in 878, Alfred was perhaps consciously acting in the tradition of his father. But here the seeds were laid of the great urban expansion in southern England which took place in the next fifty years, a planned scheme of national defence where fortified towns were laid out for permanent settlement, their military strength founded on economic success and a growing urban population. This plan was probably well under way by 890 and had far-reaching effects after Alfred's death: in fact it is probably the most remarkable achievement of the Anglo-Saxon state.

Recent discoveries by historians and archaeologists show that the recovery of urban life in England in the tenth century was the result of deliberate royal planning rather than organic growth, the conscious creation of towns as centres for refuge, defence and commercial life. They were called burhs. It entailed laying out completely new rectilinear street patterns and apportioning plots to settlers who were to provide the manning and maintenance of the defences in time of war.

WAREHAM IN
DORSET: A CLASSIC
EXAMPLE OF LATE
SAXON TOWN
PLANNING

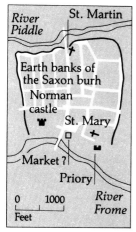

We are particularly well informed about the building and manning of
the burhs because we have a document called the *Burghal Hidage* which
dates from within twenty years of Alfred's death. It lists twenty-nine
burhs, with the units of taxable land attached to them, and this allows
us to calculate the length of wall surrounding the burh and the number
of men assigned to its defence. It is also possible to see the wider
strategy behind the system; the protection of the whole of Wessex so
that no part of the kingdom would be more than twenty miles from a
guarded centre with strongpoints on the main river routes inland which
the Viking ships with their shallow draughts had hitherto so devastat-
ingly exploited. Sometimes Alfred and his generals imitated the Frankish practice of building double forts on either river bank, completely
blocking the passage upstream.

Several of the Alfredian burhs are still well preserved today, notably
Cricklade near Cirencester (where the Thames was diverted to streng-
then the defences), Wallingford near Oxford, and in particular
Wareham in Dorset. Anyone visiting them cannot but be impressed by
the sheer scale of their ramparts. At Wareham the massive western
banks were pressed back into service as antitank ditches in 1940! In
Wareham the regular town plan also survives, a testimony to the social
engineering undertaken by Alfred and his successors; with its two
Anglo-Saxon churches, Wareham gives a fine impression of an Anglo-
Saxon town with modern urban life still contained within the ninth-
century defences.

At Winchester an important series of excavations during the 1960s
showed most clearly the royal direction at the heart of the burghal
system. Here the street plan was shown to be a development of Alfred's
reign, with a grid pattern resembling but not following the Roman street
alignment which entailed the laying of 15,000 tons of flints. In the
cathedral area, the former Roman praetorium, was the greatest collection of Anglo-Saxon royal buildings yet uncovered: the Old Minster,
chief church of the royal family, Alfred's palace, and the churches built
by his wife and son. Fragments of decoration from the stone-built royal
hall show that it contained figured wall painting of the kind known in
Carolingian palaces.

At the other end of the scale, some of the *Burghal Hidage* forts were
tiny. Lyng, for instance, near Athelney, is credited with only 140 yards
of defences. Bishop Asser also adds that Alfred built a causeway 'of
marvellous workmanship' between Lyng and Athelney and fortified
them both.

Go to Lyng today and these bare facts come to life in the clearest
possible way. Lyng is still joined to Athelney by a raised causeway,
though the land around is now drained. The long, narrow housing plots
on either side of the promontory road preserve the line of the medieval

property boundaries, and perhaps even go back to the Anglo-Saxon plan. At the western end of the village, in the orchard below the church, the remains of a massive ditch are still visible, formerly 25 feet deep and surmounted by a palisade. The defences simply cut off the approach to Athelney along the promontory from marsh to marsh, and can still be paced out at 140 yards, precisely the assessment given in the *Burghal Hidage*. The church on its raised platform may originally also have been built at this time, and its west end would have formed a solid bastion on which to anchor the defences. Lyng never developed beyond a few cottages, nor was it intended to, but it was a refuge for the people of this part of West Somerset, and it is a telling part of the story.

The seizure of London

London was the largest trading settlement in England. It was also a Mercian city, as it had been in Offa's day. In 886, according to the *Anglo-Saxon Chronicle* version sponsored by Alfred, the king *gesette* London, which means either that he occupied it, or that he settled it (that is, with West-Saxon settlers, as he had done at other burhs). Unfortunately there are other problems of interpretation involved in this, and these have considerable bearing on our view of Alfred.

As we have seen, until *c.* 880 Mercia had been ruled by a king, Ceolwulf, who had been set up as a puppet by the Danes in 874 when they wintered at Repton. The West-Saxon chronicler is openly contemptuous of Ceolwulf, calling him a 'foolish king's thegn'. This insult may have been a deliberate attempt by Alfred to impugn Ceolwulf's legitimacy as a king. In fact Ceolwulf's name could indicate that he was a scion of that branch of the Mercian royal house which produced King Ceolwulf I, though Alfred had every reason to suppress this in the record in order to justify the West-Saxon takeover in Mercian London.

Ceolwulf died around 880, but not long before that, coins had been produced by a Mercian moneyer in London for both Ceolwulf ('king') and Alfred ('king of the English'). So Alfred clearly had some authority in London earlier than he says in the *Anglo-Saxon Chronicle*. Had he seized it by violence? Some versions of the *Anglo-Saxon Chronicle* mention a siege in 883. Other writers say the seizure involved fighting, 'the burning of cities and the massacre of peoples' (Bishop Asser); Florence of Worcester's *Chronicle*, which drew from a source unknown to us, says that Alfred 'recovered London with its surrounding territories by force, and acquired that part of the Mercian kingdom which Ceolwulf had held'. And although the *Anglo-Saxon Chronicle* asserts that all the English of London and its area who were not subject to the Danes

Alfred's London coin revealing his partnership with the pro-Danish Ceolwulf of Mercia, *c.* 875–883. The reverse is modelled on Maximus' London coin (page 41).

submitted to Alfred, Aethelweard adds that this had followed 'savage internal war' in which Alfred had been unconquered 'either by guile or open opposition'. Our accounts also all agree that when Alfred had occupied London he entrusted it to his son-in-law earldorman Ethelred of English Mercia. What are we to make of all this? Clearly the fall of London to Alfred followed some sort of struggle, but against whom? Modern historians have been curiously reluctant to think that 'England's darling' might have wrested London from the Mercians, and they assume that the Danes were his enemies. But the situation may have been more complicated than that. For instance, up till his death, Ceolwulf of Mercia may have been able to call on Danish military aid *against* Alfred if the occasion arose, and it may have done so in *c*. 880. In this case the chronicle account of the occupation of 886 may deliberately conceal a bitter piece of power politics some years before. We should never forget that to some Mercians in the 880s, defeat by their ancient foes, the West Saxons, may have seemed as unpleasant a prospect as Danish overlordship.

London restored

The London triumph of 886. A London monogram on the reverse of the coin, and a Roman imperial portrait on the obverse. The West-Saxon hold on the richest city in western Europe was now assured.

Soon after 886, under Alfred's rule, the walls of London were repaired, the town was repopulated with new settlers who received regular plots of land bounded by new streets, inaugurating the street plan we know today between Cheapside and the river Thames. Here a network of streets survived unchanged until the Great Fire, and the shape of Alfred's plots (established between 889 and 898) can still be seen in the *A-Z of London*.

Other evidence of Alfred's interest in London has recently been discovered by archaeologists on the waterfront around London Bridge. Immediately downstream from the bridge the quay was rebuilt in this period with a boxed structure of heavy timbers erected in front of the Roman jetty which in one place was cut up and removed. At the bridgehead itself (which linked London with the burh in Southwark) the adjoining river-bank was reinforced with a hedgehog of wooden stakes which probably served a twofold purpose: first, to encourage silting and prevent erosion of the bridge supports, second, to make a landing at the bridgehead from the river impossible.

The archaeological evidence for Alfred's London is slight, but it conforms with the known fact that the city boomed as a commercial centre in the tenth century, and it encourages us to think that the early markets and the wharfs at Billingsgate and Queenhythe which are only mentioned in the later tenth century, date back at least to the late ninth century.

'They considered the youth of this age happy, who could have the good fortune to be trained in the liberal arts . . .'

Alfred's second great revolution is the one which has most impressed posterity, and indeed it is the one which enables us to get nearer to the man himself. The educational system of Anglo-Saxon England, which was founded on the great monasteries, was virtually totally destroyed by the Viking invasions. Though it has been fashionable in recent years to play down the destructive effect of the Vikings and to stress their role as traders and craftsmen, there is not the slightest doubt that in the ninth century the disruption they caused was tremendous. We do not need to rely merely on the testimony of Alfred's own words to know that there was a decline of learning. The evidence is clear in the falling standard of book production, in the deterioration of handwriting, the decline of the charter as an instrument of royal government. It is also apparent in the increasingly poor quality of the Latin, the language of government. Manuscripts of the late ninth century and the early tenth are often characterised by ludicrous misconstruings and specious word divisions; popular taste in fiction in churches of the time centred on the most pathetic and threadbare kind of eastern fairy tale – *Solomon and Saturn, Marvels of the East, Alexander's Letter to Aristotle* – which lacked any insight about foreign lands and cultures. Most of all a low standard of learning is implied in their audience by the additions that Alfred had to make in his translation of Bede's *History*: their world had narrowed so much that the average thegn or cleric in Wessex no longer knew the location of some of the most famous sites in Christian Northumbria.

The loss of education signified a decline in rulership. As Charlemagne had recognised, learning is power, and the relation of education and language to political life is central to Alfred's second revolution. It had become essential to restore the language, and it is interesting to see how this recovery of literacy complements the extension of the West-Saxon empire after Alfred's time.

Latin had been the instrument of government and of literate culture, but, says Alfred in the preface to his translation of the *Pastoral Care*:

> So general was its decay in England that there were very few on this side of the Humber who could understand their rituals in English or translate a letter from Latin into English; and I believe there were not many beyond the Humber. There were so few that I cannot remember a single one south of the Thames when I came to the throne.

Alfred pointedly ignores the Mercian tradition of scholarship built up under Offa which was still vigorous enough in the ninth century to provide Alfred with the scholars he needed to make his translations for him. But he felt disinclined to praise the Mercian achievement. He was an ambitious man with a purpose. His aim was simple enough. He

123

would translate from the Latin into Anglo-Saxon a handful of books he thought it 'most needful for men to know'.

The books he chose all had relevance for his time. There was Bede's story of the conversion of the pagan English to Christianity, the *Ecclesiastical History of the English People*; Gregory the Great's *Pastoral Care*, a handbook for bishops explaining their duties (though reading Alfred's additions it is difficult to avoid the impression that he saw the jobs of kings and bishops as similar – a king should also teach his flock). There was a work of history written by a Spanish priest Orosius in order to explain the fall of the Roman empire which early Christians had believed was founded, in the divine scheme of things, to propagate Christianity and usher in the millennium. Orosius showed that history is full of terrors and that humanity suffers, and his narrative must have appealed to Alfred in that it went beyond a traditional Anglo-Saxon heroic view of the past and tried to make sense of the human condition in Christian terms: a potent message for the war years of the 890s. Other works were philosophical, St Augustine's *Soliloquies* and Boethius' *Consolation of Philosophy*. To these books we might also add the *Anglo-Saxon Chronicle* itself, the story of Alfred's own dynasty and their unbroken success story leading up to the battle of Edington. Even today, you could do worse than be left with this handful of books with their wealth of moral and historical knowledge.

> I began amid the manifold troubles of this kingdom to translate into English the book called in Latin *Pastoralis* and in English *Shepherd's Book*, sometimes word for word, sometimes according to the sense as I learned it from Plegmund my archbishop, Asser my bishop . . .

So they and their other helpers made the translations in a kind of seminar, speaking the text out loud, working it into Anglo-Saxon which a secretary would note down. Copies were then made in the scriptorium of the Old Minster in Winchester and sent to all the bishops in the kingdom. The copy of the *Pastoral Care* in the Bodleian, Oxford, went to Worcester and charred fragments of the original 'office' copy survive in the British Library: two copies written in Alfred's lifetime under his direction.

Why do it? Why did a middle-aged, sick man who acquired literacy only painfully in later life feel impelled to take on this laborious task? Partly, of course, there was the influence of the Church. By Alfred's time the Church had a considerable say in the style and even the ideas of kingship, and it was thought paradoxically that a king who promoted learning (and, *ipso facto*, Christianity) would prosper at home and in warfare abroad. But there must be more to it than that. Although their clerical biographers liked to claim otherwise, men like Alfred and Charlemagne were not ruled in every aspect of their lives by the Church.

124

They were men of pragmatic intelligence, and they understood that if your concept of kingship is wider than tribal relations, if you wish to make law, impose taxes, create longer-term provisions and obligations in social life, then you must correct the language. Otherwise your meaning is unclear, your purposes are not understood and justice goes astray.

To embark on such a systematic programme of instruction at such a time was the act of a remarkable man, practical, resolute, and ruthless: he took on himself not only the strain of defence but also concern for the future lives of his subjects. That is why, alone among English kings, he is 'the Great', and why he has rightly never lost the esteem of the English-speaking world.

'Both for the living and for those yet unborn'

Because of modern archaeological discoveries we are now coming to understand more about Alfred, not merely as a warrior, or even as a thinker, but as a far-sighted man who was capable of carrying out long-term administrative reforms which had the widest implications. When near his death he composed his preface to the *Consolation of Philosophy*, he had come a long way from the neurotic and impulsive youth of Ashdown. Through the fire of Athelney and Edington he did more than become a man. He became a man who saved the essential Englishness of our culture and language.

> What I set out to do was to virtuously and justly administer the authority given me. I desired the exercise of power so that my talents and my power might not be forgotten. But every natural gift and every capacity in us soon grows old and is forgotten if wisdom is not in it. Without wisdom no faculty can be fully brought out, for any thing done unwisely cannot be accounted as skill. To be brief, I may say that it has always been my wish to live honourably, and after my death to leave to those who come after me my memory in good works.

A silver disc brooch of Alfred's time depicting the Five Senses. 'You each have something divine in your soul,' he wrote, 'namely Reason and Memory and a discerning Will to make choices in life.'

—— CHAPTER 6 ——

ATHELSTAN

The very celebrated king who by the Grace of God ruled all England, which prior to him many kings shared between them.

From a list of relics given by Athelstan
to the Church of St Peter in Exeter

Of all the characters in this book, Athelstan will be the least familiar to the general reader, merely another name from the satirical history, *1066 and All That*. But in the Middle Ages he was more famous than any of the people referred to here. For the twelfth-century antiquarian harking back to a golden Anglo-Saxon past, Athelstan was the great king par excellence, an English Charlemagne whose court was a byword for glamour, glory and gold. After the Norman Conquest there were popular sagas and stories about him. In the fourteenth century he figured in several Middle English poetic romances and was the protagonist of one, *Athelston*. He even trod the boards of Shakespeare's stage, in Thomas Dekker's *Old Fortunatus*, revelling with 'the great Cham of Tartarie' before Elizabeth I during Christmas 1599. (This was ironic because the Tudors claimed to have restored the ancient British line which Athelstan had subjugated.)

The reason for the king's long-lasting fame in popular tradition and his relatively poor showing in modern history books make a fascinating story. The explanation might lie in the nature of his accession, for like Offa, he came to the throne in dubious circumstances, but unlike Offa he did not rewrite history to justify the fact. As a result the traditionalists of the West-Saxon royal house in the churches of Winchester, the men who shaped the historiography and the genealogies of the Alfredian royal line, seem to have maintained an ambivalent attitude to him and played down his achievements in favour of the true Alfredian-Edwardian line. Indeed were it not for the historian, William of Malmesbury, having excerpted parts of a now lost life of the king in the 1130s, we would know very little indeed about the king's military achievements, or of the great prestige he had in Europe. As it is, we know enough of his deeds to see that his reign was of central importance in the development of the Anglo-Saxon 'state'.

Athelstan is also of particular interest to us because, although it

Athelstan presents a book to St Cuthbert; our earliest royal portrait, of *c*. 935. Modelled closely on continental imperial pictures, this suggests how much the king wanted to be seen as a new Charlemagne.

would be fruitless to try to write a biography of him in modern terms, a number of 'biographical' artefacts survive which bring us close to his life. For instance, many of the books and some of the treasures he owned and gave away as gifts can still be seen today. A contemporary painting of him exists – the first of any English monarch. We know he was a connoisseur and collector of books, art and relics – in fact he has been called the Pierpont Morgan of his age! From these works, and his

127

'Queen of hilltop towns': Malmesbury seen from the far side of the Avon. The monastic precinct covered the whole of the hill as far as St Paul's spire; the defences of the burh ran where the upper row of houses lies today.

inscriptions in them, we can find out something of his beliefs and tastes. We have too his personal comments taken down by a secretary during the process of law making, the drawing up of law codes, which perhaps give us a truer insight into the difficulties medieval kings had in promoting justice than the ideal enunciated by Alfred. These passages in the laws show that Athelstan is the one Anglo-Saxon king, who, for cast of mind, will bear comparison with Alfred. We could wish to know more of a man who so dominated his age, but the fragmentary evidence we have is enough to demonstrate that if Offa gave form to the idea, and Alfred laid the foundation, Athelstan turned their aspirations into fact, a kingdom of all the English.

A royal burial mystery

To uncover the tangled web of intrigue behind Athelstan's accession in 925 we go first to Malmesbury in Wiltshire, on what was then the border between Wessex and Mercia. This is where Athelstan is buried. In the tenth century it was a burh in the Alfredian system of forts, a fine natural stronghold on a steep hill in a loop of the Avon. Here was one of

128

the most famous monastic sites in Anglo-Saxon England with three churches built in the seventh and eighth centuries. The place had been a great centre of learning, and its monastic library had in part survived the Viking raids. Athelstan was especially devoted to St Aldhelm who was buried here in 709. Claiming the saint as his ancestor, Athelstan gave the church land, rebuilt the monastic buildings, commissioned a costly shrine for the saint, and gave it Breton relics along with a piece of the True Cross sent him by Hugh the Great, Duke of the Franks. As he had instructed in his will, Athelstan was interred here. But the burial was unusual since almost all the kings of the Alfredian line were buried in Winchester or Glastonbury. Why wasn't Athelstan?

The ruined fragment of the great abbey at Malmesbury finished in 1180; this replaced the earlier church rebuilt by Athelstan. As elsewhere, the Normans were quick to remove the Anglo-Saxon legacy.

Athelstan's birth and ancestry

He was born around 895, the first child of Alfred's eldest son Edward, the future king. Before his death, Alfred had given his young grandson regalia of kingship, a Saxon sword and belt, with a royal cloak. But such gestures did not mean much in a world where succession crises were the stuff of royal life. Athelstan's mother was noble, perhaps Mercian, but whether she was married to Athelstan's father is doubtful and certainly Athelstan was not 'born in purple', that is, when Edward was king. Edward later married twice, and these wives were successively acknowledged as queen where Athelstan's mother had not been. Later legends grew up in plenty about this, with tales that the king's mother was a beautiful shepherdess who foresaw in a dream that her illegitimate son would one day be king of England. But at the time it was widely known that Athelstan's birth was doubtful. In Germany, for instance, it was said that Edward's other sons and daughters were the children of queens of royal descent, whereas Athelstan's mother was not of high birth; she was 'an inferior consort', that is, not a wife.

Succession crisis

Athelstan was brought up in the house of his aunt Aethelflaed, Alfred's daughter, who was married to ealdorman Aethelred of Mercia, so his background and his contacts were Mercian not West-Saxon, and this explains much of his success. His education was also Mercian, presumably in the school attached to the monastery at Worcester, and he is the first king of his line who we know was literate from childhood. It is possible that his father intended Athelstan to be a 'Lord of the Mercians' rather than king of England, for according to Winchester sources (one of which omits Athelstan's reign altogether) Edward had made Aelfweard, the eldest son of his first queen, king in his own lifetime. This seems confirmed by a later king list which gives Aelfweard a reign of four weeks. So it would appear that our history books have failed to mention a West-Saxon king. Edward died on 17 July 924, and Aelfweard lasted only sixteen days after him, though whether or not his death was through foul play we have no means of knowing. A succession crisis now developed. Evidently the West-Saxon councillors were more disposed to favour another of Edward's sons (perhaps Aelfweard's next brother Edwin) but the Mercians felt Athelstan was their man and at a great meeting at Offa's old centre of Tamworth attended by the Mercian bishops and all their magnates, they elected him king. Athelstan was the oldest and the most experienced in warfare of Edward's sons; perhaps he was the obvious candidate, but events took time to resolve themselves. It was not until the summer of 925 that he was generally accepted as king, the West-Saxon councillors having overlooked the other brothers and elected him. Even so, Athelstan narrowly escaped an attempt to seize and blind him which took place in Winchester with the alleged connivance of his brother the atheling Edwin.

Over thirteen months after his father's death Athelstan was crowned.

He was now in his thirtieth year. Remarkably, there seems to have been a careful effort to preserve the legitimate Alfredian succession. The story brought back to Cologne by a German ambassador in 929 was that Athelstan was a kind of caretaker king, bringing up the princes born to the true queens, and in Malmesbury there was a tradition that Athelstan deliberately remained celibate and brought up the young athelings, his half-brothers, grooming them for the kingship and then raising them as joint-kings in his lifetime, as his father had done. But even this did not stop attempted coups against Athelstan.

In 933 Athelstan's brother Edwin, who may have had the title of 'king', was involved in some political disturbance and drowned while escaping to exile in France. In the event the sons of Edward's second queen succeeded in their turn, so just as the West-Saxon royal family in the ninth century had made provision for the succession and the integrity of the royal property, Athelstan in his turn seems to have protected the blood royal and literally husbanded the patrimony. His burial at Malmesbury rather than at Winchester or Glastonbury is a symbol of his anomalous position in the royal house. But even the most grudging of the Winchester hard-liners would have to admit that he did them proud.

'Consecrated with holy oil': the coup legitimised

The coronation at Kingston on 4 September 925 was therefore as much a public demonstration of the result of a power struggle as a smooth changeover stage-managed by the West-Saxon establishment. As we saw with Offa and Alfred, no early medieval king ever simply succeeded to his kingdom as a matter of course. You might be born of the royal line, be the acknowledged heir even, but you still had to be made into a king. When the personal power of the previous king ended with his death, more often than not 'hungry athelings began to prowl' as one modern scholar has put it. Athelstan's coronation in 925 showed he had won the 'political' victory; the other prowlers would remain athelings, although 'born in the purple'. Not surprisingly then, Athelstan's advisers, the men who had backed him against his brothers, followed the line of ninth-century Frankish thought on kingship by anointing him, by making the king (like a bishop) in a special way consecrated to God; emphasising that the man and the job were not the same thing, and that the job carried great responsibilities. The Carolingians thought that anointing was indispensable to kingship, that you were 'anointed to rule', and that if you were not anointed, you were 'a sword without a handle'. The bishops therefore played an important role in augmenting the power and charisma of kingship, and it was natural that in Athelstan's case, with his disputed succession, his bishops should adopt Carolingian practice, both to boost and to bind him.

Of the coronation church at Kingston, archaeology has yielded few details. It lay in a typical Carolingian-style complex consisting of royal and episcopal palaces on a great royal estate with a sheep farm, mills and a stud. The church was built of stone, probably on the continental pattern with a western balcony-chapel on the second floor where the kings could be shown to the people. A version of the actual order of service used by Athelstan survives in Paris in the National Library, and shows that the king was consecrated as 'king of the Anglo-Saxons', anointed with holy oil and bestowed with the royal regalia, finger ring, sword, crown, sceptre and staff: in pictures he is later portrayed with crown and sceptre. Athelstan also made a threefold promise: to keep his people in peace, to forbid robbery and wrongdoing by all men, no matter how high in society, and to promote justice and mercy through the rule of law. These were not merely pious hopes; they touched on the biggest social problems Anglo-Saxon kings faced in the tenth century.

Before he left the church, Athelstan performed other symbolic acts, which were not actually part of the coronation ceremony. First he restored to the cathedral church of Canterbury an estate in Thanet which had been taken from them during the emergency requisitioning during the Viking wars: a tacit acknowledgement of the help afforded him by the head church. Then at the high altar he freed a slave called Eadhelm and his children, a public act of royal humility and generosity often performed by Dark Age kings for the good of their soul.

After this the king could be shown to the people in full glory. Then he retired to the great hall of the palace for the coronation banquet,

> overflowing with splendour, resounding with tumult, wine being poured everywhere, pages scurrying to and fro, servers speeding on their tasks, stomachs filled with delicacies, minds with song.
>
> (William of Malmesbury *On the Deeds of the English Kings*)

Some parts of the service used in Athelstan's coronation were employed in the same ceremony for his distant kinswoman Elizabeth II over 1000 years later. There has not in fact been continuity of use: the twentieth-century ritual was revived as a deliberate expression of the Victorian empire at the coronation of Edward VII, a conscious piece of antiquarianism. Few would claim today that the political, legal and religious concepts of 1901, let alone those of post-war Britain, are expressed in the Anglo-Saxon inauguration ritual apart from the generalised emotions of patriotism, the appeal to a glorious past, and the colour of the ceremonial. But these beautiful and complex rituals, so rich in symbolism, were the subject of intense interest to the participants in 925, and can be seen as a precipitate of the beliefs and aspirations of Athelstan's supporters, both in a 'political' sense, and in the way they conceived of their relation to the divine order.

When Athelstan went to bed that night in the royal chamber at Kingston, surrounded by his armed followers (remembering there had been an attempt to blind him at Winchester before the coronation), he was a different man. He was now a 'warrior of God', an 'athlete of Christ', not quite king and priest, perhaps, but not far off it, the orthodoxly consecrated 'friend and guardian of all the Christians in Britain'. But he was also king in the traditional Anglo-Saxon way, 'ring-giver', 'plunder-lord', 'shelterer of warriors'. The secular *and* church lords who had heard his praises sung at the feast now wanted Athelstan to act 'according to their expectations . . . not to fall short of their desires'. Now he had to prove himself a 'deed-doer'.

And what was it that Athelstan's backers wanted? The extension of the kingdom, the accretion of their own wealth and status, that much seems clear. Athelstan did not disappoint them. In 927 he began a *blitzkrieg* which took West-Saxon arms over the whole of Britain.

The Conquest of Britain

> First king of the English to subdue all the nations within Britain under his arms, though none of his successors extended the boundaries of the empire further than he did.
>
> The 'Altitonantis' charter (964?)

In the north there had been dramatic changes since the Danish invasions of Alfred's day. New waves of Norwegian and Norse-Irish Vikings had inundated the north-west, altering for ever the racial characteristics of Cumbria and Westmorland. In 919 a powerful Norse-Irish Viking dynasty from Dublin, known as the Clan Ivar, had seized York and now ruled there, minting their own coins and engaging in diplomacy with the North Welsh kings, and those of Scotland, Cumbria and Strathclyde. All these kings were alarmed by the rise of the powerful kingdom of Alfred's line in southern England. Soon after his coronation Athelstan met the Viking king of York, Sihtric of the Clan Ivar, at Tamworth, and gave him his sister in marriage, procuring Sihtric's adoption of Christianity as part of the bargain. But when Sihtric died early in 927 it became clear that Athelstan had never intended an independent Viking Northumbria to continue. He invaded Northumbria, expelled Sihtric's son Anlaf and his brother Guthfrith, and entered York, demolishing the Danish fortifications and seizing huge booty which he distributed to his army. It was a historic moment, for a southern king had never directly ruled in York before, and entries in their chronicles show that even Anglo-Saxon traditionalists north of the

Humber viewed the turn of events in the same way as we feel about the Russian invasion of Czechoslovakia. 'We were never subject to any of the kings of the South Angles before Athelstan'.

York was only the beginning. That summer Athelstan rode up the Great North Road, attacked Bamburgh and drove out the Anglo-Saxon earl Ealdred Ealdulfing, who had ruled north of the Tees almost like an independent king. Ealdred became Athelstan's man and was reinstated. Meanwhile ambassadors had been sent to the north British kings who had given help to the Viking fugitives from York. Under threat of war they too submitted – Constantine, king of the Scots, Owain, king of the Cumbrians, and probably (though he is not mentioned) Constantine's brother Donald, king of the Strathclyde Welsh. Their submission was the prelude to 'all the kings of the island' becoming Athelstan's men.

12 July 927. *Aurora Borealis*: 'fiery lights in the northern sky'. Eamont Bridge in Cumbria, the site of the first great 'imperial' council of the tenth century. The northern kings and the Bamburgh dynasty gave up their kingdoms and were reinstated as tributaries in a ceremony on what was the northern border of the English kingdom. Eamont was a great Roman road junction twenty miles south of Carlisle, and Athelstan was establishing his frontier along the Eamont, Ullswater, and across the fells and down the Duddon to the sea. In so doing he was cutting back the expansion of the northern kings who had reached their rule deep into northern England during the Viking era. 'They established a covenant of peace with pledges and oaths,' says the *Anglo-Saxon Chronicle*, 'and then separated in concord.' The kings gave each other rich gifts, and Athelstan received Constantine's son from the font having ordered him to be baptised.

The kings of Wales surrender: 'The English are over-proud'

From Cumbria Athelstan rode south during July and launched an attack on the North Welsh kings, who, having given nominal submission to his father, seem now to have come out in open hostilities. They resisted him for some time but then risked warfare and were defeated and driven into flight. (Some of them, that is. For the Welsh kings included the Anglophile, Hywel Dda, 'the Good', who always cooperated with the English kings. Hywel's kinsmen fought a bitter struggle for supremacy within Wales throughout this period with the anti-English line in Gwynedd, and this dynastic rivalry was cynically exploited by the West-Saxon kings to aid their domination of the Welsh kingdoms.)

The king who led the resistance against Athelstan in 927 was Idwal Foel of Gwynedd, grandson of the 'nationalist' Rhodri the Great and the protagonist of contemporary anti-English poetry (Idwal was eventually killed by the West Saxons in 942). The upshot of these events was that all five kings who ruled within Wales met Athelstan at Hereford, acknowledged his overlordship as 'mechteyrn' (Great King) and agreed to pay him a huge yearly tribute: 20 pounds of gold, 300 pounds of silver, 25,000 oxen, and as many hawks and hounds as the king wished. Nothing could be more indicative of the crushing scale of Athelstan's victory over the Welsh than the size of this tribute, and an inflamed, astonished Welsh reaction to it appears in the contemporary poem 'Armes Prydein'.

The last of the kings of Cornwall: 'sorrow springs from a world upturned'

Athelstan had not finished. He now attacked the 'West Welsh', the Britons of Cornwall, crushed their opposition, deported the dissident minority, established a new boundary at the Tamar, and refurbished the Roman walls of Exeter. Here we have some measure of what he did in the city. In his father's day the circuit was assessed at 1200 yards, which probably represents an enclosure in the north-west corner of the Roman city, bounded by Queen Street and High Street. Apparently Athelstan now restored the whole of the Roman circuit, though no late Saxon work has yet been identified in Exeter's walls. Perhaps also at this time the city was replanned and resettled with West Saxons: according to William of Malmesbury Athelstan actually expelled the Britons from the city. This smacks of modern social engineering, yet Athelstan was remembered in Cornwall not as a conquering warlord but as the benefactor of their churches. He created a new bishopric for Cornwall at St Germans, and visited Exeter several times in the next twelve years, building a new minster there and richly endowing it with lands and holy relics.

'Guardian of Britain'

Historians have thought that these campaigns may have taken place over a number of years. But if the order of events given by William of Malmesbury is right (and his source was the now lost life of Athelstan), then they were completed between July 927 and April 928. A great court was held at Exeter over Easter 928, and this probably signifies the successful conclusion to Athelstan's conquest of Britain. 'At Eastertime in the royal fortress called Exeter, rejoicing with great festivities, King Athelstan and his subkings, bishops, earls, judges, chiefs and dignitaries . . .' The dating clause of the charter which records this meeting asserts that this is, 'there is no doubt', the third year of Athelstan's reign. Among the witnesses were not only Idwal Foel of Gwynedd, but a subking, Wurgeat, and a Howel who may be the well-known king of Dyfed, but may be the 'Huwal, king of the West Welsh', that is, of the Cornish, mentioned in the *Anglo-Saxon Chronicle*. Wurgeat signed a charter in 932 on which two British bishops, Mancant and Conan (of Cornwall) attested, so perhaps we have here a last glimpse of the dynasty which (as we know from memorials like the stone of Ricatus in Penzance) persisted into the tenth century. The last independent kings of Cornwall.

It was 50 years to the week since Alfred the Great had built his stockade at Athelney, when the West-Saxon royal possessions were reduced to a few square miles of marsh in Somerset. Now his grandson was 'Emperor of the world of Britain'.

'Holy King Athelstan, renowned through the wide world'

Sitting on his throne in Exeter that Easter, Athelstan could permit himself a sigh of relief. There was, as his secretary wrote, 'no doubt' who was in charge now. He had made a clean sweep of his enemies and achieved what no king before him had done: the subjugation of the whole island. He was, in short, the most powerful man to rule in Britain since the Romans. Abroad, foreign rulers were impressed by what they

An Evangelist figure from a book given to Athelstan by Otto of Germany. Such gifts hastened the reception of foreign ideas and learning.

heard and sent him ambassadors bearing fantastic treasures to beg for his sisters in marriage: they brought the Holy Lance, the sword of Constantine, a classical vase of onyx 'carved so subtly that the corn sheaves seemed to stir, the vines to sprout, and the figures of the men to move' (William of Malmesbury *On the Deeds of the English Kings*). The books exchanged by Athelstan and Otto of Germany on the occasion of Otto's marriage to the West-Saxon Edith still survive in Coburg and in London, inscribed with the kings' names. Other foreign kings showed their respect by sending their sons to be fostered in the English court, among them Harald Finehair of Norway whose son Hakon was accompanied by a truly Viking gift: a splendid ship with gilded shields and, appropriately for an emperor, a purple sail.

These exchanges undoubtedly accelerated the relationship between Britain and Europe. At this time we find German clerics in several English houses, notably Abingdon, Canterbury and London, and the English translations of the Old High German epics based on the Old and New Testaments are perhaps to be associated with them. In Athelstan's service we find Irish bishops, a Breton soldier, an Icelandic poet, and the greatest continental scholar of his day, Israel the Grammarian.

Poets in particular were attracted by the kind of success that surrounded Athelstan, and the victories of 927 induced one German cleric to praise Athelstan by reworking a ninth-century poem on Charlemagne. It was a sign of the times. Kings with *magnanimitas* – greatness of soul – were few and far between on the continent, and their demise is lamented in Frankish legal and historical writing of the early tenth century. But our author sends his message across the sea to the royal palace, saluting the king, his chiefs and the 'Heavily armed troops' who by their warfare had subdued all Britain: 'King Athelstan lives, glorious through his deeds!'

Indeed this writer may not have been the only contemporary of Athelstan who thought him a new Charlemagne, for at about the same time a Frankish cleric wrote to Athelstan describing him as 'excelling in fame and honour all earthly kings of modern times' because he was among other things 'an exaltor of the holy Church, a smasher of enemies, a subduer of wicked barbarism'. In Norway he gained the nickname 'Athelstan the Victorious' and was called 'the greatest king in the northern world'. In Ireland, with whose churchmen Athelstan maintained close contact, he was remembered as the most honoured figure in the west. All of which was doubtless just what the king wished to hear.

An initial from a royal calendar produced in Athelstan's Winchester: classical styles return to insular art.

The king as lawmaker: 'father and lord'

Meanwhile Athelstan and his advisers had to respond rapidly to a new situation. They had come to a kingdom far larger than any predecessor's, and the problems of government were enormous, especially in a world where criminality was rife, secular magnates often resentful of interference, and life in general was nasty, brutish and short. What survives of his decrees suggests that Athelstan and his bishops attempted to rectify these abuses by holding great mixed councils, not merely to enforce the attendance of hostile subjects, but to confer over policy and make laws. We see, too, that no matter how successful a king was in the eyes of outsiders, he sometimes had to be told, bluntly, by his local representatives that law and order were being undermined and that he should do something about it: 'I have learnt that our peace is worse kept than I should like it . . . and my councillors say I have borne it too long.'

Lawmaking in particular was a crucial aspect of 'barbarian' kingship in the Dark Ages, and Athelstan's law codes are an important advance on the Mosaic, Old Testament, eye-for-an-eye brand of legislation created by Alfred. Here we see clearly the difference between 'tribal' thinking and the need to enact justice on a wider scale for a kingdom embracing different peoples, though whether Athelstan's laws were ever meant to apply in the Danish Midlands, let alone Northumbria, is unclear. Despite harsh penalties, and the ruthless transportation of persistent offenders, there is also the mitigating touch of humanity:

> The king has sent word to the archbishop by Bishop Theodred that it seemed too cruel to him that a man should be killed so young (ie, twelve years), or for so small an offence, as he had learnt was being done everywhere. He said then that it seemed to him and to those with whom he had discussed it, that no man younger than fifteen should be killed unless he tried to defend himself or fled . . .

Athelstan's law codes certainly reflect the desire to strengthen royal control in England, and other aspects of his work support this. The restriction of buying and selling to burhs was an important stage in developing urban life in places which had often begun life simply as strongpoints. Some of his father's forts disappear from the record altogether at this time, and it may be that conscious decisions were made by Athelstan not to encourage town life in some forts. Pilton and Halwell, for instance, were replaced as boroughs by Barnstaple and Totnes, which are in more favourable positions. The Alfredian burh at Eashing was closed down and a town was founded on a better site at Guildford. Hamwih was moved and refounded on the site where Southampton now stands. Like Exeter, Dorchester was probably restored by Athelstan, and we find him holding Christmas and Easter courts there. Other Alfredian and Edwardian boroughs seem to have been refurbished with new ditch systems and stone walls: Cricklade, Wareham, Lydford, Oxford, Wallingford, and possibly places in Mercia too, such as Hereford. All this can be seen as a continuation of a carefully thought-out long-term royal policy the origins of which, as we have seen, may have begun even before Alfred's time.

Of other changes in the English landscape we have no clear record, although it is probable that between the later years of Edward the Elder and the end of Athelstan's reign, the whole of Midland England was organised into shires, crystallising hundreds of years of local organisation into a fabric which lasted until the government reorganisation of 1974. In Western Mercia everything Offa knew was swept away though for a long time people still said that they lived in the Hwicce or the Magon saete. In the East Midlands the areas of settlement around the Danish towns were consolidated as shires, this being part of the process by which the Danish settlers of East Anglia and the east Midlands came by Athelstan's death to regard the West-Saxon king as their natural lord.

One coinage

The clearest example of this 'centralising' tendency is found in the

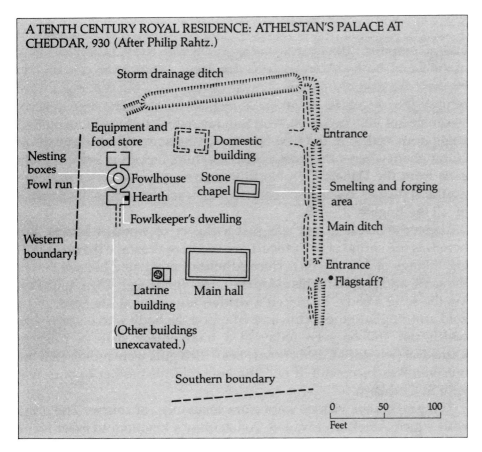

A TENTH CENTURY ROYAL RESIDENCE: ATHELSTAN'S PALACE AT CHEDDAR, 930 (After Philip Rahtz.)

Storm drainage ditch

Equipment and food store

Domestic building

Entrance

Nesting boxes

Fowl run

Fowlhouse

Hearth

Stone chapel

Smelting and forging area

Fowlkeeper's dwelling

Main ditch

Western boundary

Entrance

Latrine building

Main hall

Flagstaff?

(Other buildings unexcavated.)

Southern boundary

0   50   100
Feet

Below A silver penny minted by the moneyer Burdel of Norwich, *c.* 935. In York this type carried the legend *Rex To Bri* ('King of all Britain'), first ruler of an independent world of *Britannia* since the days of Magnus Maximus.

coins. Athelstan's coinage laws which controlled the number of moneyers at each city and borough and gave severe penalties for dodging the law, are the first in English history. 'There is to be one coinage over all the king's dominion, and no one is to mint money except in a town.' Although the coinage was organised on a regional basis, and differences in type were allowed to conform to local custom, Athelstan was able to keep a strong over-all control of weight and standard of silver. The king's determination to have a firm grip on the coinage is also reflected in his introduction through most of the country of the mint-names on the coins, a measure which made it easier to lay at the door of the guilty moneyer any of his products that fell short of the prescribed standard. That Athelstan was able to maintain such an organisation of currency is an obvious demonstration of his real power. It also backs up the archaeological evidence that town life was now beginning to pick up, and a monetary economy to be widely used for exchange; the privation and fiscal burdens of the war years under Alfred were now bearing fruit. 'From this period,' says an English writer of the 980s, 'there was peace and abundance of all things.'

Athelstan invades Scotland

Like all empires, Athelstan's was aggressive. In 934 Constantine, king of the Scots, broke his treaty with Athelstan. Whether he was already plotting Athelstan's overthrow we cannot say, but he must have refused to pay tribute. Athelstan's response was swift. A great army assembled at Winchester on Whit Sunday, which included four subject kings from Wales. In the next few days Athelstan rode northwards to Nottingham where other contingents met him, including Scandinavian earls from the Danelaw. In Northumbria he stopped off at the main northern shrines to solicit support from their saints as a fighter on behalf of 'all the English'.

Chester-le-Street in 934 was just a cluster of wooden hovels. But here was the shrine of St Cuthbert, moved here to escape the marauding Vikings of Alfred's day. Here Athelstan prostrated himself before the saint, and prayed for his aid in the forthcoming war. Then, uncovering the saint's body, he placed a written testament at his head, put a gold arm ring into the coffin, and wrapped the body with eastern silks which can still be seen today in a fragmentary state in Durham Cathedral (where St Cuthbert now lies). Rich gifts were promised if the outcome was successful; if not, the king told his brother to bury him with St Cuthbert.

The prayers for victory were extra insurance, of course. The army with which Athelstan invaded Constantine's kingdom to exact fealty and retribution was overwhelming. It was 'an army drawn from the whole of Britain' according to the cleric at Chester-le-Street who wrote an account of the war. The Welsh subkings had brought their own contingents to war, as was their due to their overlord. As they rode north they were accompanied by a powerful fleet of West-Saxon and Mercian sailors moving up the coast. Athelstan led his army deep into Scotland, Pictland and Cumbria, ravaging them from land and sea. An expression in a later Irish source indicates that the devastation included a 'preying' of stock to compensate Athelstan for the breach of faith. The expedition penetrated as far as Dunnottar, the dramatic rock-fortress of the Picts on the coast south of Aberdeen, and the English fleet reached the northernmost point of the mainland, striking at the Norse settlements in Caithness. There was no battle. The northern kings realised they could offer no resistance and surrendered their kingdoms to the English king. The sequel was only sketchily recorded in the south, but evidently there was a formal ceremony where Constantine and Owain were restored as tributaries in the presence of Athelstan and his allies in the pan-British coalition. Constantine gave his son as a hostage, renewed his submission and exchanged gifts. That done, 'the peace restored', Athelstan rode south, taking Constantine with him at least as

A detail from one of the stoles given by Athelstan to St Cuthbert's at Chester-le-Street in 934, discovered in the saint's coffin in 1827. Embroidered in gold and coloured threads on a silk base.

PICTS
Dunnottar
SCOTS
WESTERN ISLES
Perth (Fleet to Caithness)
STRATHCLYDE
WELSH
St. Andrews
Dumbarton
Edinburgh
LOTHIAN
Bamburgh

ULSTER
CUMBRIANS
Chester-Le-Street
Eamont Bridge
Armagh
NORTHUMBRIA
MAN
Ripon
York

Dublin
Chester
Lincoln
GWYNEDD
Derby
Nottingham
POWYS
Leicester
Tamworth
Stamford
Wexford
MERCIA
Thetford
Waterford
Hereford
EAST ANGLIA
St. Davids +
Brecknock
Buckingham
GWENT
DYFED
Gloucester
London
+
Malmesbury
Kingston
Llandaff
WESSEX
Winchester
WEST-WELSH
Exeter
+ St. Germans

0   50   100
Miles

THE ANGLO-SAXON EMPIRE UNDER ATHELSTAN
Showing the route of the Anglo-Saxon army in 934, from Winchester (28 May) back to Buckingham (12 September).

far as Buckingham, where the expedition watched Athelstan reward one of his army on 12 September, with the consent of Constantine 'underking'.

The events of 934 confirmed Athelstan's position at the apex of the hierarchy of rule in Britain. He was an emperor, a king who ruled other kings. He was, splendidly, '*basileus* and *curagulus*' (Greek titles used by the Byzantine emperor in Constantinople) of the whole world of Britain. To a Welsh writer he was a 'mechteyrn' or 'Great King' (God being the

141

mechteyrn of the universe; Athelstan would have devoutly accepted the analogy).

'Durbar' at Cirencester

Cirencester 935. The king held a great imperial assembly in the city which was 'formerly built by the Romans'. Five Celtic kings acknowledged his supremacy: Constantine, king of the Scots, Owain of Cumbria, and the Welshmen Howel, Idwal and Morgan, 'rejoicing under the wing of royal generosity'. What happened at these ceremonies is as yet unclear. We have the famous example of the 973 coronation at Bath and the submission at Chester when six kings rowed King Edgar on the Dee, but it has always been thought that this event was somehow unique. However, the events in 973 may not have differed so much from other 'hegemonial' ceremonies of the period. Excavations at Cirencester in 1965, for instance, discovered an unexpectedly large Anglo-Saxon church west of the present abbey, its massive foundations measuring 180 feet long by 52 feet wide, and which, therefore, is about the same proportions as Brixworth. Most interestingly, at the west end was found the foundation of a formidable structure – a tower, perhaps, with dimensions of about 22 feet by 28 feet. Like Brixworth, the church also had a ring crypt at the eastern end which probably dates it to not later than c. 850. Could Athelstan's ceremonies then have taken place in this church, and was this westwork used, like that at Bath, for a royal appearance?

If so, there was a special reason for their being in Cirencester. It was of course a Roman city with visible Roman walls and structures. It was a royal city, with a royal church. But it was from here according to a Welsh poem that the royal stewards collected their tribute from the Welsh. It may even be that the payment of tribute was one of the acts which the subject kings had to perform, in addition to 'bowing' to Athelstan, taking him 'as father and lord' and swearing to 'be his co-worker by land and sea'. This, along with the hostages, the baptisms, the enforced attendance at court, was the cement of the empire.

The grand alliance: 'we will pay them back for the 404 years'

It could not go on, of course. It was inevitable now that Athelstan's enemies would try to overthrow him. But as had been shown in 927 and 934, the Welsh kings and the North British kings could not do it alone. So a plan was formed to combine all his opponents in a grand alliance. The instigator was Constantine, king of the Scots, whom the English remembered as 'the hoary-headed traitor'. There was precedent for the cooperation of some of these mutually antagonistic peoples. Asser tells of the threat of Welsh alliance with the Northumbrian Danes in Alfred's day; the Dublin Danes had joined forces with the Scots kings on several occasions. Far back in the early Dark Ages, Penda of Mercia had brought East Angles and North Welsh against Oswy of Northumbria. But nothing of the scope of 937 had ever been attempted. Even the logistical problems seem daunting. Their aim was nothing less than to crush Athelstan with the manpower of the Celtic peoples and the Scandinavian settlements within the British Isles:

> There will be reconciliation between the Cymry and the men of Dublin,
> The Irish of Ireland and Anglesey and Scotland,
> The men of Cornwall and of Strathclyde will be made welcome among us
> . . .
> The Men of the North in the place of honour . . .
> The stewards of Cirencester will shed bitter tears . . . as an end to their taxes they will know death.

Such were the hopes of a Welsh cleric in Dyfed as the news of the coalition spread. The Welsh would drive out the 'Iwys', the West Saxons, and their allies the 'Mercian incendiaries', as far as Sandwich, where they first landed. And 'the foreigners of Dublin', the Vikings, 'will stand with us'. These lines are taken from the poem, the 'Armes Prydein', the most remarkable statement of the later Welsh heroic age. Here is not the elegiac lament of Catraeth or Pengwern, but a passionate revanchist prophecy speaking for a united Cymry. United, however, the Cymry proved not to be.

News of such moment must have passed quickly through the Irish Viking ports, Dublin, Wexford, Waterford, to Athelstan's rich entrepôt at Chester; from the Welsh citadels in Gwynedd and Powys to St David's and on to English frontier posts like Hereford and Shrewsbury. The manner in which these stories circulated is revealed in an imaginative school exercise written at precisely this time by a Celtic scribe in the

Part of the Celtic school exercise of c. 935 which tells prematurely of success in the 'Great Battle' against Athelstan (lines 2–3: *bellu(m) ingens*).

south-west. It is a classic Celtic scholastic dialogue, the schoolboy practising his Latin, the teacher asking questions. Asked where he has been, the boy says he has been studying in France, Ireland, and Celtic Britain. And what is the news? 'A great battle between the king of the Britons and the king of the Saxons' in which the latter suffers a catastrophic defeat, his friends left slaughtered on the battlefield. 'God gave victory to the Britons because they are humble and poor and confide in Him; the English however are proud and on account of their pride God humbled them.'

The plan

The plan of Constantine and Anlaf of Dublin depended on Northumbrian hostility to Athelstan's rule. They would not land their forces in southern England but in Northumbria where they knew they had supporters among the Anglo-Scandinavian aristocracy, men like Earl Orm and Archbishop Wulfstan of York himself (a resolute northerner whose story is told in more detail in the next chapter). Unfortunately there are no primary sources to tell us how they combined their armies, and the only apparently reliable fact – that they landed a great fleet in the Humber – has been disputed by many historians, though with no good reason (this detail derives from a chronicle written in York *c.* 1000).

The attack

The invaders' line of attack is uncertain. We cannot prove the story of the Humber landing, but it is probable. We can safely assume that they moved on traditional Viking routes. They certainly established themselves in Northumbria. The lost life of Athelstan quoted by William of Malmesbury says that the Northumbrians 'gave willing assent' to the invaders, 'the natives submitted, the whole region submitted . . .', and this fits with an Irish account of cooperation of Vikings within England.

It was late in the year. The weather was bad. 'Terrific winds', wrote one Irish monk in his tables. Anlaf Guthfrithson had still been in Ireland at the start of August when he pressganged a pirate fleet into his service, 'breaking their ships'. So the invasion came late in the year, and the final battle itself took place some time after 23 September (the exact date is unknown). In their campaign headquarters in York the invaders' plan seems to have been to consolidate themselves in Northumbria and then disaffect the Danish settlers in the eastern Midlands by ravaging south of the Humber. The lateness of the season suggests that they did not intend to strike into southern England until the next campaigning season. A final conjecture: we have no definite evidence on the movements of Idwal and the North Welsh; was the plan that he should attack

Athelstan's western flank? We cannot say, but the operation was grandly conceived. All depended on Athelstan now. What would he, 'the thunderbolt', do?

'Always before he had conquered by terror of his name alone'

Athelstan played a waiting game. At this point the poem quoted by William of Malmesbury surprisingly accuses him of nothing less than dereliction of duty. It says he 'spent idle hours' while the invaders ravaged his land, 'deeming his duty done'. What could have been the motive for such criticism? It is not impossible that the account was written as an exemplar for one of Athelstan's less effective successors, and the author obviously wanted to drive home his opinion that a king should be armed and vigilant, ready to immediately protect the 'farmers and poor people' who thought of him as their guardian and who were now being afflicted. A king should be, as another tenth-century poet put it, 'seated on a high watchtower, provident, wise and militant' keeping a lookout in readiness for war. This passage reminds us how much war was seen as a test of toughness and luck for a king. Vigour too was a prime quality in military expertise and the king was no longer young by the standards of his time. Maybe his contemporaries saw him as a hard-bitten and successful king who was having to display his nerve and his luck.

We can, though, explain the king's delay in moving north in terms other than idleness. We know from different sources how difficult it was to raise a large army unless the king travelled through his shires personally. Athelstan's agents will have told him the size of the invasion force, and he obviously took time to bring together as many West-Saxon and Mercian levies as he could. Unlike Harold in 1066 he was not lured into precipitate action as the news came of the allied mounted columns devastating the crops, burning down houses and driving off refugees, with 'complaining rumour' everywhere.

The 'Great Battle'

The battle was fought at the end of the year, later than 23 September and perhaps a good deal later. It was fought at a fort called Brunanburh which northerners said was on a hill called 'Weondun', 'holy hill', where there had been a heathen sanctuary or temple. This site has never been identified, but it may have been among the frontier forts on the southern border of the Northumbrians along the Don valley in Yorkshire. Athelstan eventually made a fast attack, in the tradition of his father and grandfather. The battle opened with a dawn assault around

The terror of war. Wars could be just and unjust, but in 937 Athelstan was felt to be 'defending the laws of Christ against an immense pagan army'; so it was right for his warriors to 'lust exceedingly' and to 'become enraged' in killing their enemies: 'The West Saxons pursued the hated peoples all day, hacking down the fugitives cruelly, with blades whetted on grindstones.'

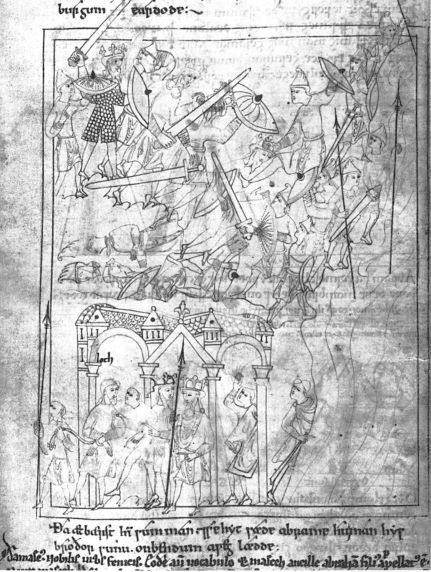

the burh by the English, fighting in separate armies, West Saxons against the Celts, Mercians against Scandinavians. The poem in the *Anglo-Saxon Chronicle* describes savage hand-to-hand fighting in regular battle order, the famous but mistitled 'shield walls'. The Irish *Annals of Ulster* say the struggle was 'immense, lamentable and horrible and desperately fought', so there was no rout. But the well-armed and equipped frontline troops of the southern English won the day. There was a long pursuit until nightfall, the West-Saxon mounted companies cutting down fugitives 'cruelly, with blades whetted on grindstones'. The allies escaped under cover of night and made their way back to their ships, which were a considerable way from the battlefield. The English losses had been heavy: two of Athelstan's cousins, two earls, two bishops, and, according to the *Annals of Ulster*, 'a multitude' of lesser men. But the invading army had been destroyed. Five kings, seven of Anlaf Guthfrithson's earls and a son of Constantine are named by English sources. Among the kings were the Viking king of the Western Isles and Owain of the Cumbrians. Two sons of Sihtric also fell. Anlaf Guthfrithson's arrival back in Dublin 'with a few' is noted early in 938.

'Victorious through God'

Not surprisingly the battle was viewed as the great event of the era. According to the chronicler Aethelweard, writing in the 980s, the man in the street still called it simply 'the great battle'. After it, he says, 'the barbarians were overcome on all sides and held the superiority no more . . . the fields of Britain were consolidated into one, there was peace everywhere and abundance of all things'. An exaggeration of course, but Aethelweard clearly saw Athelstan's warfare as providing the foundation for his nephew, King Edgar's, peace and the high noon of the Anglo-Saxon empire.

Athelstan's contemporaries too were quick to see the battle in a historical perspective. A Norse poet in England saluted the king as 'noble born son of kings' (a pointed flattery) and compared the triumph to the coming of the English and the first bretwalda: 'Athelstan has done more [than him]: now all bow low to him.' A German cleric resident in Christ Church Canterbury went to the Old Testament and Joshua's slaughter of the kings of the Amorites for his parallels: 'King Athelstan . . . whom God set over the English as king and as leader of his earthly armies plainly so that the king himself, mighty in war, might conquer other fierce kings and crush their proud necks.'

In the royal court the victory was celebrated as a national triumph. The cleric who composed the Anglo-Saxon poem on Brunanburh placed the deeds of 'the sons of Edward' in the long line of the race of Cerdic, kings who had carved themselves a kingdom in Britain. Deliberately recalling Bede on the state of Britain in 731, he already claims the authority of the history books for his statement that this was their greatest victory:

> Never before in this island, as the books of ancient historians tell us, was an army put to great slaughter by the sword since the time when Angles

and Saxons landed, invading Britain across the wide seas from the east when warriors eager for fame, proud forgers of war, overcame the Welsh and won themselves a kingdom.

Anglo-Saxon Chronicle

'King and teacher'

An illustration of Christ in glory from Athelstan's own private psalter. To many of his book gifts he added a request that 'whoever may read this will pray for my sins'. Like most Dark Age kings he was a serious man.

At this point let us pause as we did with Offa and Alfred, to see if a picture of the king has emerged, stressing the danger of anachronism in trying to make 'modern' judgements about medieval personality. Recent historians have asked many questions about what was expected of a king in the Dark Ages, and it is obvious at the outset that much of his success depended on the individual force of the man. We shall see this more noticeably with Ethelred the Unready. But what impressions would the journalist or anthropologist have of a reception in Athelstan's court? We have seen Offa taking food rents, Alfred making comments on political power. What of Athelstan? What made the king great apart from his wars, his enriching of churches, his ability to guarantee peace? What made the impression that stuck, so that even after the Norman Conquest, 'the opinion was firmly held among the common people that no one more just or learned had ever ruled the country'?

'His manner was charming and well disposed to churchmen, affable and kind to laymen, serious with magnates out of regard for his majesty.' Athelstan put aside the 'pride of kingship' only with the poor, to whom he was 'approachable and serious minded . . . out of sympathy for their poverty', a suitable enough sentiment on the part of the rich. His spirit we are told was 'audacious and forceful, much beloved by his subjects for his courage and his humility and like a thunderbolt to rebels with his invincible steadfastness' (William of Malmesbury *On the Deeds of the English Kings*).

These virtues – fortitude, humility, constancy – appear in so many royal biographies in the Dark Ages that they have almost become clichés, but just like modern princes, Anglo-Saxon athelings were groomed for the job, and our imperfect sources on Athelstan suggest a man possessed of such qualities in good measure. 'Medium in height, slender in body, his hair flaxen, beautifully mingled with golden threads' writes William of Malmesbury, Athelstan's 'greatness of mind' was what distinguished him; it was what foreign rulers saw in him, and it was what his followers wanted. He 'graciously bestowed courtesy on all' and that was how a king should be; it was not the most important thing, but it mattered.

But ultimately, as we have seen, it was bravery in battle and generosity after it which still marked out the successful Anglo-Saxon king. And none was more successful in warfare than Athelstan. In his youth he

The king's place: in the saddle ready to lead his army. No wonder continental writers praised the English who 'drove out the pirate armies in violent warfare'.

had a reputation for audacity and courage. It was by boldness that he wrested his father's kingdom from his brothers. Brought up in Mercia he must have fought in most of the campaigns which conquered the Danelaw, and his strength in war later became proverbial. 'Very prudent, mature, far sighted and hard to overcome in any strife', Athelstan could rule 'by terror of his name alone'; he 'implanted the nations around him with dread' and 'instilled terror into all enemies of the fatherland'. In a world where the individual strength of the king and the fear he personally excited mattered so much, it was of the essence that he should be dread-inspiring, *ondraedendlic* as he would have put it.

In his last years Athelstan was an elder statesman in the eyes of Europeans and pre-eminent within Britain. His court was a haven for guests, scholars, pilgrims, poets and churchmen. At different times he sheltered the exiled royal families of Brittany and Francia, and Alain of Brittany and Hakon of Norway were his foster sons. Four of his half-sisters married leading Europeans. In 936 he had supported the restoration of the Breton and Frankish royal families (the latter using his coronation service, brought by English bishops). In 939 he even sent an English fleet to Flanders, the first case in history of English intervention on the continent.

King Athelstan died on a sickbed in the royal chamber of the palace at Gloucester on 27 October 939. He had reigned for fourteen years and was probably forty-four. Perhaps he had been exhausted by the exertions of kingship, though none of his line lived to a ripe old age. In the last month of his life, his old friend Cenwald, bishop of Worcester, expressed Athelstan's supremacy in these terms: 'King of the Anglo-Saxons, Emperor of the Northumbrians, ruler of the pagans and guardian of the Britons.' The tone was set for the tenth-century empire. In

Athelstan's tomb at Malmesbury. 'The firm opinion is still current among the English,' wrote William of Malmesbury in the 1130s, 'that no one more just or learned administered the state.'

Ireland it was the king's prestige which struck an Ulster chronicler, who recorded his death in terms used for high kings like Charlemagne or Brian Boru, and before them the Roman Emperors: 'Athelstan king of the English died, the roof tree of the honour of the western world' (*Annals of Ulster*).

150

CHAPTER 7

ERIC BLOODAXE

King Eric was treacherously killed by Earl Maccus in a certain lonely place which is called Stainmore, with his son Haeric and his brother Ragnald, betrayed by Earl Oswulf, and then afterwards King Eadred ruled in these districts.

Roger of Wendover *Flowers of the Histories*

Soon after 954, a northern cleric sat down at his desk in the library of St Peter's church in York, the Anglo-Saxon minster, and wrote the above words in Latin.

The king whose death was thus recorded had been the most famous Viking of the era. Briefly king of Norway, sometime king of the Hebrides, ruler of Viking York for two short but intensely dramatic reigns in the 940s and 950s, Eric's career took him from the White Sea to Spain, shooting across Scandinavian history like a meteor, but it has only been in modern times that historians have pieced together his role in British history. Nicknamed 'Bloodaxe' for his ruthless bravery, Eric lived most of his life a pagan, a true son of Odin. He probably died a pagan too. But why then should a priest in the church of York, one of the greatest centres of Northumbrian Christianity and learning, have noted his death with sympathy? Why did our annalist view his downfall at the hands of the English earl of Bamburgh, Oswulf, as a treacherous betrayal? And why was the accession of Eadred, grandson of Alfred the Great, and like the annalist, an Englishman, greeted with tight-lipped resentment? Eric's is an intriguing story, but more than that, it takes us to the root of how the Vikings were assimilated in England.

Eric Bloodaxe was a true saga-hero. Unfortunately, his own saga does not survive today, but its gist is preserved in others written by Snorri Sturluson: they are those of his father Harald Finehair, his half-brother Hakon the Good and that of his enemy the poet Egil Skallagrimson. These sagas are late, written in the first part of the thirteenth century, and in general they are unreliable as history. They are a marvellous entertainment though, and should be read by everyone interested in the Viking story. These sagas do, however, preserve early poetry in praise of Eric, written by poets in his entourage, and this tells much about the way he thought of himself.

The synoptic histories of the twelfth century written in Latin and Old

Norse, which were available to the saga-writers, add only the odd detail; in fact, Eric's story seems to have been preserved in Iceland and Norway by oral tradition, and it was obviously a story which seized people's imagination. But to get to the real events of his life we must turn to the lost chronicles written in the north of England in the tenth century, fragments of which are only now being untangled from much later authors who assimilated them. We also have now the testimony of archaeology to colour our picture of Eric's career. Especially in Viking York, this evidence is giving us a new insight into the Anglo-Scandinavian civilisation over which Eric ruled in the mid tenth century.

To contemporary observers it must have seemed that Athelstan's conquest of Northumbria and his great victory at Brunanburh had sealed the fate of an independent kingdom of Northumbria. But his death at the end of 939 threw everything into the melting pot. It led to a fifteen-year struggle for power in Northumbria where the last energies of the Northumbrian kingship attempted to resist the trend of English history and the military power of Athelstan's successors, his young half-brothers Edmund and Eadred. Between 939 and 954, seven different kings ruled in York, Scandinavian and English, in nine separate reigns. Between 939 and 948 seven major military expeditions are recorded to have occurred in the zone between York and the Five Boroughs, the armies of the West-Saxon overlord and the Norse king of York attacking each other across the Humber borderland. Something of a Dark Age Vietnam then, where the instruments of war were great mounted raids to devastate the land, burn crops, drive the population away from their homes – the Dark Age equivalent of modern saturation bombing or chemical warfare. It was a war of attrition, where the southern kings systematically set fire to areas, demolished strongpoints and arrested suspects. There was propaganda too: both sides wrote histories of their ruling dynasties from their own point of view. Inevitably, the Northumbrians lost, and became a province of the kingdom of England, albeit a recalcitrant one. Eric was their last king, and that fact – coupled with the manner of his fall – left a nostalgic mark in their history books: 'from that time to the present, Northumbria has been grieving for want of a king of its own, and for the liberty they once enjoyed' (John of Wallingford's *Chronicle*).

The years during which Eric ruled York, then, are a most violent phase of British history. York was the racial melting-pot of the north and north-west of Britain and it saw constant change. As the biggest city in the north, York was at the centre of these movements. It was the ancient 'capital' of Northumbria, former Roman city, catalyst in a diplomatic, political and trade nexus which extended from the Viking ports of Ireland, the Viking settlements in the Western Isles and North Britain, through Viking Scandinavia and further east by the rivers of Russia. In these years successive kings of the Norse family of Dublin were accepted as king in the city, only to see it captured and recaptured by the southern English successors of Alfred. No sooner had the southern kings been accepted as 'father and lord' and tribute paid to them, than the Northumbrians invited another Norse king to rule them.

Eric's backers

At the centre of these intrigues was the enigmatic Archbishop Wulfstan of York. A more unlikely partner to Eric Bloodaxe could scarcely be imagined, but their careers are bound together. Wulfstan was a man unto himself, a resolute northerner to the end. It was he who had ridden south with the York Vikings in 940, devastating the Midlands, sacking Tamworth and fighting against the Anglo-Saxon King Edmund at Leicester. It was Wulfstan's diplomacy which secured the east Midlands Five Boroughs for Viking rule after his 'victory'. But he was no puppet; he was for instance instrumental in removing two Dublin Viking kings from York in 944. We find him in a remarkable annal for 947 leading the 'witan', the council of wise men, the 'chiefs of the Northumbrians', negotiating with the southern King Eadred like a king on the borders of his own kingdom: in this way the ancient Northumbrians had dealt with the bretwaldas of old.

We know something about the citizens of York, the chief men who supported Wulfstan. Enough to know that they included men of English, Danish and Norwegian descent. Earl Orm, to whose 'help and advice' the Northumbrians owed the victory of 940, was a great landowner of Norwegian descent, but his daughter whom he married to King Anlaf Guthfrithson bears an English name, Aldgyth, suggesting that Orm had an English wife. Although he clearly kept in touch with Vikings outside Britain, Orm signed southern charters from 929 to 956, never entirely losing the favour of kings like Athelstan: a slippery customer then, and one who rode changes of regime with a sureness of touch remarkable even in this age of shifting loyalty.

The master moneyers too were men of substance, rapidly adapting to changes of regime. Athelstan's old master moneyer Aethelferth (who has an English name) minted coins for the Viking kings as soon as they took over in York. He minted the large and handsome issue of coins of Anlaf Guthfrithson which bore a raven with the legend 'Anlaf Cununc' (king) and on the reverse the moneyer's name and city. Another English moneyer, Rathulf, was brought down to Derby by the Vikings as soon as the Five Boroughs fell in 940, and brought dies with him from York to use with the captured dies at Derby bearing the characteristic Derby flower design. We shall find further innovations in Eric's coinages in York, made by English moneyers. These were important men, and the value the Norse kings attached to them also proves the significance by this time of coins as a means of trade. After a coup in York coinage was almost the first thing to be regularised. Nothing was left to chance there. The moneyers' careers show we should be wary of attributing 'national' characteristics to race: an Englishman in Northumbria did not see the world in the same way as an Englishman in Winchester, and might be happy to serve a king like Eric.

The Norse kings in Northumbria generated their own styles of kingship, their own coinages, their own literature. At times York was the centre of a Scandinavian empire which included Dublin and the Norse settlements in Ireland, the Western Isles, the archipelagos of north Britain, Northumbria and the Five Boroughs. Kings like Anlaf Guthfrithson gave themselves 'imperial' titles just as the southern English kings did – 'King of Ireland and of many islands', 'King of all the Scandinavians of Ireland and Britain', 'Unconquerable king, a terror by land and sea, who by his force of arms has brought several countries under his sway'.

The arrival of Eric: his background in Norway

The protagonist of our story, Eric Bloodaxe, was such a man, perhaps the most famous of them all. He arrives out of the blue having no ancestors in Britain, unlike the Norse kings of Dublin whose pedigree in York went back to the ninth century. In 947 Wulfstan and the Northumbrian 'witan' submitted to Eadred king of the West Saxons and 'Caesar of Britain' at Tanshelf on the hill where Pontefract now stands, a Northumbrian settlement of a few hundred people, with a hall and mills, above the river Aire. There in the hall they formally acknowledged Eadred 'father and lord', bowed to him and gave him tribute and gifts. But a few months later news reached the archbishop's palace in York of a new and unexpected development, a new element in the politics of the North. A king to bring back the great days. Southern historians recorded it bluntly: 'Within a short space of time the Northumbrians were false to their pledges and oaths'. 'They do not know how to keep faith,' said one. 'They set up over themselves a certain man of Danish line called Eric.'

Who was he and where had he come from? How had he come to be in Northumbria at this moment? He was in fact not Danish but Norwegian. His father was the first king who had subdued all the petty chiefdoms of Norway, Harald Finehair. Eric's mother was Ragnild, daughter of a King Eric in Jutland, and he was married to the beautiful

Gunnhild, daughter of Gorm the Old, king of Denmark. King Harald seems to have set his hopes on Eric, for a later tradition in Norway was that in his old age Harald had raised him to the kingship. But if he did, it proved a meaningless gesture. At Harald's death his numerous sons began to fight for their inheritance. Eric killed two of them and was momentarily successful, but his violent personality had not endeared him to many in Norway. His fifteen-year-old half-brother, Hakon, who had been brought up by Athelstan in the English court, was brought back from England and set up as king by a powerful group of land-owners opposed to the strong and wilful Eric. The takeover was expertly stage-managed, and with his support dwindling away Eric sailed westwards from Norway with his ships, his movables and treasure, his wife and a small army of friends, family and supporters who had stuck by him.

Eric Bloodaxe's name entered among the Christian benefactors of the church of St Cuthbert.

Initially his journey into exile was a mere plundering expedition. Later Norwegian sources say he touched in at Orkney and perhaps there he heard from Viking traders of events in Northumbria. There, at any rate, many joined him, and after plundering in Scotland and North Saxonland, he arrived in Northumbria. The sagas are unclear about the chronology here and should not be taken literally in much of what they say. But clearly Eric was invited to be king in York. The magic of his name, his lineage and reputation was perhaps paramount in the eyes of men like Earl Orm, Norsemen who were in touch with events in the wider Norse world. The Norse synoptic histories say Eric accepted baptism along with his wife, children and supporters and became king with his residence in Jorvik-York. This account squares perfectly well with the English annals. The same men who had submitted to Eadred at Tanshelf – Archbishop Wulfstan and the Northumbrian 'witan', English, Danish and Norse – were within months asking Eric to be their king. Here, they thought, was a man who could restore the great days of Ragnald and Sihtric in York, perhaps even of the bretwaldas of old. To see why they thought this, and why the Church of York backed them up, we must go to Viking York and see for ourselves the rich and volatile society which existed there in the mid tenth century.

The Northumbrians: 'a treacherous and violent race'

A Dark Age observer might have remarked of the Northumbrians, as they did in classical times of the Sicilians, that they were a mixture of different races, always changing their constitution. Here was a very traditional society with deep-rooted social customs and means of worship, archaic tenurial systems which nonplussed the compilers of *Domesday Book*, and which probably represent the failure of the Anglo-

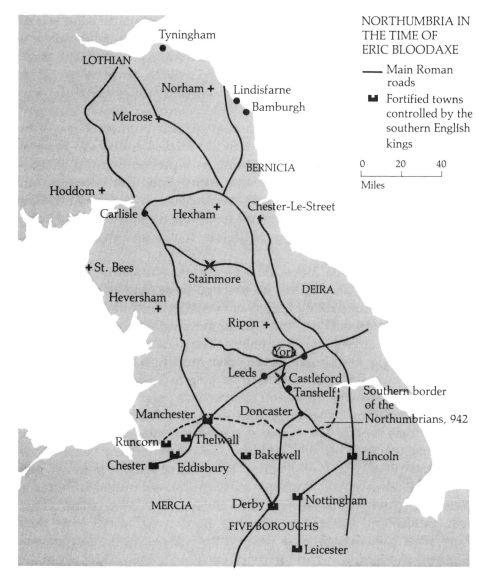

NORTHUMBRIA IN
THE TIME OF
ERIC BLOODAXE

—— Main Roman
roads

◪ Fortified towns
controlled by the
southern English
kings

0   20   40

Miles

Saxon kings to rule effectively north of the Humber. To the southern
English they were treacherous, stubborn, violent and rebellious. Their
accent was uncouth and incomprehensible to the southerners. They
also drank too much. If you were travelling there it was best to ride in a
party and take guides and escorts from one border to the next. In the
eleventh century merchants were recommended to go in groups of
twenty. Most people did not travel far. A journey from Northumbria
into Scotland or Mercia was the exception, unless with an army. Merchants came and left by sea. For locals, six miles was as far as you would
be expected to go to buy and sell goods. The Northumbrian Priests' Law
shows that the usual Sunday observances were waived to allow people

to pass through carrying goods by wagon, horseback or on their own backs, 'for their own needs'.

Hints of the unstable nature of the times are evident in the provision in the laws for times of war – 'in case of hostilities one may travel because of necessity between York and a distance of six miles on the eve of festivals'. It suggests that different levels of war existed in such a society, that when the army of the 'south English' was not devastating the land, Norse warbands foraging, or forces from Ireland or Scotland on expeditions into Northumbria to seize cattle and slaves, there was still brigandage and banditry; life was brutal and unstable. What is surprising in the face of all this is that York in the tenth century was populous and wealthy, with thriving commercial trade, a boom town second in size only to London, and comparable to the great continental trading towns. The picture of York we get from the sagas and confirmed by archaeology and the author of the tenth-century *Life of St Oswald* who lived there is a thriving town 'packed with people of all races', with colonies of Frisians and Britons as well as the Danish merchants who flocked to the city; men accustomed to political instability, and used to following in the wake of the armies to make a quick killing.

Northumbria was sandwiched between the English kingdom to the south and the kingdoms of the Scots, Cumbrians and Strathclyde Welsh to the north and north-west. So anyone who was king in York in the tenth century had to be adept at playing off the West-Saxon and British imperialists, or allying with them. They all moved in the same world, of course, and at one level it is the cultural unity of their world which strikes us. You could ride from Perth in Scotland to Kent in the mid tenth century, through British, Norse, Danish and English lands, and be welcomed and entertained in all the kings' courts on the way, which suggests that the hazards of travel did not prevent the reception of learned men and travellers, and exchange of news and ideas. Language was no barrier among learned men, nor among nobles who, though illiterate, were trained for diplomacy and spoken contact.

A journey to York

We can ride with one traveller to Eric's court in York. A pilgrim's account survives of a journey there from Abernethy in Fife in the 940s, a journey which took him on to Francia. Preparations for such a ride were thorough: mortgaging your property, procuring good horses, buying travelling clothes, packing purses of gold and silver to buy accommodation. Catroe and his twelve companions were escorted by his kinsman King Constantine to the border of the kingdom of Strathclyde where the king's brother, Donald, king of the Strathclyde Welsh, received the travellers and entertained them at his court (perhaps on the rock at Dumbarton). Then Donald accompanied them on the long journey south. The kingdom of Strathclyde and its dependency, the kingdom of the Cumbrians, extended deep into what is now England for a period in the 940s, and it was best for the pilgrims that they had the king's escort through the mixed Norse and British hills of Galloway to Carlisle, possibly the centre of the kingdom of the Cumbrians. Here there were still impressive Roman walls, a working aqueduct and fountain at least as late as 685, and a temple of Mars and Victory which was still standing in the twelfth century. Here they could rest in church establishments, the early church of St Alban, or the church of St Cuthbert. Perhaps they even engaged in a little tourism; for Dark Age men, Roman ruins exerted an unending fascination.

Then, instead of taking the route along Hadrian's Wall into 'North Saxonland', or the route over Stainmore, they passed through the mixed Anglian, British and Norse population of Westmorland, maybe staying at the Anglian monastery of Heversham on Morecambe Bay, and over the Pennines into the Aire valley with its churches at Ilkley and Otley, and the archbishop's residence at Addingham. King Donald conducted them to the 'civitas' of Leeds (perhaps the present city; an elaborate tenth-century carving is preserved in the church) and here they parted, for this, says the *Life of Catroe*, was the boundary between the Cumbrians and the Norsemen (of York). This had been doubted by historians, but political boundaries (or zones of control) advanced and receded rapidly in the Dark Ages, and in the 940s, with the constant changes of regime in York, there is nothing improbable in the idea.

At Leeds the travellers were met by a nobleman called Gunderic (an English name) who took them to York. Obviously it was best to make prior arrangements with a sponsor: unidentified travellers off the main roads ran the risk of being killed out of hand if they did not shout and blow their horns. Gunderic rode with them to York itself and into the court of Eric, whose wife is stated to have been a kinswoman of Catroe. What Eric made of Catroe we are not told, except that he received him as any king would a distinguished guest. It had been a long journey, and doubtless at this point the pilgrims rested for a few days before carrying on south. There were many places to stay in the city, for York was used to receiving a great influx of travellers and merchants. They might stay as guests of nobles or freemen in the city in their houses. They might, if they were important enough, be received in the Archbishop's house. They might find space in the 'hospitium' near St Peter's where Celtic holy men, 'culdees', worked among the sick and poor. Or there was a host of other places where travellers could stop, whether churchmen going south to the West-Saxon court, pilgrims, pedlars or salt sellers, merchants from Scandinavia or the Danelaw, or even travelling warriors on the tracks of news that a king like Eric was looking for men and generous with his gold.

York: 'metropolis of the Northumbrian people'

The city the pilgrims woke up to was one of the richest and most exciting places in the northern world. A place where old and new existed side by side. Towns, as Fernand Braudel has said, are electric transformers. 'They increase tension, accelerate the rhythm of exchange and ceaselessly stir up men's lives.' They have the best foods, the luxury industries, currency, trade with the outside world bringing new ideas, produce and artefacts. York had all this. 'Once nobly built (by the Romans) and most solidly constructed with walls which are now decayed by age, indescribably rich, packed with the goods of merchants who come from all over but especially from the Danes, a multitude of people numbering 30,000, not counting infants', says a tenth-century writer. His estimate has provoked disbelief, for the *Domesday Book* population would appear to have been around 10,000 in 1066; but by then the city was past its heyday, and may have been much larger in the 940s.

The first thing that would strike the visitor about the city was its Roman character. This was what struck Alcuin in the eighth century, and William of Malmesbury in the twelfth. Along the river was a massive eight-towered frontage built in the early fourth century. Where the Minster stands today stood the principia, the headquarters building where Constantine the Great and other emperors had sat in state, and which stood roofed as late as the Viking era. The whole area of the Roman fortress was inhabited, with ribbon development to the northwest and southwards over the Foss, and the area now within the medieval walls west of the Ouse, centring on Micklegate, also had a large population. In the tenth century there were at least eleven churches with new ones being built to cater for the booming population and the spread of Christianity among fourth-generation Danes and second-generation Norse settlers.

Viking industry

The Viking quarter of the city lay south of the fort on the Ousegate axis, extending to the Foss, where there were wharves, fortified with an extended bank, gritstone revetment, palisade and ditch: this had been partly demolished by Athelstan in 927. The Danish sector was densely populated, damp, squalid and dirty, an industrial quarter with timber walkways onto which the long, narrow timber-framed houses were built with gable ends facing onto the streets. The houses were made of

Domestic buildings in Coppergate, a street in Eric Bloodaxe's York. The scale by the timber wall is 1 metre. An average room might be 7 metres by 3, and would have a partition.

vertical planks with clay daub, or wattle and daub, and were probably thatched. Some of these have been discovered recently, preserved in the waterlogged soil to a height of six feet. There were craftsmen's enclosures, earmarked as such, and recent archaeological evidence supports the early place-names of York which suggest that this goes back to the Viking period. The name Coppergate, for instance, shows the presence of carpenters (*koppari*), who were most necessary to the town, since they were the men who put up the wooden housing. Parts of the town will have turned the noses of visitors from the rural north. The area of leather workers' tenements was uncovered in the dig beneath Lloyds Bank and the coffee house in Pavement. They lived and worked in flimsy wattle and daub buildings where they did all the processes of their trade: skin stripping with bone strippers, rotting them with chicken dung (which covered the floors of their shops), curing them with elderberry ferment, dyeing them with heather dye, stretching (remains of wooden stretcher frames have been discovered), finishing and working into shoes, jerkins, belts and so on (masses of scraps and cuts have been found). These shops stank, and swarmed with flies. Leather workers were numerous in Eric's York, and their goods must have formed an important part of the city's trade. A large number of their shops have been found along Pavement, which was probably the main thoroughfare of Viking York.

Apart from leather goods you could buy most things in the shops of the Viking quarter. There was a comb factory with a huge turnover of plain and carved bone combs. Knives, axes, buckles, shears, hooks and nails found all over York were probably made by smiths near the tanneries in Coppergate. Here too Danish bronze foundries have been found which provided pins, brooches, buckles and suchlike for both the luxury and the mass trade: everybody needed cloak fastenings, belt strap ends and buttons. There was a glass bead workshop in Clifford

160

Street in Pavement, and in the same area amber workshops cut great lumps of raw amber from the Baltic and turned them on lathes into beads, finger rings, spindle whorls, chessmen (chess was a very popular Viking game) and pendants like coiled serpents.

The city was the gateway between Scandinavia and Anglo-Saxon England, and its trade routes reached out to Ireland, the Shetlands, the Rhineland, the Baltic, and further afield: one of Sihtric's York Vikings lost his purse in Bangor in 925 with coins minted in Samarkand. At the Foss, wide-bellied Viking cargo ships tied up to discharge amber, furs, whalebone, cable, skins from the Baltic, whetstones, hones and soapstone from Norway, pottery from the Rhineland, lava querns from the Rhineland, and even wine from France. And here they took on treated leather, textiles, wool, jewellery, and if the sagas are right, agricultural produce: if there was famine in Iceland, corn could be bought from merchants in York and shipped north. The impression is of a Viking centre like Dublin, Hedeby, Birka or Trondheim, only far bigger, and with a larger and more mixed population, and a more settled sense of urban life, as befitted a former Roman city.

Christianity

The head church of York was St Peter's, the ancestor of the present York Minster. We are not certain of its site, but it probably lay between the west end of the Minster and High Petergate, and there are few sites in Britain on which archaeologists would rather get their hands. Here had been the wooden church of King Edwin, and the stone church of St Wilfrid which was rebuilt in the eighth century, 'A paragon of lofty beauty, supported by massive pillars,' says Alcuin, who was educated there. In that part of the city there were many other chapels as well as the parish churches, clustered around the huge Roman principia which was only demolished in the Viking era (its foundations can be seen in the undercroft of the present Minster). To the north of the principia was the archbishop's house and court, where according to Northumbrian tradition, he gave bread to the people. Nearby was another magnificent late eighth-century church, that of the Holy Wisdom, and a 'hospitium' attached to St Peter's where Celtic holy men tended the poor and sick. St Peter's was still a royal burial place: King Guthfrith, a Danish convert to Christianity, had been buried inside the church in 895, 'in the high basilica'. An important Viking-age cemetery with carved grave covers and markers has been found under and near the present Minster, presumably from the old cathedral graveyard, and the style of carving has suggested an 'Anglo-Scandinavian' taste on the part of wealthy York citizens. By the 940s there must have been numerous Christian

The intact tenth-century tower of St Mary, Bishophill, in York, a church of Eric Bloodaxe's day.

A tenth-century cross shaft from Kirkleavington, Yorkshire. Perhaps the man is Odin with his two ravens, symbols of the mind of the seer or shaman: an ancient motif found in early Sweden. A typical blending of Christian and Viking traditions.

Vikings in York, and these probably included members of the upper classes. At this time English, Danes and Norsemen intermarried, and a common culture and language developed which mingled Scandinavian and English words. One Anglo-Scandinavian noble of the period, Regenwold, appears in the confraternity book of the continental monastery of Pfäffers around 940. Earl Orm was perhaps at least nominally Christian, if, as we think, he had an English wife. Another Norse earl in Yorkshire, Gunner, was favoured by the West-Saxon kings and may also have been Christian. The tenth-century inscription of St Mary's Castlegate is written in Anglo-Saxon and Latin but says that 'Grim', and others with Norse names, established the church *on naman drihtnes haelendes*, in the name of the Lord Saviour; the church was founded to serve the growing Danish population in the industrial quarter around Castlegate, and though Grim need not be the man who is sometimes found in Athelstan's court, we can see this may well have been the background of such men. The church of St Peter doubtless also had benefactors among the Scandinavians in York, and they would be among those buried in the cemetery. The impression they make is a far cry from the traditional one of uncouth pagan pillagers; here we have relatively sophisticated city-dwellers.

This kind of attitude can also be seen in the monuments of the period. The carvings in the York cemetery, the cross heads found at Ripon, the elaborate cross shafts at Middleton, were all done by English sculptors for Scandinavian patrons to satisfy Scandinavian Christian tastes. Most remarkable of all is the tomb monument at Nunburnholme near Beverley where a chief in Viking dress and war gear is portrayed with his patron saint and a holy lady with a book satchel, complete with cornucopia and centaurs. (The allusion is to the classical myth of Cupid and Psyche.) The aspirations of the landed Viking nouveaux riches could hardly be better shown up. The patrons of such a work may not have got the point of its subtler iconography, but the sculptor obviously thought he was following the best models: Norse hero stories, classical paintings and religious motifs off portable ivories from the Ottonian empire.

A sculpture in St Mary's Museum in York shows us what these prosperous York 'gentry' looked like to meet in the street. It dates from the ninth century, but doubtless the members of the Northumbrian council in 947 wore the same kind of gear. The first man has a long skirted tunic with a girdle (its strap ends might be decorated with interlace and gilded), he carries a hunting horn, and over his head a voluminous hood fastened with a small brooch at the front. The other has a heavy woollen cloak down to his ankles with a collar probably of fur. They both wear shoes of the kind found in the artisans' shops in Coppergate. They look prosperous. The kind of personal adornments they wore can be seen in the Museum too: a silver disc brooch with

intertwined animals in the Danish style; a silver armring with a punched decoration; an animal-headed comb; a sword with a decorated bronze scabbard chape; a silver brooch incorporating a cast of a coin of Valentinian. But if one artefact could be chosen to represent their taste it would be the beautiful gold finger ring which someone lost in Fishergate in the early tenth century. Its front shows two animals clasping a man's head in their paws; an ancient northern motif, but here a reference to St Edmund of East Anglia, whose cult was enthusiastically fostered by the Danish settlers of East Anglia in the time of Alfred the Great, and which spread rapidly to Northumbria through the merchants and travellers who coasted up to York. Any of the wealthy citizens of Viking York might have worn this: Earl Orm, Aethelferth the moneyer, Grim, Archbishop Wulfstan, Eric himself.

Beleaguered Christianity. The ancient sees of Northumbria lapsed during the Viking era. But small local houses survived, like this Anglo-Saxon church at Escomb in the Wear valley.

The king's home: 'Eric went to table as usual, and there were very many men who sat with him'

The royal hall where Eric sat in state and which is mentioned in the sagas, the 'king's garth', was near King's Square, whose name recalls it. It was still known as *Kuningsgard* in the thirteenth century, at which time the memory of the *Koningsgarthr* of Eric was still current in Iceland. Hereabouts was the south-eastern gatehouse of the Roman fort with its great arches and an inscription commemorating Trajan's rebuilding which was discovered here in 1970. It may be that the Norse hall was built around and incorporated the still massive remains of the gatehouse: indeed there is nothing against the idea that the structure was still roofed in the tenth century, as the principia was in the ninth. If this was indeed the case, then it would be typical of the Viking ability to use the past, as it would of their sense of political style. This has been called one of the most important sites in the Viking world, and would repay intensive excavation. As yet, the digs around King's Square have revealed little, save that the Norse hall was right in the middle of the most populous area of the city, with wooden tenements right up to it; the numerous finds there of this period have been domestic – cooking pots, pitchers, the ubiquitous bone combs, wooden bowls, whetstones, antler horns, a stone spindle whorl, a skate. Living cheek by jowl with the crowd, kings like Eric could keep themselves in the know, for York was a place where political intrigue, instability and violence ran hand in hand. Everyone who came here – merchants, craftsmen, poets, sailors, mercenaries, traffickers – all were accustomed to revolution and followed in the wake of the armies to profit by every change of regime. It is easy to imagine men like the moneyer Aethelferth playing it by ear and living to a rich old age!

And what of Eric himself, seated in the high chair of the royal hall in York, surrounded by his armed following? The description of him in the sagas may go back to the lost Eric saga: 'A big man and handsome, strong and valiant, a great warrior and victorious in battle, very impetuous in disposition, cruel, unfriendly and silent.' Like other Norse kings, Eric surrounded himself with poets; they recorded his battles in Bjarmaland by the White Sea, and among those who told of his deeds in England were the skald Egil Skallagrimson and the anonymous poet of the *Eiriksmal*, his last elegy. In the fragmentary remains of this skaldic verse we can read of the ideals and hopes of Eric's Norse followers, and perhaps some of his English supporters too. As we would expect, what they wanted differed little from the *Anglo-Saxon Chronicle*'s portrayal of Alfred or the Brunanburh poem's of Athelstan: except that Eric was a pagan, and moved in the old-fashioned world of Norse kingship. 'I have spared no deed or word which might make your glory greater,' says Egil, 'I will display to men the leader's glory . . . this high lord gives gold freely . . . rules his land strongly and deserves praise.' The poems are full of references to the giving of gold, or 'hawkstrand's goldshower' as Egil puts it in one of the elaborate kennings so beloved of the Norse poets. Eric's prowess in war is held up: he is an 'artist' in battle, a 'whetter of swordplay' and his reputation spreads far and wide: 'across the sea leaps his fame . . . most of mankind have heard what battles the king has fought, and Odin saw where the dead lay . . . I have praised the king's merit and brought it forth so everyone might hear it . . . high minded mighty king's son.' That was evidently what Eric wanted to hear when he sat at table in York, and in Old Norse the technique of Egil's poem was clever stuff, not exactly avant garde, but something for a sophisticated audience used to the poet's art.

The *Eiriksmal*, the great poem in praise of Eric's valour, by contrast is a very traditional piece. Composed within a few years of his death, perhaps in Orkney rather than at York, it was commissioned by his widow to commemorate Eric's deeds. The images of the poem invoke the warlike ideals of Eric's rule, the pagan's ultimate hope for eternal life, the nature of his mortuary beliefs, presided over by the shamanistic figure of Odin. It also invokes a sense of material wealth which may not be out of place in York: it starts with the raising of the house of the wealthy to prepare for the great feast, a formula as traditional as the *drapa* in praise of the king. It pictures the royal hall, the benches spread with cloths and furs, the walls hung with tapestries, and it glorifies the warlike, aristocratic ideals of that society.

From the sagas and poems we can picture Eric and his kin in the hall with guards on the gates and surrounded by their armed following, quick to exact vengeance. A dramatic picture, but how true it is difficult to say. The archaeological evidence suggests the Norse kings in York were preoccupied with controlling trade, minting coins and engaging in diplomacy. But it is the images of Egil's poems which linger on:

A silver penny from Eric's first rule in York, minted by Rathulf, one of the city's wealthy English moneyers (*c.* 948).

> Mighty king, son of the Ynglings . . . Under a helmet of terror the all powerful lord of the people sat over the land and gave lavish gifts. The king ruled in York with harsh thought for his sea-washed shores.
>
> It was not safe, nor without terror, to look at the light of Eric's eye, when serpent keen, the eye of the all-powerful shone with terrifying light.
>
> *Egil's Saga*

War in the north: the burning of Ripon

Eric's first rule in York was brief. As far as we know it lasted from late in 947 into 948. In that time coins were minted bearing his name – *Eric Rex* – by the moneyer Rathulf who had minted coins for Eadred. They were a purely English design and would have circulated with ease beside English coins of the same date, and York merchants who we know sailed down to Thanet to sell their goods could use them as easily as the coins of Eadred. But the clash with the southern king could not long be put off. The Northumbrians and Archbishop Wulfstan had after all broken their faith with Eadred in making Eric king, and his response

was inevitable. In the summer of 948 he collected an army of South-Angles, and like a bretwalda of old rode into Northumbria to 'subdue their pride'. The campaign of 948 was etched on people's minds in Northumbria for a long time to come. Eadred used terror as a tactic to force the Northumbrian council to reject Eric and submit to him: he 'burned down towns, razed fortifications, slaughtered opposition and arrested suspects' (John of Wallingford). The route of his ravaging took him up the Great North Road, 'and in that ravaging the glorious minster at Ripon which St Wilfrid built was burned down' (*Anglo-Saxon Chronicle*).

In the north the burning of Ripon had the same effect that the shelling of Reims had in 1914. The northerners were outraged, the English were embarrassed. One southern version claims the Danes were responsible, but the York source of the 'D' version of the *Anglo-Saxon Chronicle* shows what really happened. Indeed there is nothing improbable in the idea that Eadred burned the place down deliberately, for this ancient centre of learning may have been a focus for Northumbrian separatist feeling. Archaeologists have uncovered some traces of the pre-948 settlement here. Like all small towns, and most cities, it was completely rural in character, wooden houses and barns clustered around the church and protected by a dry ditch 18 feet wide with a wooden palisade and gates. The population was tiny, probably only two or three hundred, swelled by travelling stonemasons and sculptors who worked on the church and by seasonal shepherds and farmers who worked the summer months in Wensleydale: transhumance remained the way of life in many of the dales for centuries. The church itself had been built by St Wilfrid in the seventh century, in the style of an Italian basilica with long arched side aisles, and its crypt can still be seen, the relic niches empty now, the only part which survived the destruction of 948 and the rebuilding later in the century. An insight into Scandinavian patronage of St Wilfrid's Church was provided in 1975 when a hole was driven through the crypt revealing pieces of tenth-century cross shafts which may be from the wreckage of the 948 destruction. The heads were carved by English masons on Scandinavian themes including the legend of Sigurd and Fafnir. In Viking Yorkshire the greater glory of God came from diverse sources!

Archbishop Oda of Canterbury was with the English army at Ripon and took the opportunity to 'kidnap' what he thought were the bones of St Wilfrid and remove them to Kent. This was ostensibly to protect them from the 'innumerable upheavals of the English kingdom', as Oda said. But is it not just as reasonable to think that in abducting the remains of the Northumbrian saint, Oda was depriving Wulfstan's party of a focus for both their political feeling and their prayers for celestial aid from the 'heavenly battalions' in whose ranks Wilfrid now stood? His action certainly appears to back up the claim that the church was deliberately destroyed.

The battle at Castleford

With the ashes settled at Ripon, and the harvest burned away, Eadred rode south, away from the columns of smoke and the streams of refugees. Fearful of ambushes he spread the army out, setting a rearguard to cover his retreat. At Castleford, on the Aire, the main ford of the Roman road out of Northumbria, the Northumbrian army from York cut off the rearguard and annihilated it. They had lain in wait at the narrow approach to the crossing where the most damage could be easily inflicted, and, says the northern annalist, 'they made great slaughter there'. In a much later source, the notebook of John of Wallingford, we find this additional note: 'the author of this ambush is said to have been Eric the son of Harald.'

Eric had confirmed his reputation as a cunning and victorious general. It was the first time the West Saxons had been defeated in a stand-up fight since 902. Survivors who escaped the debacle struggled across the river and somewhere between Castleford and the Northumbrian frontier caught up with Eadred and the main army. He took the news badly. 'The king became so enraged that he wished to march back into the land and destroy it utterly.' When the Northumbrian witan understood this, they backed down. They hastily met and deserted Eric. Ambassadors were despatched to Eadred bearing gifts, and 'by their entreaties and many rich presents, and by their entire and final submission they mitigated his anger (John of Wallingford). The deaths of a large number of the southern nobility who were in the rearguard had to be compensated too, and the Northumbrians agreed to hand over a great sum of money, presumably calculated on the wergelds of the dead men, that is, their rating in the tariff for injuries which existed in Old English law. The year 948 ended with Eadred again acknowledged as king in Northumbria, and Eric and his followers setting sail for exile none knew where, the second time in his life he had faced exile. Many kings had done the same, of course – the Northumbrian Edwin, Aethelbald of Mercia, Egbert of Wessex – and it had not been an impediment to their future greatness. The Northumbrian submission was not 'final', and nor was Eric's exile.

Exile and the slave trade: 'a pirate voyage to Spain'

We cannot recover Eric's lost years between 948 and 952, for no primary sources survive which throw any light on them. The sagas record plundering expeditions in Scotland, the Hebrides, Wales and Ireland at this time, and there was a tradition that Eric was king for a while in the Sudreys, a favourite stopping-off place for disappointed Viking freebooters. But in the synoptic histories of Norway written in the late twelfth century an unexpected twist emerges. Here we find garbled accounts of a pirate expedition by Eric to Spain, which was then under Arab control. The Spanish Arabs engaged in a very lucrative slave trade with the Dublin Norse at a slightly later time. Could it be then that Eric followed the Viking route to Cordoba and North Africa to sell British and Anglo-Saxon slaves in exchange for silver, with which to pay his followers? If this is so, it adds a dramatic new dimension to his story.

Apart from war, slavery was the best business in the Dark Ages. Even the Church was economically dependent on slaves, though naturally churchmen spoke out against the seizing of Christians and their sale abroad. From the mid ninth century thousands were taken captive from Ireland in particular. The Vikings planned their descents with cunning cruelty, often raiding on major Church festivals when they knew towns would be thronging with pilgrims. Armagh, for example, was raided at Christmas 926 and at St Martin's Eve 933. The Irish annals of the ninth century present a grim catalogue of misery which goes through Eric's day: 'three thousand or more captured with great booty and cows, horses, gold and silver' (around Kells, 951).

The Irish Viking towns were clearing houses, exchange ports for this trade. At first glance if you landed at the quay of Viking Dublin in 950 you might see little difference from the Viking quarter of York, the familiar streets of laid split timbers, the dirty industrial quarter, the narrow planked houses jammed close together. But Dublin was quite different in character from the settled city life of York. The Dublin Norse colonists lived on the edge of Irish society, never occupying the land to any great extent; they were fewer and wealthier than in Britain, entrepreneurs, 'nabobs rather than settlers' they have been called, men with a diplomatic and exploitive relation with the interior. By the late tenth century in Dublin they were minting large coinages modelled exactly on those of the Anglo-Saxon kings, and the widespread trade in England implied by this was probably slaves, young Britons and Anglo-Saxons shipped to Dublin, Wexford and Waterford and then sold to Spain, North Africa, or down the Russian river route to eastern Islam.

Only aristocrats stood a chance of being ransomed. Most people who were abducted never saw their home villages again. Indeed for many it was their last sight of the British Isles. An Arab traveller of Eric's time who came to Spain remarked on the great numbers of European slaves in harems and in the militia. The palace of the Emir of Cordoba in particular had many white girls, though chiefly Frankish and Italian. Of these unfortunate people the Vikings were undoubtedly a major source of supply: they had the easiest access to Christian captives and they had no scruples about enslaving them. The Arabs in Spain saw the long-term potential of this trade, and as early as the 840s sent a diplomatic mission to Scandinavia to put it on an organised basis. Most British slaves though seem to have ended up on the Russian river route to eastern Islam. The *Laxdael Saga* mentions an Icelandic chief who visited a slave mart off the coast of Sweden, again in Eric's day. There he purchased an expensive, aristocratic Irish girl from Gilli 'the Russian' who was said to be 'the richest man in the league of merchants', and who did his buying and selling in a plush tent 'wearing velvet clothes with a Russian hat on his head'. Gilli obviously got his nickname from his trading in Russia: his name is Norse-Irish.

The extent of this commerce, and the speed with which it spread are astonishing. We find Swedish dealers on the Caspian in 922 and by the 940s they had penetrated to Bukhara, Merv and Samarkand. No wonder that as early as the 920s a wealthy York Viking should carry in his purse coins only recently minted in central Asia! The numbers involved are also eye opening. From eastern Europe where Otto of Germany was ruthlessly extending his *reich*, thousands of captives came west from the defeated Slav tribes (the word 'Slav' is derived from 'slave'), to be 'processed' by rich Jewish and Syrian merchants in Verdun, many made into eunuchs for the Spanish market. A frightened pilgrim in the late ninth century in Taranto saw nine thousand Italian captives being loaded onto ships, making up just one consignment to Egypt.

With so many people available as victims of war, famine and natural disaster, and with so much profit to be made, the story of Eric's journey to Spain makes sense and enables us to fill partially in the lost years. In York itself he can have heard details of the sea journey to the Mediterranean, for the sons of Ragnar Lothbrok had made an expedition to Spain and North Africa in 859–861, before they established themselves in York. There they had carried off a great host of 'blue men' from Mauretania, and brought back to Ireland and York geographical information on the situation of Morocco and the Balearic Isles. If anywhere, old salts on the Foss quay in York would remember stories of the tides in the Bay of Biscay, the dangerous northern coasts of Spain, and the watering places in North Africa. They would tell, too, of the treasures the sons of Lothbrok brought back with them: gold and silver, jewels, decorated Arab saddles, woven cloths, beautiful satins and silks 'variegated, scarlet and green', gold embroidered gloves, 'a head band studded with gold'.

So at some point around 950 we can imagine Eric's longships edging up the Guadalquivir, or standing off the coast of Tangier. And perhaps the much-travelled Eric saw the voyage as the tenth-century author of the Viking proverbs of the *Hávamál*: 'Only the man who makes far journeys and has travelled extensively, who knows the kind of mind any man has, can truly be self-possessed.' Like his slaving, his proverbs show the Viking's mind to be pragmatic, not romantic.

Eric may have gathered news of events in York during these years, from a passing merchant ship off Ireland or Brittany. In 949 Anlaf Sihtricson had come back there from Dublin, and King Eadred, while anxious to keep Eric out, may have been less worried about Anlaf. The Norseman's reign of three years (until 952) can only be explained by his having cooperated with the southern English king, and acknowledged his overlordship. It may be that the Northumbrians paid tribute again, and in return were allowed to mint English-type coins.

Eric's return: Archbishop Wulfstan arrested

In 952 the storm broke. In this year, says *Chronicle* 'E', 'the Northumbrians drove out Anlaf and received Eric, Harold's son'. There was evidently exasperation in Winchester. Court rumour was that Archbishop Wulfstan was once more at the root of things. When the archbishop next came south he was immediately placed under house arrest, 'because accusations had often been made to the king against him,' says the chronicler; 'He was said to have connived at the shifts of allegiance by his compatriots,' adds William of Malmesbury. Eadred and his advisers had had enough. They decided to imprison Wulfstan 'in close custody' in the fort of Iudanbyrig. The place of his confinement has not been certainly identified, but was doubtless the site known to Bede as Ythancaestir, the former Roman Saxon Shore fort of Othona, now Bradwell-on-Sea in Essex. It is a desolate spot, suitable for such a prisoner, a marshy promontory by the sea, with 14-feet-thick Roman walls, inside which were the seventh-century monastery of St Cedd and the chapel of St Peter which still stands intact on the site. Perhaps Eadred's advisers hoped that the troublesome priest would catch marsh fever or pneumonia and solve a thorny problem! For the whole period of Eric's second reign in York Wulfstan kicked his heels in this remote part of East Anglia.

With Eric back in the king's garth in York, Eadred was at first unwilling or unable to do anything himself. But perhaps his diplomats were at work in North Britain, spending English silver to procure Eric's downfall. This is conjecture, but at the end of the year a great battle rocked North Britain. An alliance of English (probably the North Saxons from Bamburgh), Scots and Cumbrians was defeated with great loss by the Norse. The event is only known from Irish sources. The Scottish king, Indulf, had been on the throne a matter of weeks. Some important realignment was taking place in relations between the kings of the north.

It is hard not to associate these events in northern England with Eric, especially in view of the alliance which eventually brought him down. At any rate the battle of 952 must have consolidated Eric's position in Northumbria, and his second and last reign in York lasted the best part of three years from 952 to 954. The tradition of the Norse synoptic histories was that he reigned alone for two years and for the third jointly with his brother. Their rule marks the end of the Scandinavian heroic age in Northumbria.

'The last king of the Northumbrian race'

This last period of Northumbrian greatness was looked on nostalgically by the later Northumbrian annalists in their backward-looking summaries and genealogies, and the eleventh-century conclusion, the *History of the Earls*. That something different happened at the time is suggested first by the coinage. The coins Eric issued now were quite distinct from the standard English types of his first rule. The silver penny minted by Ingelgar in York evoked the conquest of York of 919 by resuscitating the old obverse design of a sword, with the inscription Eric Rex. Some scholars have seen this revival as a bid for Norse-Irish support in York (that is, followers of the deposed King Anlaf Sihtricson whose kinsman from Dublin had ruled in York intermittently since 919). It was also a gesture of defiance, a restoration of the old order.

Eric's final rule: the enigmatic sword coin minted by Ingelgar in York c. 953.

Eric acted as an old-fashioned king of the Northumbrians in other ways too. Just as Athelstan, Edmund and Eadred had done, he made a journey to Chester-le-Street to visit the shrine of St Cuthbert and make his personal pact with the saint. In the *Liber Vitae* of the community his name is still to be seen among the kings and hundreds of obscure Christians who entered into confraternity with the saint in the Viking era. It conjures up an image of Eric, secure after the victory of 952, coming to the shrine, at the instigation of his advisers, to ingratiate himself with the traditionalist Bernician aristocracy. Here perhaps he opened the coffin of the saint and added an arm ring and a Kufic silk to those which Athelstan and Edmund wrapped around the body, and which are still to be seen in a fragmentary state in Durham Cathedral Library. And here too, perhaps, he was accompanied by the 'High-Reeve of Bamburgh', earl of Bernicia, Oswulf, son of Ealdred Ealdulfing, and chief man in the Saxon lands north of the Tees, the head of a family which ruled in these parts from at least the ninth century until after the Norman Conquest. The Ealdulfings made alliances with anyone who held power in the north, Scots or Vikings; they had been defeated in 952, and may have then acknowledged Eric's overlordship north of the Humber. But when Eric came out into the sunlight after keeping his vigil with the saint, he may not have suspected that Oswulf was again plotting his overthrow. If anything our northern annalist implies that Eric trusted him.

With so many opposed interests at stake in the north, why did the Church of York stand by the Norse-Irish kings and Eric Bloodaxe so long? It is too much of a coincidence that Wulfstan was imprisoned in East Anglia for the whole of Eric's second reign: the archbishop must have been his supporter, as he had been in 947. Wulfstan was a Northumbrian Angle to the core. His eventual burial at Oundle where St Wilfrid died suggests he was a Wilfrid man, and indeed like Wilfrid he lived like a great secular lord, leading the Northumbrian witan, riding with the army into the Five Boroughs in 940 and securing their surrender, expelling Anlaf Sihtricson, dealing with Eadred at Tanshelf as a king does on the borders of his kingdom, and eventually being imprisoned, like Wilfrid in exile. Wulfstan was part of a society which cared for show and power, and he dominated Northumbrian politics from 931 until the fall of Eric, running the diocese of York like an ecclesiastical empire. This was the tradition of being a bishop in Northumbria, and it is no wonder that the later Anglo-Saxon bishops of York were all drawn from south of the Humber. He spoke for the power of the Northumbrian church and kingship, crowning Norse kings 'with the approval of the bishop and the whole army, Angles and Danes'; the same expression we find in the Five Boroughs, reflecting the custom and nomenclature of a Viking republic. But Wulfstan made it something more.

Enough fragments of the northern annals survive to show that the monk who wrote his chronicle in tenth-century Northumbria (and it is a fair assumption that he wrote in Wulfstan's church) saw the wars of the 940s in the context of the ancient wars with the South Angles fought by the bretwaldas Edwin, Oswald and Oswy. For him and the men who supported Eric, men like Earl Orm, these wars were fought for the lordship of the lands north of the Humber. Only this can explain Wulfstan's extraordinary career in which he led the witan of the Northumbrians in matters of allegiance. The Humber was the greatest cultural and political divide in early English history, and the reality of this in the tenth century explains the tenacity with which the Northumbrians clung to their concept of their history and kingship, and the way in which the Viking kings were readily adopted to preserve this, and came as Eric did to be seen as fitting upholders of the old order. In the fragments of these northern annals we detect vestiges of an attitude which seems to regard Wulfstan as representing the interests of the Church and the landowning class, Anglian, Danish and Norse, against the West-Saxon kings. Their interests and those of Eric Bloodaxe were clearly not incompatible. To read between the lines of Wulfstan's 'political' career is to suspect that the point of view of the head of the Church of York was that of a northern English aristocrat who saw Norse *condottieri* like Eric, and not

A Crucifixion scene from the cross at Gosforth in Cumbria; a 14½-feet-high masterpiece in stone. Scandinavian religion told how Odin 'hung on the windswept tree for nine days and nights, wounded with a spear, and they offered no horn to me'. Here, in another guise, is Odin; the woman with the horn could be Mary Magdalen; equally, it could be Odin's handmaid. In Viking Northumbria the Church found no more difficulty in making the leap from paganism to Christianity than it does in Brazil today, or in Angola with its shamanic black female St Anthonys, and its crucifixions of a black Christ.

the hated *Suthangli*, as best representing the aspirations of his class, his region and his Church.

The final battle

Wulfstan had plenty of time to fret over these thoughts while he paced the compound at Iudanbyrig. Meanwhile Eric's enemies were combining against him. The events which ended his rule are still shrouded in mystery, and the Norse sources give us few clues. In the main the story of Eric's death as told in the sagas has all the marks of a tale reconstructed in the thirteenth century. According to *Fagrskinna* Eric's downfall was his own hubris: 'Eric had so great an army that five kings followed him because he was a valiant man and a battle-winner. He trusted in himself and his strength so much that he went far up country, and everywhere he went with warfare. Then came against him King Olaf, a tributary king of King Edmund. They fought and Eric was routed by the army of the land; and he fell there with all his force.' The *Saga of Hakon the Good* adds little detail but lends to Eric's impetuosity the inexorable momentum of tragedy: 'A dreadful battle ensued in which many English fell. But for every one who fell three came in his place out of the country behind, and when the evening came on the loss of men turned against the Norsemen and many were killed.' The saga also names some of the famous dead: three kings, Guttorm, Ivar and Harek, Sigurd and Ragnvald, and Arnkel and Erlend, sons of the Norse Earl of Orkney. Where these stories came from is uncertain, but in the main they are probably novelistic inventions of the twelfth century, and it is perhaps significant that the synoptic histories from that time have no details of his death. The *Anglo-Saxon Chronicle* is also singularly unhelpful: 'the Northumbrians expelled Eric, and Eadred succeeded.' It is only with the York annal which begins this chapter that part of the veil of mystery is lifted, with the lines telling of Eric's treacherous betrayal and death in the 'lonely place called Stainmore' with his son Haeric and his brother Ragnald. (The similarity of these names to Harek and Ragnvald in the saga is immediately obvious.) His betrayer, Earl Oswulf, is obviously the English earl of Bamburgh. His killer, Earl Maccus, is identified elsewhere as 'the son of Olaf' and may well be a son of one of the Norse-Irish Anlafs. This information was recorded by Roger of Wendover in the early thirteenth century but must derive from a lost tenth-century York chronicle. So the sagas have got some of the details wrong, but not totally so. That this story was later in circulation abroad as an ordered chronicle, such as I have suggested, is proved by Adam of Bremen, writing *c.* 1075. Adam cites a chronicle, a '*Gesta* of the English' for the sequence of kings who ruled 'England' for almost a century:

Guthfrith, his son Anlaf, Sihtric, Ragnald, and finally the son of Harold who went with an army to England and 'having conquered the island was however betrayed and killed by the Northumbrians'. The same Latin word for Eric's betrayal shows Adam had the same source as Roger of Wendover: a Northumbrian historian whose point of view was that the Norse kings of York had been pre-eminent in the tenth century. If only we possessed it today!

As Sir Frank Stenton has said, the story sounds like the last stand of a deserted king on the edge of his kingdom. Whether the saga tales of a terrible battle are right we cannot say, but it is hard to imagine Eric leaving the security of his residence in York for the wild heights of Stainmore without his warband, and he would never have given up without a fight. Warfare had been his métier since he fought in his teens by the White Sea over thirty years before.

The other actor in Eric's drama, Archbishop Wulfstan, was released from his imprisonment, and 'restored to the episcopal dignity at Dorchester', but he may never have been allowed back into Northumbria again. According to William of Malmesbury he rejected the proffered pardon and died, a proud and embittered man, two years after Eric. He was buried in the diocese of Dorchester in Wilfrid's church at Oundle, where the saint had died.

We hear no more from the anonymous clerk in York who made his few remarkable notes through the 940s and 950s, out of which this story has been reconstructed. The death of the last native archbishop and the passing of the last king of York perhaps took away the point of continuing. The lost *History of the Ancient Northumbrians* ended with Eric's death, and was rounded off with the king lists: 'Ever since, the Northumbrians have been mourning their lost liberty.' And of course, some of them still do!

'A certain lonely place called Stainmore'

Go up to Stainmore today. The modern road between Brough and Bowes follows the line of the Roman road which Eric took that day in 954. From the top there is a marvellous view with Edendale sweeping away below, and the Lakeland mountains towards the west. Here was the boundary between the 'Westmoringas' and the Northumbrians, the old Glasgow diocesan border, and before that the frontier of the Cumbrians and Northumbrians. The place is marked by the stump of a cross, still called the Rey Cross, from the Norse word *hreyrr*, meaning 'boundary'. Some seventy years ago Prof. W. Collingwood identified this as an English-style wheel-cross with figured decoration, and suggested that it was done by an English sculptor and commissioned by sympathisers

'A certain lonely place': Rey Cross on Stainmore, the site of the death of Eric Bloodaxe.

in York to commemorate their king. Too romantic? If Collingwood was right, then this stump is one of the strangest memorials in Britain.

Eric's other monument survives in a more intelligible form. When his wife and family fled by sea from York to Orkney, a poet in their entourage composed his epitaph, the *Eiriksmal*. It is redolent of the old Scandinavian world, thoroughly pagan, soaked in the shamanistic inspiration of Odin. It is also an anachronism, just as Eric's rule had been. For despite all the vicissitudes, the future of a united kingdom of England, incorporating the descendants of the Danish and Norse settlers of the ninth and tenth centuries, was decided by Alfred, Athelstan and Edgar, and not by the kings who sat in the royal hall of York, no matter how charismatic they may have been. It is, though, a magnificent anachronism. Hotfoot from the battle on Stainmore, his death wounds displayed, Eric enters Valhalla, the hall of the gods, a hero above heroes. Odin greets him with: *'Heill thu nu, Eirekr! vel skaltu her kominn! ok gakk i haoll, horskr'*.

'Hail to you Eric, be welcome here and come into the hall, gallant king!'

CHAPTER 8

ETHELRED THE "UNREADY"

> Summer has dried the Cheviot tract;
> the Pictish chief rides south
> to cram the steaks his winter lacked
> into his hairy mouth.
> But who comes here? A monk? astride
> an armour-plated neddy?
> and murmurs: 'Men, the war is off –
> for Ethelred's unready . . .'
>
> *Ethelred! Ethelred!*
> *spent his royal life in bed;*
> *one shoe off and one shoe on,*
> *greatly loved by everyone.*
>
> Christopher Logue

Ethelred the Unready has acquired the poorest reputation of any English king. Even the villainous Richard III of Tudor tradition, or the capricious King John come nowhere near the image of national degeneracy, incompetence and treachery with which Ethelred's reign is synonymous. According to the authors of the satirical *1066 and All That* he was 'the first weak King of England and was thus the cause of a fresh Wave of Danes'. Nor is this a modern myth. Even Christopher Logue's hilarious poem, published in 1977, has its antecedents; this, for instance, is how the usually temperate William of Malmesbury viewed Ethelred a century after his death:

> The king, eager and admirably fitted for sleeping, put off such great matters (that is, opposing the Danes) and yawned, and if ever he recovered his senses enough to raise himself upon his elbow, he immediately relapsed into his wretchedness, either from the oppression of apathy or from the adverseness of fortune.

But can a king who reigned for 38 years have really been that bad? What were the events that brought about the collapse of Europe's richest and most prestigious kingship and brought in the young Viking 'terrorist', Canute? Was it all due to Ethelred? And in what sense was he 'unready'?

High noon of empire

The decline of England under Ethelred was both astonishing and perplexing because it followed what educated men at the time thought was the golden age of Anglo-Saxon England, the reign of Edgar. During Easter in the year 973 Edgar had been ritually anointed and made head of the 'Anglo-Saxon empire', a king over many peoples, not just the Anglo-Saxons. This event made a great impression on people. It took place not at the coronation church at Kingston, but at Bath, whose Roman buildings still stood during the tenth century with all their connotations of Rome, Britannia and the imperial past. It was the culmination of the hegemonial imperialism we have seen developed by Athelstan – a British Empire, tenth-century style. There was even a special issue of coins minted at Bath for the coronation. Indeed Edgar's subsequent reform of the coinage has been associated with the second great event of that year, when Edgar was rowed on the river Dee at Chester by six or eight subkings including five Welsh and Scots and a sea king from the Western Isles. With such a carefully stage-managed piece of political theatre, Anglo-Saxon political ideology reached its apogee. Writers like Abbot Aelfric and Archbishop Wulfstan II, Ethelred's adviser, looked back on it as a golden age.

The Vikings return

Edgar's strategy in controlling his empire was to enlist the leaders of allied peoples for the purpose of defence. One of the promises a subking swore to his overlord was to be his 'co-worker by land and sea', in return for which he could call upon the overlord's aid when threatened by an enemy. The need for collective defence was once more being forced on the people of the British Isles from the 960s onwards by the reappearance of Viking invaders.

Edgar and his advisers responded quickly to the renewed threat. The introductions to the king's charters in the late 960s are full of dire warnings against complacency over threats to peace. In a more practical response, annual naval exercises were held in summer around the coasts of Britain by three fleets of about 120 ships each. (Presumably the kings who rowed Edgar at Chester were participants in these manoeuvres, members of a sort of pan-Britannic alliance.) No one could mistake the purpose here: as the chronicler Aethelweard wrote at this time, 'no fleet remained here, having advanced against these shores, except under treaty with the English'. Edgar's Britannia literally did rule the waves.

'979. In this year on 18 March King Edward was murdered in the evening at Corfe passage: he was buried at Wareham with no royal honours'

This determined maintenance of the supremacy came to a sudden crisis in 975 when Edgar died unexpectedly at the age of 32. The court was thrown into tumult. Infighting between rival factions of the large royal house came to the surface in the next three years. Edgar's teenage son Edward was crowned that same year, but the omens which were still thought to attend a lucky king were absent. A comet, which was considered an unlucky sign, appeared in the autumn. The next year the crops failed and famine struck: 'Hunger reigned over the earth,' wrote Wulfstan, who later became Ethelred's archbishop of York. Worse, civil disturbances spread as factions quarrelled. Many of the monasteries which Edgar had founded were destroyed, 'and afterwards,' says Archbishop Wulfstan, 'things went from bad to worse.'

Like many of his predecessors Edgar had married more than once as well as taking young concubines, so there were two royal mothers who laid claim to the throne on their son's behalf, and two factions to support them. Early in 978 or 979, Edward was murdered by the retainers of Queen Aelfthryth at the royal residence of Corfe in order that his ten-year-old half-brother, Ethelred, should become king. Edward had been violent, unstable and quick-tempered, sybaritic, petulant and quick to make enemies – indeed a thoroughly unpleasant character – but he was an anointed king, and the Church was quick to find saintly virtues in him and to transform him into another English royal martyr when Ethelred's reign plunged into disasters. In fact even in Ethelred's lifetime men seem to have ascribed these disasters to the murder which brought him to the throne. Certainly it was no time for a ten-year-old to ascend the throne of the richest country in western Europe. As if to cover up the deed as fast as they could, the royal advisers consecrated Ethelred 'very quickly afterwards', a fortnight after Easter at Kingston, 'amid great rejoicing of the councillors of England'. But there was a shadow on the horizon. 'This same year a cloud red as blood was seen frequently with the appearance of fire and it usually appeared about midnight: it took the form of rays of light of various colours, and at the first streak of dawn it vanished.' Even the most determined rationalist among the 'confident sages, wise seers, astronomers and sage scholars' in the West-Saxon court must have taken notice. Like the comet it presaged evil. 'Throughout the nation the vengeance of the Lord was widely evident.'

The renewal of the raids

In 981, the *Anglo-Saxon Chronicle* notes, 'for the first time seven ships

Cain Enthroned: when things started to go badly for Ethelred homilists were quick to point out that he too had come to the throne through a brother's murder.

179

SOUTHERN
ENGLAND IN THE
REIGN OF ETHELRED
THE UNREADY
(Dates signify the
presence of Ethelred
himself; unlike many of
his predecessors,
Ethelred rarely left
Wessex)

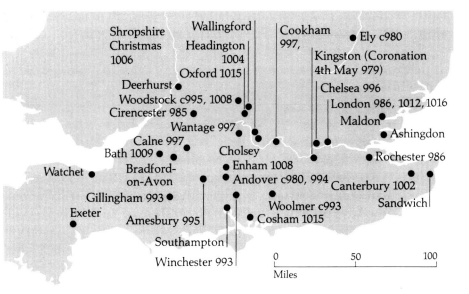

Shropshire Wallingford Cookham Ely c980
Christmas Headington 997,
1006 1004 Kingston (Coronation
Oxford 1015 4th May 979)
Deerhurst Chelsea 996
Woodstock c995, 1008 London 986, 1012, 1016
Cirencester 985 Maldon
Wantage 997 Ashingdon
Calne 997 Rochester 986
Bath 1009 Cholsey
Watchet Bradford- Enham 1008
on-Avon Andover c980, 994 Canterbury 1002
Gillingham 993 Woolmer c993 Sandwich
Exeter Cosham 1015
Amesbury 995
Southampton
Winchester 993

0   50   100
Miles

came and ravaged Southampton'. Most of the citizens were killed or taken prisoner. It was virtually two centuries since the first fateful landings at Lindisfarne and Portland which preceded the wars of Alfred the Great. In 980 Thanet and Cheshire were ravaged. The next year Padstow was sacked and 'much destruction was done everywhere along the coast of both Devon and Cornwall'. In 982 Portland suffered the same fate, and to make matters worse, there was a great fire in London.

During the next few years the young Ethelred, not yet twenty, saw nearly all the great men pass away who had guided England through the mid century, some of whom, like Archbishop Dunstan and Aethelwold, bishop of Winchester, were old enough to have known King Athelstan intimately back in the thirties. The loss of such men, and of great secular leaders like the army chief, Aelfhere of Mercia, may have deprived Ethelred of the political and moral advice he needed at this crucial time in his reign. In twenty years' time he would have Archbishop Wulfstan to advise him, a man versed in the techniques of Carolingian kingship. But by then it would be too late. From the latter half of the 980s the *Chronicle* opens out into a devastating indictment of the Anglo-Saxon government, a tale of treachery, indecision and mindless cruelty by its leaders and especially, it alleges, by Ethelred.

Maldon

In this year Ipswich was harried and very soon afterwards ealdorman Britnoth was slain at Maldon. In this year it was decided for the first time to pay tribute to the Danes because of the great terror they inspired along the sea coast. On this occasion it amounted to 10,000 pounds. This course was adopted on the advice of Archbishop Sigeric.

Anglo-Saxon Chronicle

So laconically the events of 991 are told by the chronicler. From other manuscripts we know that a fleet of 93 ships under Olaf Tryggvason, later King of Norway, devastated the towns and villages along the eastern seaboard from Sandwich up to Ipswich, which was burned, and then turned south to Maldon. At Maldon they were met by ealdorman Britnoth with his troops, presumably East-Saxon local levies. A life of Bishop Oswald of Worcester, written only years after the event, says that, in spite of their victory the Danes were so badly mauled in the fighting that they could hardly man their ships. In an Ely church calendar the date of Britnoth's death appears as 10 August. The battle was a small event on the wide canvas of the chronicler, another local defeat which in this case led to the payment of Danegeld. But a poem about the battle survives in Anglo-Saxon, and this, which is perhaps the greatest battle poem in English, reveals another dimension altogether.

According to the poet the Danes landed on an island off the Essex coast which is thought to be Northey Island near Maldon. It is surrounded by great expanses of tidal mudflats, with narrow deep channels running up to the Hythe at Maldon; a typical island base of the type favoured by Viking armies. This one, says the poet, was joined to the mainland by a causeway which was covered by the sea at high tide, in fact over which the sea 'locked' at high tide: a phenomenon which can still be seen at Northey and which despite recent objections surely makes it the likely site of the dramatic events which are described in *The Battle of Maldon*.

Britnoth came up with his forces on the landward side, a towering figure of a man, grey-haired (he was then around 65 years old), and as befitted one of the leading English nobles of the old school, he pointedly refused their request for tribute. 'We will give you spears for tribute . . . you shall not win treasure so easily; point and blade shall bring us together first, grim battle-play, before we pay tribute.' When the tide went out a handful of Saxons held the causeway and defeated Danish attempts to cross and join battle. Eventually, the poet claims, the Danes asked Britnoth to allow them to cross, and amazingly he did so. What are we to make of this? The overconfidence of the hero appears as a literary motif in other hero stories, a grand gesture by the protagonist before his fall, but this does not necessarily make the causeway story a fiction. If there is any truth in the allegation that Britnoth voluntarily allowed his enemies to cross to him, it may be that because of the destruction of Ipswich he did not want to let them escape, he wanted battle. The lie of the land, the state of the mudflats and channels of

'The streams locked together. They stood in battle array by Pant's water.' The causeway at Northey covered by the tide. The river Blackwater here is still also known as the Pant.

Maldon, make it improbable that the Danes could simply have brought their army to the mainland in their boats. The Danes had to cross the causeway or there would be no battle.

At any rate the Danes crossed, the armies ordered themselves and the battle began. Britnoth made an easy target, towering head and shoulders above his men, and the Vikings went for him, killing many of his kinsmen and friends who surrounded him before they cut him down. His death was followed by flight on the part of many of the English army, but the poet raises the whole fiasco to true heroism in recounting the decision of Britnoth's hearth companions and friends to fight on around his body. As it happens the ideal of dying by the side of one's lord was something which probably struck a tenth-century Anglo-Saxon as an archaic and primitive practice, a fitting and moving motif for a heroic poem but hardly civilised behaviour in everyday life. But for whatever reason part of the army fought on and was destroyed to a man. The end of the poem tells of the heroic deaths of the group of friends and Essex landowners who died in this forlorn spot, their unavailing struggle 'for their country' (as a contemporary said) immortalised in the words of the old retainer Byrhtwold:

Thought shall be harder, heart the keener, courage the greater, as our strength lessens. Here lies our leader all hewn down, the valiant man in the dust; may he lament forever who thinks now to turn from this warplay. I am old in age; I will not hence, but I purpose to lie by the side of my lord, by the man so dearly loved.

The Maldon poem is so powerful and moving that it is easy to accept it as a historical record accurate in all its detail. It is not. It is a literary work based on fact and undoubtedly uses literary devices to heighten the heroism and the tragedy. However, it is now argued by some that the poem has no basis in history at all and that the poet was writing forty

'The time had come when doomed men must needs fall. Then clamour arose . . . bitter was the rush of battle.'

years on with no source but the short Latin account mentioned already, the *Life of St Oswald* composed in Ramsey in 997–1005. In short, the details of the island, the tide, the reason for the battle, the names of all the people in it, and the last stand are all fairy tale.

All these criticisms are wildly overstated. It is true that Scandinavian personal names appear among those on the English side but this is entirely to be expected by 991 because Vikings had been living in East Anglia since Alfred's day. The presence of a Northumbrian hostage in Britnoth's ranks may well be explained by a valuable but difficult account from Ely, where the earl was buried, which claims that Britnoth had authority not only in Essex but also in Northumbria. The assumption of one critic that because none of the English are mentioned in the *Life of St Oswald*, and because it is unlikely that their names would be preserved by oral tradition, 'it is best to accept that all are fictitious', is disproved by the circumstantial detail available to us concerning some of the indubitably historical characters in the poem. What after all was the poem written for? In what milieu? Britnoth's widow commissioned a tapestry to commemorate her husband's deeds, and the poem similarly has the marks of having been produced for an audience who knew the men who died in the battle. Is it likely that a poet, writing within living memory of the event which he describes, would invent and falsify the key moments of a famous local battle? He might have used poetic motifs to ennoble the action, but that does not mean that the battle did not take place. His chief source, we may feel confident, was the oral memory of friends and people who fought in the battle 'for their country', as the *Life of St Oswald* says. The epic ideal of dying unquestioningly for one's lord was by then an anachronism, but clearly for the poet, as for the authors of the *Life of St Oswald* and the Ely account, something heroic happened at Maldon; it was not merely another squalid brutal struggle ending in yet another ignominious defeat. This was why the poem was written, a fitting device to elevate the sacrifice to a higher plane. This pointed critique of the heroic versus cowardly behaviour remains most likely to have been written in East Anglia in Ethelred's time, where we know such heroic resistance still continued under local leaders until 1016, contrasting strongly with the pathetic failures of the royal army in Wessex. Like Ulfcytel 'the Valiant' of East Anglia, Britnoth of Essex gave the Danes tribute in the form of spears. That was the message for the generation of 991–1016. Unhappily Ethelred and his advisers did not heed it.

The Chronicler

In the 990s the raids against England grew in intensity as large royal fleets from Scandinavia and Denmark descended in the hope of rich pickings. From this point it is obvious that the weakness of the English government had become common knowledge abroad, and that its wealth was regarded as easy prey. In 994 Olaf Tryggvason of Norway and Swein of Denmark launched a concerted attack on London itself, and though the city held out, their army burned towns and villages in Essex, Kent, Sussex and Hampshire. The raids were no longer mere plundering attacks, but destructive forays designed to achieve the maximum damage and to extort the largest amount of tribute possible. The Danish armies were thoroughly professional in outlook, operating from specially constructed bases at sites such as Fyrkat and Trelleborg. When a second Danegeld of 16,000 pounds was paid in 994, two years after the first, the course of the next twenty years was determined.

The story of those years unfolds through the eyes of an anonymous chronicler who lived through these events. His account, which is part of the *Anglo-Saxon Chronicle*, is one of the most vivid pieces of English historical writing. It is biased, geographically, politically, personally. It was written by a man rehearsed in the homiletic style of sermons we find in Ethelred's reign and so gifted that we may wonder whether he had come into contact with Archbishop Wulfstan, the most famous sermon writer of the period who was a close adviser of Ethelred. Our chronicler is bitter, acerbic, with a fine eye for telling irony, a technique full of taut antitheses as his frustration grew at the ineffectiveness of the English resistance. 'In the end it effected nothing' (999); 'It effected no more than it had often done on many previous occasions' (1006); 'No more than on previous occasions were we to enjoy the good fortune or the honour of naval operations which would be advantageous to this country' (1009). Nine times between 993 and 1013 he tells how the Danes 'worked the greatest evil any army could do'; fifteen times in the same period he adds that the Danes did 'as they pleased' or 'as is their custom', always highlighting the inability of Ethelred to get to grips with the enemy.

When was this invaluable account written? Evidence for retrospective drafting shows that the whole narrative was put into its final form after Ethelred's death in 1016 and before 1023. Very probably it was done in 1016 or soon after. But other features of the text show that it was written at the same time that the events described took place. And indeed it would be unrealistic to think that such a detailed story could have been composed without the benefit of a contemporary chronicle to work from. Accordingly it would seem that the author himself (or possibly another annalist) kept a record throughout the period which was written down after the eventual triumph of Canute in 1016. The evidence for retrospective drafting does not mean that we do not possess a contemporary source, even though the bias of the writer enables him, with hindsight, to paint a cumulative picture of collapse which may not have been apparent to contemporaries until late in the reign.

In what part of England did our unknown chronicler actually write? Unlike the story of Alfred's wars, his account is not easy to pin down geographically. One of its most important qualities is its national consciousness, its identification with the suffering of the people of England as a whole, the feeling for the poor and helpless left in the lurch, the conviction that everyone was betrayed by the leadership. There has consequently been a long controversy about where this man wrote. The most likely place seems to be London. The chronicler often shows local knowledge; he frequently emphasises the heroic fight put up by the citizens; above all he expresses audible relief that London continued to survive repeated attacks ('praise be to God it still stands undamaged' he writes in 1009). If he was indeed a Londoner, then who was he? He was clearly a churchman because he was literate and also proficient in the sermon style of writing. But we cannot tell whether he was a monk, a member of the bishop's household at St Paul's, or a parish priest in one of the city's churches. He may have known Wulfstan when the latter was bishop in the city; it is certainly tempting to think that he had contacts in the royal household.

Ethelred: why 'Unready'?

Despite the chronicler's strictures he is a loyalist. He rarely attacks the king personally, although he constantly harps on his errors of judgement. The people would have forgiven Ethelred, he says in 1014, if only he would govern more justly than before. His criticisms were implicit in the narrative. The blinding or killing of nobles, desertion of his troops, failure to pursue a policy to its end: so many entries indicate that the king had acted with cruelty and folly. Nothing illustrated this more than the Massacre of St Brice's Day in 1002 when the paranoiac Ethelred gave orders (sent by letter to all his agents in the burhs according to a later tradition) to massacre the Danes living in England on the grounds that they intended to depose and kill him, along with all the members of his witan. Scholars now believe that this move was only aimed at Danish mercenaries in the king's pay, but as often happens events got out of hand. In many Danish parts of England this could never have been carried out, but traditions survived from Oxford, for instance, that the Danes there had taken refuge in the church of St Fritheswide, where they had been burned alive by a mob inflamed by the government's anti-Danish rhetoric. The Danish invaders had committed many cruelties, but the average Danish farmer or shopkeeper whose family had lived in Oxford for over a century could hardly have posed a threat; they had freedom to settle among the English in English lands for around seventy years, and in ordering this terrible act of racialism, Ethelred was undoing the work of his great predecessors. How did he come to act so thoughtlessly? What was the character of the king like?

Our chronicler never talks of Ethelred personally, only once evincing some sympathy for his difficulties at his death when he speaks 'of much hardship and many difficulties' that he had to endure. Later sources contain the tradition that the king was 'graceful in manners, beautiful in face, comely in appearance'. As for his personality, the royal charters, the soberest of sources, show a man unable to punish offenders, constantly self-justifying, a man prone to act with impulsive cruelty at the wrong moment, a man who chose his advisers badly. The *Anglo-Saxon Chronicle* account, which forms the basis of our view of Ethelred, bears this out and can be supported in much of its detail. Writing in the 1120s, William of Malmesbury preserves an interesting tradition about the king. 'After deep reflection it seems extraordinary to me that a man who, as we have learned from our elders, was neither very foolish nor particularly cowardly, should have passed his life in such wretched terror of so many calamities.' But William's other comments may also be taken to reflect the story handed down by his elders, namely that Ethelred was lethargic, sybaritic, vicious, wilfully violent, arrogant, and torn by the adversity of his fortune. The nickname *Un-raed* from which

This magnificent Roman sardonyx cameo, 6 inches long, was given by Ethelred to St Albans. It shows an emperor with Victory in his hands: doubtless how Ethelred would have liked to see himself.

the modern corruption 'Unready' is derived is only recorded in the twelfth century, but there seems no reason to doubt that the pun was thought up by some wit at the time. 'Ethelred' is a compound of two Anglo-Saxon words *aethel* and *raed*, meaning 'noble counsel'. *Unraed* means 'no counsel', with connotations of evil counsel, treachery and so on. The pun then could mean that Ethelred was given bad advice, did not take advice, or simply that he was unwise; it could mean worse, that he was guilty of acts of evil. Certainly *unraedas* were what England was plagued with: all these disasters befell us through *unraedas*, 'bad policies', says the chronicler in 1011, and does so again in 1016. The pun is a clever one and there is no reason to think it only arose nearly two centuries later, as some have thought. The nickname is quite in keeping with the irony displayed by the chronicler. Why, then, did people think him a 'bad king'?

Good kings and bad kings

We know well enough what people thought made a good king in later Anglo-Saxon England. Old English accounts of Alfred, Athelstan and Edgar provide us with ample material on which to base our opinions. And even though the really damning accounts of Ethelred's reign of nearly forty years were put together near its end and had the advantage of hindsight – the *Sermon of the Wolf* by Wulfstan, and the *Anglo-Saxon Chronicle* itself – we can see here too how much the personal magnetism of the king mattered in Anglo-Saxon England. Athelstan ruled 'by

'The Christian king must severely punish wicked men,' wrote Ethelred's adviser Wulfstan: 'He must be both merciful and austere; that is the king's right, and that shall accomplish most in the nation.'

'The levies would not be satisfied unless the king was with them': part of the king's job was to lead the army.

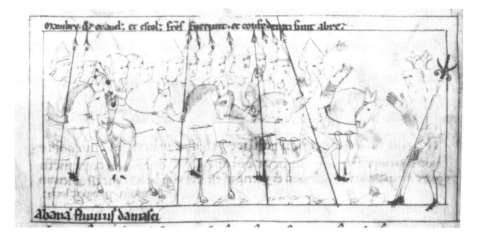

terror of his name alone', he 'struck all the peoples round about with fear' (Asser had said the same of Offa); he had *constantia* but was 'like a thunderbolt to his enemies'. As for Edgar, 'no host however strong was able to win booty for itself in England while that noble king occupied the royal throne'. And why? Because hostile kings, 'fearing his *prudentia* submitted without fighting'. The virtues of these kings were plain. They were hard but just, they had 'greatness of soul'. Like Alfred they were battle winners and like him they had *fortuna*, luck on their side.

Ethelred had no luck: he was unlucky to become king in the way he did; unlucky that Danish attacks should come so hard on the heels of his accession; unlucky in the strength, skill and staying power of the Danish leaders who attacked him. Even so, the successful kings of the Dark Ages had contributed to their own luck. And the English, as they were to show later, could still fight and win under a good leader. It is Ethelred's lack of any of those qualities which his contemporaries really felt to count, which is so damning. It is not modern research which has condemned him. The fact that recent historians have been able to reveal the efficiency of the Anglo-Saxon administration under Ethelred does not prove that he was himself efficient. On the contrary the strength of the national kingship organisation built up by his predecessors demonstrates the weakness at the top in Ethelred's time. Moral failure in a king had drastic results in early medieval society, and that is exactly what Ethelred's own adviser Wulfstan wrote in his numerous theological and political tracts which reflect his whole experience of the Danish wars: 'There are eight columns which firmly support lawful kingship,' he wrote in his *Institutes of Polity* (c. 1020), 'truth, patience, liberality, good counsel, formidableness, helpfulness, moderation, righteousness.' Ethelred failed in no small measure because he lacked these qualities, and for all his words, the enigmatic Wulfstan was unable to make the king act up to them.

'In every way it was a hard time'

The ten years between 997 and 1007 were spent in constant hostilities. Year by year the *Anglo-Saxon Chronicle* gives us a record of devastation: Cornwall, Wales, and Devon (997), Dorset (998), Kent (999), Hampshire and Devon (1001), Exeter and Wiltshire (1003), Norwich and East Anglia (1004), Kent and central England (1006), punctuated by famine (1005: 'the most severe in living memory') and increased payments of Danegeld (24,000 pounds in 1002, 30,000 in 1007). There were heavy defeats for the local levies, despite sometimes stubborn and brave resistance especially under Ulfcytel of East Anglia. And always the chronicler's lamentations. 'Time after time the more urgent a thing was the greater the delay . . . so in the end these naval and land preparations were a complete failure and succeeded only in adding to the distress of the people, wasting money and encouraging their enemy' (999); 'in every way it was a hard time, for they never ceased from their evil deeds' (1001).

According to the chronicler, things had reached such a pass by the Christmas of 1006–07 that 'the terror inspired by the host grew so great that everybody was incapable of devising or drawing up a plan to get them out of the country, or of holding this land against them'. The solution reached by the king in council was to negotiate a truce between them and pay further tribute, supplying the Danes with provisions requisitioned from all over England. In the New Year the Danegeld was paid, 36,000 pounds according to the 'C' and 'D' manuscripts of the *Chronicle*. It was at this nadir of his fortune that Ethelred seems to have been cajoled into action.

'I Ethelred the king considered first how I could most surely promote Christianity and just kingship': so began the official version of a law code issued at the royal residence at King's Enham in Hampshire in 1008. How much the law code was meant to be acted upon, how far merely being seen to make law was what counted in the eyes of men like Wulfstan, are still disputed by historians. But this text, which was actually written by Archbishop Wulfstan, surely reflects the mounting fears and preoccupations of the Anglo-Saxon bishops and others of their class at this moment. They were frightened of a lapse into paganism – especially in the semi-Christianised province of Northumbria where the worship of magic stones, trees and wells was prevalent, where witches and spell workers influenced people's lives and where the priesthood was worldly, polygamous and illiterate. They feared an upsurge in slavery; already many of the poor had been sold to the Vikings, and women had been bought for sex and then sold as slaves to the invaders. They feared disloyalty and desertion from the army where, charters show us, there were many traitors to the king from the landed aristocracy, as far back as 994. They feared the depletion of the Church's power through alienation of its estates, incomes and treasures to pay the increasingly huge Danegelds, the 'infinite tribute' paid for 'the freedom of the kingdom'. Above all they feared dissolution of the bonds of the social hierarchy. The King's Enham code shows that the people believed that God was no longer with the nation. The land must be purified. The last line of the code says it all:

> We must all love and honour one God and completely cast out every heathen practice.
> And let us loyally hold to one royal lord, and defend life and land together as well as ever we can, and from our inmost heart beseech Almighty God for help.

Disaster off Sandwich

Help they would need. Soon after issuing the Enham code Ethelred 'gave orders that ships should be built speedily through the whole of England; a large warship from every 300 hides with a cutter from every ten while every eight were to provide a helmet and suit of mail'. This was the most positive military initiative of the reign so far. What happened next cannot be paraphrased; it is best left in the words of the chronicler:

> 1009. In this year the ships about which we spoke above were ready, and there were more of them, according to what the books tell us, than there had ever been before in England in the days of any king. They were all brought together off Sandwich, to be stationed there to protect this realm against every invading host. But no more than on previous occasions were we to enjoy the good fortune or the honour of naval operations which would be advantageous to this land. About this same time or a little before, it happened that Beorhtric, the brother of the ealdorman Eadric, made an accusation to the king against Wulfnoth, a nobleman of Sussex, and he then fled the country and succeeded in winning over as many as twenty ships, and went harrying everywhere along the south coast, and did all manner of evil. Then information was brought to the fleet that they [Wulfnoth's ships] could easily be surrounded if the opportunity were seized. Then the aforesaid Beorhtric procured eighty ships, and thought to win great fame for himself by taking Wulfnoth dead or alive. But when his ships were on their way, he was met by a storm worse than anyone could remember: the ships were all battered and knocked to pieces and cast ashore. Then that Wulfnoth came straightway and burned the ships. When news of the fate of these ships reached the rest of the fleet under the command of the king, then it was as if everything was in confusion, for the king, the ealdormen, and the chief councillors went home, abandoning the ships thus irresponsibly. Then those who remained with the ships brought them back to London, thus inconsiderately allowing the effort of the whole nation to come to naught, so that the threat to the Danes, upon

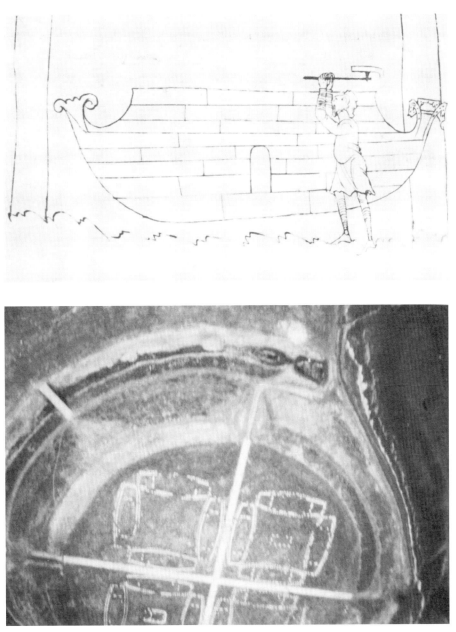

Left Shipbuilding, from an English manuscript of *c.* 1000.
Below The camp at Trelleborg in Denmark, showing the long huts where King Swein's Vikings lived and trained before leaving to terrorise England.

which the whole of England had set its hopes, turned out to be no more potent than this.

Anglo-Saxon Chronicle (translated by G. N. Garmonsway)

Almost as soon as this fiasco was consummated an immense Danish fleet came to Sandwich, extorted tribute from Kent and ravaged through Sussex, Hampshire and Berkshire down to the Isle of Wight. While these disasters happened the king and his witan seem to have

191

The unusual stepped structure with centre doors shows a mis-understanding of his models by the artist, but the general impression of ornamental prows and expensive fittings accurately reflects the huge investment involved in constructing the royal fleets of Ethelred's reign.

met in Bath, but their solution to all this was to issue a penitential edict ('decided on when the great army came to the country'), declaring a kind of moral state of emergency and calling for prayer and fasting to make the Vikings go away.

To supplement this there was an experiment in the coinage, the so-called *Agnus Dei* type with the lamb of God and the Holy Spirit on the reverse, which, it was hoped, would bring the wisdom of God to the English. This iconography, and the Bath edict related to it, bear the unmistakable signs of Wulfstan, now the dominant spiritual figure at court. In fact it is uncertain whether the type was ever issued. Only thirteen examples from widely separated mints have survived to modern times of what is perhaps the most beautiful of all English coins. Small as this number is, it is enough to suggest that the coin was indeed put out, but only as a limited issue, possibly as a royal donation to local churchmen, to show the king's renewed spiritual determination. But by the end of 1009 we may surmise that events had taken such a turn for the worse that the gesture was seen as meaningless:

The *Agnus Dei* silver coin, *c*. 1009, by Blacaman of Derby. Thirteen of these survive from eight different mints. A limited issue donation presumably intended to 'exalt Christian faith and kingship'.

> 1010 . . . And when the enemy was in the east, then our levies were mustered in the west; and when they were in the south, then our levies were in the north. Then all the councillors were summoned to the king for a plan for the defence of the realm had to be devised then and there, but whatever course of action was decided upon it was not followed even for a single month. In the end there was no leader who was willing to raise levies, but each fled as quickly as he could; nor even in the end would one shire help another . . .
>
> 1011. In this year the king and his councillors sent to the host and craved peace, promising them tribute and provisions on condition that they should cease their harrying.
>
> They had by this time overrun (i) East Anglia, (ii) Essex, (iii) Middlesex, (iv) Oxfordshire, (v) Cambridgeshire, (vi) Hertfordshire, (vii) Buckinghamshire, (viii) Bedfordshire, (ix) half of Huntingdonshire, and to the south of the Thames all Kent, and Sussex, and the district around Hastings, and Surrey, and Berkshire, and Hampshire, and a great part of Wiltshire.
>
> All these misfortunes befell us by reason of bad policy, in that tribute was not offered them in time; but when they had done their worst, then it was that peace was made with them. And notwithstanding all this truce and peace and tribute, they went about everywhere in bands and robbed and slew our unhappy people. Then in this same year between the Nativity of St Mary and Michaelmas, they besieged Canterbury, and made their way in through treachery, for Aelfmaer, whose life archbishop Aelfheah had saved, betrayed Canterbury to them. And there they seized the archbishop Aelfheah . . .

Anglo-Saxon Chronicle (translated by G. N. Garmonsway)

Martyrdom at Greenwich

The army retired with their prisoner to Greenwich and remained there from the autumn of 1011 until Easter 1012. During this long period there is no evidence that even this extremity raised Ethelred to the decisive action which the chronicler (and others) seem to have hoped for. Before Easter the chief members of the witan met in London (curiously there is no mention of the king) and remained there over the festival until all the Danegeld they had agreed to pay had come in from the shires. The week after Easter 48,000 pounds in silver was paid to the Danes in their camp at Greenwich: about twelve million coins if it was paid in money. Then on the Saturday things became even worse. Despite the huge payment made to them, the Vikings became incensed against the archbishop because 'he was not willing to offer them any money and forbade any ransom to be given for him'. The chronicler adds that they were drunk, for French wine had been brought to them, presumably from plundered merchantmen in the Thames. On the Saturday night, 19 April, they led the archbishop to their tribunal and pelted him to death with bones and the heads of cattle, one of the Vikings striking him on the head with the blunt end of an axe head. This crime probably took place on the spot where Greenwich church now stands, for when Aelfheah was canonised the Church would no doubt have taken pains to find out exactly where the martyrdom took place and to build the church on the very place. The church is dedicated to St Aelfheah today.

Ethelred's fall

The next year, 1013, the English empire which had existed since Athelstan's day finally came apart. Swein of Denmark opened his campaigning season as usual in August when his fleet arrived off Sandwich, but this time he sailed round East Anglia into the Humber and up the Trent to Gainsborough, which was to be the chief Danish base for the next two years. In rapid succession there then submitted to the Danish king the Northumbrians, the people of Lindsey, the Five Boroughs, and finally all the Danes north of Watling Street. Swein then took hostages, provisions and horses from all the shires, and leaving the ships and hostages in the charge of his teenage son Canute, he struck south forcing the surrender of Oxford and Winchester. However he failed with London, because once more the citizens resisted 'with the utmost valour, because king Ethelred was inside'.

Ethelred was now virtually a king without a country. Swein turned westwards and at Bath the thegns of the western shires met him and submitted, giving him hostages. After this, Swein returned to his ships and the whole nation accepted him as king. Nothing remained for the unbowed, obdurate and resourceful citizens of London but to submit too and pay tribute. 'At this time nothing went right for this nation,' says the chronicler. Ethelred himself remained for a while with his fleet in the Thames, sending his wife and sons to his brother-in-law in Normandy, and after a forlorn Christmas in the Isle of Wight he joined her there in exile. The line which extended through Edgar and Alfred to Cerdic, the oldest and most prestigious pedigree in Europe, seemed to have lost its patrimony for good.

'Nothing was ever done': hard on Ethelred?

We have followed the narrative of the *Anglo-Saxon Chronicle* this far, but had Ethelred really been as ineffective as the chronicler says? Recently other kinds of sources – archaeological finds, coinage, charters – have revealed that in the second half of Ethelred's reign practical decisions were taken by the king to improve the worsening military situation. There was for example the creation of 'emergency burhs', transferring mints from less well-protected towns to reoccupied Iron Age hillforts. In this way the king's coinage continued to be issued and renewed in the customary six-year cycles right up to Ethelred's exile – an indication of the underlying efficiency of the administration.

As early as *c.* 997 the mints of Barnstaple, Totnes and Lydford may have been temporarily removed to an as yet unidentified fort called Gothaburh in the interior of Devon. In 1003 the mint at Wilton was set up behind the great Iron Age ramparts of Old Sarum where it survived Swein's attack unscathed although Wilton itself was sacked. Such instances grow more frequent as the reign progresses. In 1009 the small mints of Ilchester, Crewkerne and Bruton in Somerset were concentrated within the huge banks of South Cadbury which was refortified with stone walls and gates (so the fort which had last seen action in the Arthurian wars was once more in the thick of things). In the same year the Chichester mint reopened at nearby Cissbury. Dorchester's moneyers may have worked for a time at Eanbyri (Henbury near Wimborne, Hean byrig, 'the high burh'). Others await identification, such as Brygin and Niwan near Shaftesbury, and the 'newly fortified town' of Beorchore mentioned in a charter of 1007. Archaeologists suspect that at the same time many of the old burghal defences, such as Wareham, Wallingford and Cricklade, may have been refurbished in stone. This picture surely adds up to a thought-out governmental defence policy which is not recorded in the chronicles of the time.

Nor was this kind of initiative confined to the domestic front. Chance hints in foreign sources show that Ethelred and his advisers also worked through diplomacy to combat the growing Viking threat. The papal archives reveal that Ethelred's ambassadors were in Rouen in 991, negotiating with Duke Richard of Normandy for an agreement to prevent Viking fleets sheltering and refitting in Norman harbours. A subsequent English naval attack on the Cotentin peninsula of Normandy (in *c.* 1000) was presumably to the same end. Similarly, Ethelred's marriage to Richard's daughter Emma in 1002 should be seen in the context of this foreign policy.

The Viking threat did not only exist in the Channel and the North Sea. In 1000 there was a major English naval expedition in the Irish Sea which devastated the Isle of Man. According to the *Anglo-Saxon Chronicle* this did not achieve its objective, which was a combined operation with a land attack on Cumbria; but it was an offensive campaign none the less.

These hints show us that the English government was constantly experimenting, if usually without success, and they suggest that Ethelred was not paralysed by inertia to the extent that the myth asserts. But more than that we cannot say. In the end, the inner personality of this unfortunate king eludes us.

Ethelred, Canute and Edmund: the final struggle

On 2 February 1014 Swein died at Gainsborough and the Danish army there chose Canute as king. But in London, says the chronicler, the English councillors advised that Ethelred should be recalled, 'declaring that no lord was dearer to them than their rightful lord, if only he would govern his kingdom more justly than he had done in the past'. There is no better example of the reserves of feeling commanded by an Anglo-Saxon king. Ethelred sent his young son, Edward, the future Confessor, with messengers promising that 'he would be a gracious lord to them . . . and everything should be forgiven, that had been done or said against him, on condition that they all unanimously and without treachery returned to their allegiance'. During Lent Ethelred came home, 'and was received with joy'.

At this time Canute was still at Gainsborough, holding hostages from Lindsey. With new-found military vigour Ethelred immediately led levies into Lindsey and devastated the land to punish the population for their support for Canute. Unprepared, Canute put to sea and left his erstwhile allies in the lurch, depositing the hostages at Sandwich after cutting off their hands and noses. The campaign ended ineffectually with Ethelred paying another Danegeld of 21,000 pounds to the Danish army still camped at Greenwich. To cap his misery, bad weather in the autumn brought terrible floods which drowned many and made even more homeless.

Ethelred's brief period of glory was over by 1015. In that year the king's son Edmund, who was about the same age as Canute, quarrelled with his father and struck out on his own. Other English leaders, including the powerful Eadric of Mercia, decided to throw in their lot with Canute. Ethelred tried to raise further troops, but with the air full of rumours of betrayal, he abandoned his levies and retired to London. There Edmund joined him. The way was now clear for Canute to strike the final blow. He closed in on London with all his army:

> then it happened that King Ethelred passed away before the ships arrived. He ended his days on St George's day (23 April) after a life of much hardship and many difficulties. Then after his death all the councillors who were in London, and the citizens, chose Edmund as king, and he defended his kingdom valiantly during his lifetime
>
> *Anglo-Saxon Chronicle*

And so, almost unobtrusively, Ethelred 'did his country the only service that was in his power by dying', as a nineteenth-century historian wrote, harshly. He was buried 'with great honour' according to the later writer Florence of Worcester, in St Paul's Cathedral in London. Florence also preserves details of the dramatic internecine struggle which followed. Although the council in London had proclaimed Edmund king, the bishops and chief men of Wessex assembled and unanimously elected Canute as king. Meeting him at Southampton, says Florence, 'they repudiated and renounced in his presence all the race of Ethelred, and concluded peace with him, swearing loyalty to him, and he also swore to them he would be a loyal lord to them in affairs of Church and state'.

Edmund 'Ironside'

Edmund responded to this political disaster with the utmost vigour. While Canute dug siege lines around London, Edmund himself made his way into the western shires of Wessex, and there he raised a small army of loyalists. Canute followed him with his ally Eadric of Mercia and other English leaders who had joined him. In June in battles at Penselwood and Sherston Edmund beat them off. The English now had a leader who gave them heart, and Edmund was able to raise further levies and launch the offensive: a daring attack on London to lift the Danish siege. He moved on the city not from the south-west, but kept north of the Thames all the time and descended from the woods north of the city at Clayhill Farm in Tottenham. His surprise move was entirely successful, breaking through the Danish earthworks, and driving Canute's forces to their ships. He entered London in triumph, and two days later crossed the river upstream at Brentford and defeated the

Danish army when it tried to make a stand on the south bank. Desperate for reinforcements, Edmund was now forced to return to Wessex to raise more levies, but when Canute retaliated by raiding into Mercia, Edmund followed him up and drove him into Kent. At Otford near Sevenoaks Canute stood his ground but when Edmund charged, the Danes were panicked 'at the first clash of the standard bearers' (Florence of Worcester) 'and the host fled before him with their horses into Sheppey, and the king slew as many of them as he could overtake' (*Anglo-Saxon Chronicle*).

A legend was now in the making. After thirty years of military disaster, a West-Saxon king of Alfred's line had turned things on their head by nerve, luck, magnetism and hard fighting. Seeing how Edmund's fortune had changed, Eadric of Mercia changed sides again and joined Edmund at Aylesbury: 'No greater error of judgement was ever made than this,' adds the chronicler.

The Battle of Ashingdon

For a fifth time Edmund called up his levies ('all the people of England' says our chronicler, with pardonable exaggeration, even enthusiasm). In the autumn he attacked Canute not far from the Essex coast at a place called Assandun, 'the hill of ash trees', now Ashingdon a few miles north of Southend. Here on 18 October was fought the bloodiest and most obstinate battle in the whole war.

Edmund was riding on the crest of a wave, the impetus of five victories behind him. He had a large and confident army of West Saxons, East Angles (under Ulfcytel 'the Valiant' who had been the most resolute local commander of the previous decade) and Mercians under the reformed turncoat Eadric. He immediately took the offensive. But the battle on which so much depended was a complete disaster. 'Then ealdorman Eadric did as he had often done before: he and the Magesaete [men from Herefordshire and south Shropshire] were the first to set the example of flight, and thus he betrayed his royal lord and the whole nation.' According to the Latin poem in praise of Canute's queen, Emma, written around 1035, this act of treachery had previously been agreed upon by Canute and Eadric. Eadric was by no means the only English leader to desert his royal lord during these years, in fact such double-dealing seems to have been frequent whenever Ethelred lost control over his magnates. But why Eadric acted this way, we do not know. Perhaps the answer lies in the as yet unwritten history of Mercian relations with Wessex in the tenth and eleventh centuries. The result was the destruction of Edmund's army, the death of all the main leaders including Ulfcytel, 'and all the flower of England perished there'.

Deerhurst, Gloucestershire, the meeting place of Canute and Edmund.
Left The finest Saxon font in existence, from the ninth century.
Far left Interior, west wall.

Canute 'King of all the English'

'Canute was victorious and won all England by his victory', our chronicler wrote a few months later when the outcome was clear. But despite the shattering defeat at Ashingdon Edmund refused to be beaten. He retreated into Gloucestershire hoping to raise another army and renew the struggle. No wonder that he rapidly acquired the nickname Ironside, 'for his valour'. Canute followed him and the two kings met at Deerhurst on the Severn. There they swore to be brothers, exchanging clothes, weapons and presents. They then agreed to partition the country, with Edmund ruling in Wessex and Canute in the north. (The church where this pact was made still stands at Deerhurst, one of the finest surviving Anglo-Saxon churches.) Within a month, however, the heroic Edmund died – or was murdered with Canute's connivance – and was buried with his grandfather at Glastonbury. Canute was now unopposed and the English councillors made him king in 1017. For the next twenty-five years a Danish dynasty would rule from the throne of the Cerdicings, and England would become part of a Scandinavian empire where before its contacts had been more closely tied to Carolingian Europe and Rome.

There remained the legacy of war to be paid. In 1018 the last and biggest of the Danegelds was paid to Canute. The country had to raise 72,000 pounds, in addition to which the citizens of London had to provide another 10,500 pounds. Part of the host then returned to

Denmark, Canute reserving forty ships' crews to defend him. Finally, at a great meeting at Oxford, the Danes and English agreed to observe the laws of the last great West-Saxon king, Edgar. Canute's subsequent letter to his bishops, earls and all his people, shows that through the influence of men like Wulfstan he had quickly seen what advantages accrue from an alliance with the Church in medieval kingship. Now he would be a worthy successor to Edgar.

> I inform you that I will be a grateful lord and a faithful observer of God's rights and just secular law. I have borne in mind the letters and messages which Archbishop Lifing brought me from Rome from the Pope, that I should everywhere exalt God's praise and suppress wrong and establish full security by that power which it has pleased God to give me. . . . Now I thank Almighty God for his help and his mercy, that I have so settled the great dangers which were approaching us.
>
> Canute's First Law Code

Canute as a West-Saxon king, wearing the fleured English crown. Struck at the short-lived Cadbury mint, c. 1020.

Here too the hand of Wulfstan is apparent, and we cannot but think that the Archbishop, sitting in his library in Worcester writing his treatises on just kingship, was relieved to have a young king to whom he could be father-figure at such a formative stage. Treason of the clerks? Hardly: merely another intriguing insight into how the Catholic Church shaped the barbarian kings of the west in the Dark Ages. Canute after all was a man to fear. A man who cut off ears and noses for no reason, killed Ethelred's child, Eadwig, and executed all the major secular leaders he did not trust. But the Church's influence was such that he became respected and admired as a king who was just, who was a conscious emulator of the great West-Saxon kings, a pious man who endowed the Church. The picture of him in the New Minster charter sums it up: the big tough flaxen-haired young Viking (only about 20 when he became king), former 'terrorist' turned the Lord's Anointed, it shows how easily he could move from the world of Scandinavian paganism to that of Christian European kingship. Indeed in 1027 he went on a pilgrimage to Rome, walking in the footsteps of Offa and Alfred. It may seem difficult to reconcile the two sides of Canute, but in him there is much that is characteristic of medieval kingship. Remember Alcuin's strictures about the great Offa: thinkers like Alfred were rare indeed, and the Church could never exact much more than formal demonstrations of piety from most kings. For most Dark Age kings had the inclinations of spoilt children (like Ethelred himself) and their moral sense was un-refined. Canute, you may say, was a brutal, hypocritical opportunist. But he was a second generation Christian only. His father, Swein, had hardly been Christian at all, and Canute was brought up in a world unused to Christian standards such as Alfred would have recognised.

Canute listened to his advisers assiduously, especially to Wulfstan whose pen produced Canute's laws, and who clearly directed Canute's

Canute in the *Liber Vitae* of the New Minster, Winchester. With one hand on his sword, he gives a gold cross to the church.

ideas of kingship ('He was loved as a brother, honoured as a father and frequently summoned to the highest affairs of the realm, as being the most learned of councillors,' says the Ely account of Wulfstan's relationship with the king). Canute was not, people would have said, *un-raed*. Hence the enduring English myth of Canute commanding the waves to go back. In fact, far from a sign of folly, the point of the story was to prove the king's sense and humility, showing flattering courtiers that even the greatest king cannot control the waves, that earthly authority has its limits.

Return to Ashingdon

There is a final scene in our story which brings these strands together. In the summer of 1020 Canute journeyed to Ashingdon with his leaders and with Archbishop Wulfstan and other bishops, abbots and monks. There, according to the *Anglo-Saxon Chronicle*, he consecrated 'a church built of stone and lime for the souls of those men who had been slain there'. Canute's church still stands on the hilltop at Ashingdon, with part of its original fabric, and in the little churchyard a silver penny of the king, an arrowhead and fragments of badly corroded chain mail

Ashingdon: Canute's church was longer than the present one, extending beyond the east end at the right of the photograph. There part of his church survives, incorporating reused Roman brick.

have been found recently. It is perhaps not stretching the imagination too much to picture our anonymous chronicler present at Ashingdon with the Bishop of London at the dedication ceremony by Canute and Wulfstan. His chronicle ended with the triumph of Canute: perhaps he felt there was nothing more to say. What would that bitter and ironic observer have made of the events that day on the 'hill of ash trees'? The man who had claimed to write for 'the whole nation of the English'? He would, I suspect, have sympathised with a much later writer:

> It is always a temptation to a rich and lazy nation
> To puff and look important and to say: –
> 'Though we know we should defeat you, we have not
>   the time to meet you
> We will therefore pay you cash to go away'.
>
> And that is called paying the Dane-geld;
> But we've proved it again and again,
> That if once you have paid him the Dane-geld
> You never get rid of the Dane.

Rudyard Kipling
Dane-geld (AD 980–1016)

Ethelred in a warlike mood: a unique gold coin minted at Lewes in *c.* 1003; modelled closely on a late Roman coin portrait, Ethelred here wears Roman war gear.

CHAPTER 9

WILLIAM THE CONQUEROR

Without the Normans what had it ever been? A gluttonous race of Jutes and Angles capable of no great combinations; lumbering about in pot-bellied equanimity; not dreaming of heroic toil and silence and endurance, such as lead to the high places of the Universe . . .

Thomas Carlyle *Frederick the Great*

The Norman Conquest of 1066 is the most famous event in British history. And no event has provoked more controversy. It has been viewed both as England's most lamentable defeat, and as the foundation of her greatness. In the seventeenth century when the Levellers argued about fundamental rights in the English Revolution, their starting point was what they perceived to be 'the Norman yoke', the ordinary Englishman's loss of liberty at the Conquest. In the era of Gladstonian liberalism and nationalism an even more highly coloured version of this theme painted the English witan as the origin of Parliament and 'the spirit which dictated the Petition of Right as the same which gathered all England round the banners of Godwin . . . [and] for which Harold died on the field . . . the martyr of England' (E. A. Freeman).

At the centre of these events is perhaps the most remarkable figure in the whole period, William the Conqueror. These days it is fashionable to attribute decisive historical transformations to the underlying social and economic currents in civilisations, not to events and individuals. But without William's personal force, his implacable drive, there would undoubtedly have been no Norman Conquest and that peculiar amalgam of the Anglo-Saxon and the European in English culture might never have been. But although he is the most famous king in English history, William's career in Normandy up to 1066 is still completely unknown to the general reader.

The questions we have set ourselves here are simple ones. First, what was the nature of the Norman dukedom before 1066? In other words, how was it that this small duchy on the fringe of the French kingdom was able to conquer Europe's oldest kingdom, and one of her richest? Then, second, what actually happened in 1066? Was the battle of Hastings a simple triumph of the technologically advanced over the older and more conservative culture? The naïve and backward English bowing to the hard reality of 'modern' warfare and political mastery? And after the Conquest, what was *Domesday Book* and what impact did the Normans have on the ordinary Englishman?

Normandy: 'a band of pirates'

Normandy in the tenth and early eleventh centuries was a Viking province. Its dukes were called *Duces Northmannorum* – leaders, or later dukes, of the Northmen. Its origins lay in 911 when the Frankish king, Charles the Simple, struck a deal which settled a small Viking army in the old Frankish archdiocese of Rouen. The leader of the Vikings, known to Norman sources as Rollo, was probably the same man who appears in Norse sagas as Rolf Ganger, a famous Norwegian Viking. The agreement bears many resemblances to Alfred the Great's pact with Guthrum after his victory at Edington. Rollo had been defeated below the walls of Chartres, and, so tradition asserted, Charles met Rollo in a formal interview at Sainte-Clair-sur-Epte, rather like Alfred and Guthrum at Aller. Here too Christianity was part of the bargain. As a token of his new status, as a *dux* under the Frankish king, Rollo accepted baptism at the hands of the Archbishop of Rouen.

Initially Rollo's territory seems to have been confined to an area no more than thirty miles in diameter in the Seine valley above Rouen, centring around Les Andeleys, where the later castle of Richard the Lionheart stands today. Rouen itself soon came under Norman control, and in the next generation their power expanded to the sea coast and as far west as the Cotentin, taking in what was to become the heartland of William's family, Bayeux, Caen and Falaise.

With such antecedents it is astonishing that by 1066 the Norman duchy should have been famed throughout western Europe for the extent and quality of its church and monastic life. As late as 996 their duke was referred to by the neighbouring French as 'a pirate chief' (*ie* a Viking) and around 1004 the grandfather of William the Conqueror welcomed into Rouen a Viking army which had been plundering in north-west France. But we also know from the chronicler Dudo of St Quentin that by 1025 Viking speech had died out in Rouen, although it still persisted in the more traditional centre of Bayeux. Indeed Adamar of Chabannes found that in 1030 he could emphasise how quickly the new settlers had assimilated Frankish culture, civilisation and language. And so, despite the survival of some Scandinavian traditions, when William and his followers came to England in 1066, they were French in speech, dress, culture and political ideas.

*   *   *

William's birth and early career

William the Conqueror was born in 1027 or 1028, the bastard son of Robert I, sixth duke of Normandy. His mother was Herleve, a tanner's daughter from Falaise, and father and mother were probably only teenagers at the time of William's birth. The whole of his early life was conditioned by his bastardy. When his father died in 1035 he became Duke of Normandy, though still a boy. On the horrors of the next few years much has been written, and certainly the dreadful experiences of his boyhood and early teens help to explain why, as a mature man, William was surpassingly harsh, ruthless and unlovable, a man who never showed emotion in his life save on two occasions (his coronation at Westminster Abbey in 1066 after the Conquest when he 'trembled violently'; and his deathbed when he shed tears).

In those early years the court was a nest of vipers; his guardians nearly all perished by murder or poisoning; he himself frequently had to be rushed from his home at night to be hidden from violence. Most of his life was spent in violence and war, and war seems to have brought out a brutal streak in this uncompromising, forceful man. Harsh, rapacious, courageous, possessed of tremendous physical stature and strength, he had that unique gift of being able to make even the most hard-faced men around him do what he wished, 'fluent and persuasive, being skilled at all time in making clear his will', as a contemporary said.

Val-ès-Dunes and Varaville

Duke William, a detail from the Bayeux Tapestry, an embroidery executed by English artists at Canterbury before 1082. 230 feet by 20 inches it is one of our main sources for the Conquest.

At the age of twenty he was threatened by the most serious rebellion of his life. A group of leading nobles gathered round William's cousin and rose in armed revolt. The young duke however was able to ask assistance from his nominal lord, the French king Henry I, who came in person to help him. At Val-ès-Dunes near Caen the rebels were scattered. William had tasted battle and shown his military skill for the first time.

In 1053 a larger coalition of his foes tried again to crush him. By now King Henry seems to have changed his attitude to William; perhaps the growing military strength and independence of Normandy had become a threat. At any rate Henry attempted to defeat William and add the duchy to the French kingdom. In 1054 a French army marched into Normandy in a two-pronged attack, one force devastating along the Seine while the other struck into the Norman heartland. Once again they underestimated William's skill in war, and his ruthlessness. Hearing that the northern French army was feasting in the town of Mortemer north of Rouen, William fell on the French at dawn and completely surprised them, setting fire to the town and wiping out their armed force. Panicked by the disaster, Henry withdrew.

In 1057 the last French effort to overcome William met with a humiliating defeat at Varaville east of Caen, where king Henry was forced to watch his advance guard being systematically destroyed by the Norman duke, who had cut it off on the west bank of the river Dives. Varaville set the seal on William's consolidation of the duchy, and remarkably the time span between that victory and the Conquest of England was a mere nine years.

*   *   *

Norman military power – 'modern' warfare

A number of factors had made these impressive victories possible, and were just as important in 1066. The Norman aristocracy which after 1047 provided William with such solid backing was perhaps the most remarkable secular aristocracy of the early middle ages. Families like Grandmesnil, Tosny, Beaumont were to dominate later English history. Some of the most famous names, Warenne, Fitz Osbern, Montgomery, were all young men like William in the wars of the early 1050s, and they and their retinues provided the military force which the duke led to England in 1066: a 'tightly knit group of politically motivated men' they stood to gain most in William's eventual conquest. Their society was 'feudal', a social organisation based on the holding of a unit of land in return for a stated service, normally military, with a relationship of homage existing between the overlord and the holder of the land, called a fief. Feudal society rested on the backs of the peasantry, but essentially it was about military service on the part of an aristocratic élite. Its characteristic products are knights and castles.

The knight was the essential element of William's military power. In 1066 the Norman feudal force was a kind of New Model Army, crop headed, mounted on trained, bred horses, heavily equipped, clad in chain mail; used to fighting on horseback with throwing and jabbing lances and cutting swords; accustomed to operating in squadrons, to act in concert, to respond to the movement of flags, to use archer cover; expert and ruthless in breaking up and routing a defeated host; practised in devastation as one of the arts of war. Such a force contrasted with the royal expeditionary force of the Anglo-Saxons, which although dependent on not dissimilar forms of lordship was in the main a 'national' army whose backbone (apart from mercenaries) was the thegnhood, and which, though it rode to war, fought in the traditional Anglo-Saxon way, in the 'shield wall', the dense lines of heavily armed infantry.

The Normans were also becoming masters of the art of digging fortifications, although the exact nature of these before 1066 has not yet been decided by archaeology. It has been suggested that the famous motte and bailey layout of the Norman castle – with a keep on a steep mound and a circular outer ditch – only developed under the pressure of the campaigns for the Conquest. But there are many references to castle building in Normandy before 1066, and it is safest to believe that the motte was already a feature of Norman warfare.

It was certainly a highly effective means of waging war. It was through the castle that William had built up his feudal power within his own duchy, and also the way he had extended and consolidated his power in his frontier zones. Unlike Alfred's burhs, these were purely

Crop-haired Normans: an English caricature? The English nobility wore their hair long and cultivated social graces while the Normans saw hardness as a virtue and mocked the English for being 'beautiful, like girls'. The societies also had contrasting attitudes to women: in England they had a high status and had always been able to own and dispose of land; by contrast, the Normans would probably strike us today as male chauvinists.

military in function, bases for the annexation of territory and the cowing of recalcitrant populations, and this is how they would be used in England. Unlikeable the Normans may have been to their neighbours, but as a great Anglo-Saxonist has commented, 'politically they were masters of their world'.

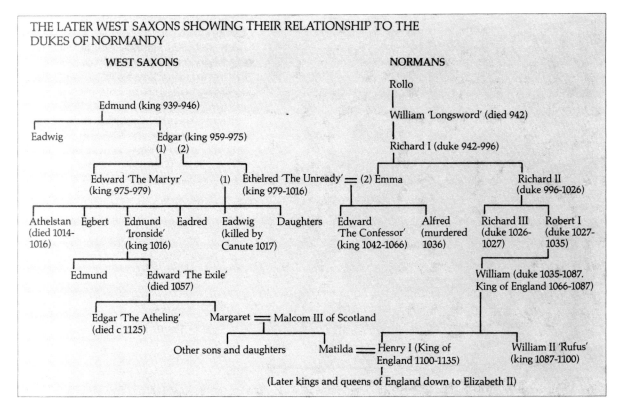

THE LATER WEST SAXONS SHOWING THEIR RELATIONSHIP TO THE DUKES OF NORMANDY

The English connection

Why did William invade England in 1066? The antecedents lie back in the troubled reign of Ethelred the Unready.

There had long been connections between Normandy and Anglo-Saxon England. For example, Norman writers give details of Athelstan's friendly relations with Duke William 'Longsword' in the 930s. But the marriage of Ethelred to Emma, the daughter of Duke Richard I of Normandy, put the connection on an altogether more intimate basis. In his early boyhood, when Canute ruled in England, William may have met the exiled sons of Ethelred at his father's court. In fact it was in the Norman court more than anywhere that the claims of Emma and Ethelred's children, the athelings Edward and Alfred, were kept alive. It was during this period that Edward's sister, Goda, was married to William's ally Dreux, count of the Vexin, and the Norman writer William of Jumièges claims that William's father actually contemplated an invasion of England on Edward's behalf. And so, when the atheling Edward (the future Confessor) was invited back to England as king in 1042, and hence the old line of Wessex restored, it must have been viewed by Edward for one as a victory for the Norman connection. From

Edward the Confessor despatches Harold to Normandy on the ill-fated embassy to William. Other versions say that Harold arranged his own voyage.

then on the Normans, under William, must have felt especially tied to the English royal family, and in particular to King Edward. Similarly, for his part Edward showed a strong partiality to Normans in his administration. Norman clerks appear in his household early in his reign, and he was soon introducing Norman bishops into England, notably Robert, Abbot of Jumièges, who became Archbishop of Canterbury in 1051. In the same year William himself may have visited Edward in England, and though that is uncertain, there seems little doubt that by 1051 the childless and chaste Edward had designated William as his heir. The crown was not in fact an Anglo-Saxon king's to give, but such a designation would have carried much weight given the ties of kinship. There was however a rival for the throne whose family had already shown their ambition to succeed Edward. This man, the other great protagonist in 1066, was Harold, son of Earl Godwin of Wessex.

The Godwin clan: patriots or nouveaux riches?

Despite the Danish names he gave some of his sons, Earl Godwin seems to have been English in origin, son of that Wulfnoth who deserted Ethelred the Unready in 1008. The family therefore had sprung only

211

from the moderate thegnly class. While still a young man Godwin had shown himself adept at going with the tide: he became one of Canute's right-hand men and rose to a position of tremendous wealth and power, concentrating virtually the whole of southern England into his family's control. That his ambitions lay further seems clear. When Edward's brother the atheling Alfred returned to England in 1036 he had been brutally murdered, a crime for which Norman propaganda later (and probably rightly) made Godwin responsible. After an unsuccessful rebellion and exile in 1051, Godwin returned to England in triumph the next year and the family's position of influence over Edward the Confessor was confirmed in 1053 when Godwin's son Harold succeeded to the earldom of Wessex. Subsequently Harold's brothers Gyrth and Leofwine received the earldoms of East Anglia and Middlesex, and Tosti the great province of Northumbria. By the early 1060s they were the dominant power in English politics. Harold is described as *Dux Anglorum*, 'chief of the English', at this time, and along with his brother Tosti led a combined land and sea attack on the Welsh in 1063 which culminated in a crushing English victory. Not since the 'army leader' Aelfhere of Mercia in Edgar's time had there been such a powerful clan. These developments must have been of great concern to William and his supporters since the Godwins were irrevocably opposed to a Norman succession in England. In 1057, the year of Varaville, the exiled atheling Edward, son of Edmund Ironside and nephew of the childless Edward the Confessor, was brought back to England, and when he died in suspicious circumstances William must have realised that Harold Godwinson intended to be king. In the next years Anglo-Norman relations crystallised into an individual rivalry between (as Professor Douglas calls them) 'two of the most remarkable personalities of eleventh-century Europe'.

Harold's accession: a right-wing coup?

It was all the more ironic that in 1064 on a boating trip from his manor at Bosham, Harold Godwinson should have been shipwrecked on the French coast and brought to William's court. There he stayed for some time participating in a military expedition against the Bretons, in which he impressed the Normans and their duke by his physical strength and chivalrous behaviour. The upshot of Harold's stay however was a famous and fateful oath sworn at Bayeux by which (so the Normans later asserted) the earl promised to support William's claim to England. Whether Harold's oath was made under duress or not it placed him in the position of a perjurer in the eyes of the Normans, and was instrumental in William's obtaining papal blessing for his war against England.

Earl Harold crowned king, with ceremonial sword, rod, orb and crown. The artist comments silently by adding in the lower margin a beast biting its tail from Aesop's *Fables*.

On 5 January 1066 Edward died in his new church at Westminster. The very next day, 'before the funeral meats were cold', Earl Harold seized the throne and was crowned in the abbey. It was alleged by some that on his deathbed Edward had put his kingdom in Harold's protection, and the Bayeux Tapestry portrays such a scene. But the unseemly haste of the earl's consecration indicates the true nature of the changeover: an all-powerful dynasty, not of royal blood, had effectively usurped the throne of the Cerdicings. It was a *coup d'état* carried off with great speed and purpose. When the news reached William he received it in silence, his face black with fury. A protest was immediately sent off to the English court asking for an explanation. But that was mere diplomatic protocol. The die was cast. William gave the order for a fleet to be constructed.

The expedition prepares

In taking the throne Harold undoubtedly knew he would have to fight to keep it. Soon after Easter a comet was seen, 'a portent such as men

Halley's Comet: harbinger of the death of kings. *Below*: spectral ships, Harold's nightmare.

Harold, king of the English. Though the reign lasted only nine months, coins survive from over forty of the sixty or so mints.

had never seen before' (it was Halley's Comet and was visible from 24 April for seven days), and the Bayeux Tapestry portrays a spectral fleet invading Harold's mind as news is brought to him of 'the long haired star'. He had troubles enough on his mind. His brother Tosti had been expelled by the Northumbrians the previous year – even in that wild province his brutality had been extreme – and had come across from his exile in Flanders to plunder on the south coast. Thinking this descent to be a precursor of the expected Norman attack, Harold decided to call out his armed forces and put them on standby. That summer he raised 'the greatest sea and land hosts that any king in this country had gathered before' (*Anglo-Saxon Chronicle*) and brought them round to Ethelred's old naval base at Sandwich to await the mobilisation of his household troops (this took a long time, says the chronicler, presumably because Harold was also recruiting short-term mercenaries from abroad, and Denmark in particular).

Over the Channel William was now assembling a great fleet at Dives-sur-Mer, where there was a good anchorage in the river Dives estuary, protected by a great sweep of sandbanks. A permanent Norman fleet existed by the 1030s, but this can hardly have been very numerous. By the early summer of 1066, therefore, plans were actively in hand for the construction of a fleet of transports capable of carrying several thousand Norman and continental knights, infantry and archers, and at least a couple of thousand warhorses, together with provisions, military supplies, mobile smithies, racks of arms, and large quantities of 'spares' – especially arrows – for the replenishment of supplies during battle. It may even be that the timbers for a small motte were taken 'prefabricated' for erection in an emergency – for instance in the event of the landing being contested: perhaps this was the 'castle'

The Norman fleet prepares.

eventually erected at Hastings. The magnates of Normandy were each required to make a contribution of ships, and these were sizeable and expensive (there were stories that the Norman nobility were initially very unwilling to undertake the expedition, on account of the strength and wealth of England, the ability of her professional troops, and the dangers of the sea voyage; but at a great meeting at Bonneville-sur-Touques, William won them over). On the Bayeux Tapestry the main transports look similar to Viking ships, but the whole fleet must have been diverse, ranging from large ornate vessels like the royal flagship the *Mora* (given by William's wife Matilda), to tiny supply craft. The construction of the ships went ahead with every speed in the Norman ports, and after May they began to concentrate in the mouth of the river

'These carry arms to the ships, and here they draw a cart bearing wine and arms.' Not a man to leave things to chance, William even took his own wine with him.

Dives, where the fitting-out was done. It may be conjectured that the fleet was ready from the start of August. But adverse winds looked like delaying the start of the expedition. Meanwhile a new element entered the story.

Harold's renegade brother Tosti, still smarting from his humiliation in Northumbria and anxious to get his own back on his brother for his expulsion, had made his way to Norway. There the king, Harald Hardrada ('the Ruthless') was probably already making his own elaborate preparations for war. Hardrada had his own claims on England through Canute and his successors who had ruled in England from 1016. His wife was a kinswoman of that line; he had also inherited rights to succeed in England based on a formal pact made between Canute's son Harthacanute, king of Denmark, and Magnus, king of Norway. Harald Hardrada was one of the great figures of the age, in prestige as well as in physical size, a warrior famed throughout the northern world. After a youth spent in exile, and a period fighting for the Byzantine imperial guard in Constantinople, he returned to Norway in 1047 with great wealth in bullion, and successfully contended for the throne. His intermittent war with the Danish kingdom now over, Harald was looking for a new outlet for his energies, and the English succession crisis provided it. In the spring of 1066, Harald assembled a great Viking fleet in Trondheim.

Harold Godwinson could hardly have found two more formidable rivals than those who now confronted him: William in the south and Harald in the north. The Norwegians were the first to strike.

Harald Hardrada lands in Yorkshire

In the summer Harald Hardrada made his way to Scotland. Here Tosti joined him and they prepared to move south. Meanwhile King Harold had brought his fleet to the Isle of Wight, a central point for naval manoeuvres used by Ethelred and Swein alike sixty years before: presumably there was a permanent fleet base there.

The southern English coastal defences were now on the alert, beacon pyres at the ready. But during July and August there was no move from Normandy. Around the end of August William shifted his base to St Valéry at the mouth of the Somme. However the north winds continued to pin him down and eventually the delay proved so expensive to Harold in provisions for his army that he was forced to send the levies home on 8 September. He then brought his fleet back to London where they would spend the coming winter. Some were wrecked on the way, but Harold must have felt that he only had to hold out a little longer and winter storms would force the Normans to abandon their plans for the year.

However fate took a hand. The winds which pinned William down brought Hardrada's longships scudding down the eastern coast of England. Early in September he appeared in the Tyne with three hundred ships. They ravaged in Cleveland, sacked Scarborough and around 15 September entered the Humber and anchored at Riccall, a mile below the confluence of the Ouse and the Wharfe. Riccall remained the Norwegian base for the campaign which followed: one of the shortest, and most dramatic, of all Viking campaigns.

Battle at Gate Fulford

On 20 September Harald marched on York. If we can accept the *Anglo-Saxon Chronicle*'s estimate of three hundred ships, then he may have been able to put over ten thousand fighting men into the field, a large army by the standards of the age. At Gate Fulford, two miles south of York, he found his way blocked by a Northumbrian force under Earl Morcar reinforced by housecarls of his brother Earl Edwin of Mercia and troops from the Five Boroughs. The English straddled the road, their line stretching from the river Ouse to the marshy low ground towards Heslington. They put up a hard fight, but the Norwegians broke them and forced their left wing into the marsh where many were drowned. A thousand of the best troops in the north were killed that day, along with a hundred of the clergy of York who had come out to support their army. The Norse poets King Harald had brought with him to record his triumphs were jubilant; the English, it was said, 'lay in the fen, hewn down by the sword, so thickly heaped that they paved a way across the swamp for the brave Norsemen' (*Saga of Harald Hardrada*). The city made no further effort to defend itself, and Harald was politic enough to keep his army out of it. The leading citizens entered into negotiations with him and surrendered on the Sunday, agreeing to accept Harald Hardrada as king and to assist him against King Harold. Hostages were given as a token of faith, and more promised from the shire. Suddenly the Northumbrian witan was acting once more as it had in the heady days of Eric Bloodaxe.

Harold of England acts

How quickly did Harold hear the news from the north? The events between the landings on the east coast and the battle of Fulford can be roughly dated between 12 and 20 September. If mounted messengers had ridden south immediately, Harold could have had news of the Riccall landing in three days. But if beacons were used, he could have heard within a matter of hours. This, not post horses, is probably what enabled Harold to act with such decisive speed. Around 20 September, he set off for the north, 'riding day and night' says the *Anglo-Saxon Chronicle*, gathering his levies as fast as he could. He must have picked up local thegns on the way, but the core of his army was the élite royal force with its housecarls and other mercenaries. He reached Tadcaster, nine miles south of York, on the evening of Sunday 24 September after a march which counts as one of the great feats of medieval warfare. That evening in Tadcaster he put his household troops into battle order, perhaps expecting an attack from the direction of York or Riccall, more likely preparing weapons and tactics for the next day with the house-carls who would be the backbone of his assault.

Stamford Bridge

With Harold of England on the south coast (as far as he knew), Harald Hardrada was in no hurry. On the Monday morning he moved to a road junction called Stamford Bridge seven miles east of York. There he would collect hostages from the shire, and more important, receive supplies for his army which had now exhausted the Riccall area.

When King Harold reached Tadcaster he must have been informed about the Norwegian plans. On the Monday morning he launched a lightning advance through York and on to Stamford Bridge, a total of sixteen miles. The plan was classic Anglo-Saxon strategy, the long-range advance by a mounted army to a prearranged rendezvous within striking distance of the enemy, and then the final advance at dawn followed by a massive assault by the heavily armed picked troops. The execution was perfect. So confident were the Norwegians that they had left a large part of their army with the ships at Riccall, and they seem to have had so little inkling of what was going on that they had even left their body armour behind because it was a hot day. According to the *Saga of Harald Hardrada* their first knowledge of the English advance was a cloud of dust rising in the hot air a mile or two off.

Harald Hardrada's fall

That is not to say that Hardrada could not put up a tough fight. He had been in tight corners before, from Byzantium to the rivers of Russia. He immediately sent off mounted messengers to Riccall to summon the rest of his army. In the meantime, the *Saga* relates, Harold of England called a parley and offered his renegade brother peace and his earldom if he would change sides. For Harald of Norway, however, he had only 'six feet of English earth' to give, 'or as much more as he is taller than other men'. Unfortunately this story is probably no more than a saga man's literary device. The English launched their attack, first of all, it seems, on a Norse covering force on the York side of the river. Was Harald trying to transfer forces to the east bank to delay the English crossing and give his reinforcements a better chance of turning the issue? According to Florence of Worcester, Harold could deploy 'many thousands of heavily armed well trained troops', which suggests an élite royal army, and Marianus Scotus at Fulda records that they attacked in 'seven divisions', strikingly recalling Otto of Germany at the Battle of the Lech. There is certainly no need to confine Harold to the simplest 'shield wall' tactics, though we cannot prove or disprove the Norse account that he employed mounted javelineers with his house-carls in the 'modern' style by now well known on the continent. At this stage the Norwegians attempted to hold the bridge, and a tradition recorded in the *Anglo-Saxon Chronicle* says that eventually a single Norseman heroically defied the English for a while before he was killed. The main battle took place after the capture of the bridge which enabled Harold to cross the Derwent and deploy his army on the east side. According to Norwegian traditions in the sagas, Harald Hardrada fell early on, struck by an arrow in the throat, leaving Earl Tosti to lead the invaders against his own brother. At this point *Morkinskinna*, an early thirteenth-century saga compilation, alleges that King Harold blew his war horn and asked the Norse to surrender, 'but they all shouted back that they would take no truce but would rather conquer or die'. Earl Tosti then fought bravely 'and he fell there gloriously and covered himself with honour'. The final phase was remembered by the Nor-wegians as the fiercest of all, in which the English suffered terrible losses. It was called 'Orri's storm' after the Norse earl who led the reinforcements to the scene, late in the day. 'It was even in the balance whether the English would fly,' says *Morkinskinna*. But the reinforce-ments were so heated by their race from Riccall that they threw off their heavy mail, and many fell through sheer exhaustion. The last stand took place 600 yards east of the river in a field still called Battle Flat where battle relics and numerous small horseshoes have been ploughed up. There most of the Norse leaders fell. Those who fled were hunted down by the West-Saxon mounted troops and killed, drowned in the Derwent, or trapped and burned in bothies and barns. The sun set on an unparalleled catastrophe for Norse arms. The survivors (including Harald's son Olaf, who had remained at Riccall) could man only twenty ships, their army having suffered perhaps the heaviest casualties of any in the Viking era.

Contrary to custom, King Harold did not share the booty won in the battle with his army, but entrusted it to Archbishop Ealdred of York. According to Adam of Bremen it included a block of gold accumulated on Harald's Greek expeditions which needed twelve men to lift it. Later

219

writers ascribed this appropriation to greed on Harold's part, but he was a hardened general in a fight against time, and the last thing he would have wished was an army encumbered with booty. There was more fighting ahead. We may conjecture that Olaf's surrender was negotiated on 26 September while the English buried their dead. (The Norse dead were left unburied and their bones were still a prominent landmark for the traveller in the Yorkshire wolds in the 1130s.) On the night of 26 or 27 September Harold probably celebrated his victory in York. At 9 am on Thursday 28 William of Normandy landed at Pevensey. The news may have reached Harold in York on Sunday 1 October. The net was closing on Anglo-Saxon England.

William: the landing in England

The weather on the French coast was probably cold and wet until 27 September when the wind changed to the east. The ships were loaded, the troops embarked and they set sail in the evening. The crossing was to be made through the night, to reduce the risk of interception by the English fleet. Dawn came around 6 o'clock, and the royal ship touched Pevensey level at 'the third hour', about 9 o'clock. There was no opposition. The hazard of war had fallen with William. The duke quickly rode into the interior to explore the by-paths with a small force, presumably reconnoitring the line of the Roman roads inland. Not satisfied with what he saw he transferred the whole army down the coast to Hastings

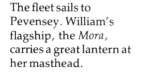

The fleet sails to Pevensey. William's flagship, the *Mora*, carries a great lantern at her masthead.

(probably rowing round) and built a fort there. From Hastings he controlled the roads inland to London, and William occupied himself for the next few days with devastating the villages round about: twenty places around Hastings are mentioned in *Domesday Book* as being wasted, and some were never rebuilt.

Harold: the English army

Meanwhile Harold was riding hell for leather down to London to assess the situation. If he left York on 2 October, as seems likely, then he may have reached the city on 6 October – 40 miles a day. The speed of this march could again suggest that he came with an élite force, the house-carls and other mercenaries with their spare mounts. In other words the royal *fyrd* which supported him in the northern campaign was discharged, and a fresh army summoned to London. Some shires of course had been heavily hit in the fighting so far. Mention of a Cambridgeshire thegn in *Domesday Book* who died at Stamford Bridge makes us wonder whether the eastern counties had been on the northern campaign, and that as at Ringmere and Ashingdon fifty years before, Cambridgeshire lost many men at Stamford Bridge. At any rate the myth of Harold having taken the same army up from the south coast to Yorkshire and then back down to Hastings cannot be sustained. One northern chronicler says Harold had five days in London to gather fresh forces but that losses in the north had been so severe as to leave him with a much smaller army than normal. This would mainly comprise the élite troops: 'apart from his stipendiaries and mercenaries,' says William of Malmesbury, 'he had few from the country'. Even more serious than this is the suggestion in the *Anglo-Saxon Chronicle*, in Florence of Worcester's *Chronicle* and in William of Malmesbury's *Deeds of the Kings*, that Harold could not count on the loyalty of all his troops, and that there were desertions in the crucial hours leading up to the battle. We will look at

The Anglo-Saxon military tradition: armies moved on horseback and fought on foot. Painting of *c*. 1000.

this in more detail below, but the build-up to the Battle of Hastings starts to look less like a great defensive national effort, as portrayed by nineteenth-century historians, but more a desperate throw of a crippled dynast with his support dwindling away: a man wearing the crown of the Cerdicings, but unable to command the allegiance of an Athelstan or an Edgar.

The Plan

What should Harold do? When he arrived in London the news he would have received was clearly that William was at Hastings and devastating the land. Should he therefore attack immediately? Or delay, as Athelstan did before Brunanburh? The troops at his disposal were very limited for an immediate attack, unless Harold had already set in motion some organisation under the shire reeves, to raise troops south of the Thames as soon as William landed, enabling him to call on a force in arms as soon as he returned south. But we have no evidence for that, and we know the West-Saxon levies had been on active service all summer. Unless the king personally called them out, they may have been unwilling to respond.

Harold's plan is clearer, and may reveal something of his resources as it clearly does about his impetuous, confident disposition. Our evidence suggests that he left London on 12 October and arrived on the battlefield not on the evening of 13 October as most authorities have alleged, but on the morning of 14 October, the actual day of the battle. The Norman writer William of Jumièges specifically says that having ridden through the night, Harold reached the battlefield the next morning. His rendezvous point seems to have been 'the hoar apple tree', which stood on what is now Caldbec Hill north of Battle village: a junction of old tracks where the London road comes out of the forest of the Weald, seven miles from Hastings. Harold was clearly trying to repeat the successful strategy of Stamford Bridge: a fast advance to take the Normans by surprise. Possibly he intended to nullify William's mounted troops by a dawn attack on their stockade, using his heavily armed axemen to storm the palisade, a tactic used many times by West-Saxon armies against the Danes in the tenth century. However the plan went disastrously wrong. According to the *Anglo-Saxon Chronicle* it was William who advanced on Harold unexpectedly and fought with him before his whole army had arrived, and before he had it in battle order. The *Anglo-Saxon Chronicle* also implies there were those who were unwilling to fight for Harold. Florence of Worcester's *Chronicle* is more precise: only a third of the English army was in order when the battle started and only half assembled at all. Florence also says the reason for

English footsoldiers with long barbed throwing spears and cutting swords.

the desertions was that the narrowness of the position chosen by Harold did not allow some of the professionals to use their weapons properly. William of Malmesbury in his *Deeds of the Kings* also blames the desertions on Harold's appropriation of the loot from Stamford Bridge; it would be a mistake to exaggerate the English numbers, he says, 'they were few in number and brave in the extreme'. Though not primary sources, William and Florence cannot be ignored on this point.

The pictures on the Bayeux Tapestry give us a further clue. They show us the housecarls, whose equipment is essentially indistinguishable from the Norman, but they also show poorly equipped troops fighting alongside them who cannot be members of the royal *fyrd*, the thegnly class, but who must be general levies, the home guard. This detail suggests that Harold had called out the shire levy of Sussex. Indeed if they had been summoned to meet at the hoar apple tree, then this could have been the reason for the failure of the plan. The rendezvous was too close to the Norman camp, and on the evening of the thirteenth William would have been alerted by his scouts to events in the Weald north of him, and would have stood his army to arms all night expecting an attack. From that moment it was William who was to be in charge, and when his scouts revealed the state of the English army, he immediately ordered an advance out to the hoar apple tree.

Harold's position

Dawn rose on 14 October 1066 at around 5.30 am with a less than half moon waning in the southern sky. The English army was in no position to launch an attack, as it was probably stretched out down the London road. The Normans, who, if William of Poitiers is right, had stood to arms all night fearing a night attack, immediately moved off when it was light and when their scouts had reported (say, around 6 o'clock). They would have caught their first glimpse of the Anglo-Saxon army from Telham Hill within an hour. Harold, not William, was taken by surprise, as the Anglo-Saxon chronicler admits, and his extremely dangerous gamble had failed. There was nothing to do now but form a battle array and meet the Norman attack while waiting for the rest of the army to come up. This is what Harold did.

A thousand yards south of Caldbec Hill and the site of the apple tree, a pronounced ridge falls away with watersheds on either flank. In front of it the road from Hastings crossed the marshy bottom of a depression which made it difficult for an army to deploy. On the ridge in the centre of which the abbey now stands, Harold placed his standards – the famous dragon of Wessex, and his own banner depicting a fighting man (a warrior saint or a figure from classical myth, an Ajax or a Hector?).

Around him were his housecarls and other Danish mercenaries, and the retinues of his brothers with other thegns and supporters, along with the terrified members of the Sussex levy, men with no body armour, 'straw hats' and wielding 'stones fastened to pieces of wood'. The heavily armed were grouped round the king, but also formed the front line, so that the best trained and equipped took the main onslaught.

THE BATTLE OF HASTINGS, 14 OCTOBER 1066 The armies in position at the start of the battle.

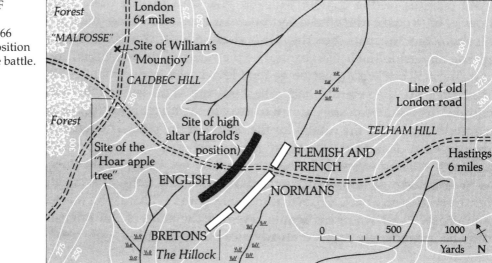

There was no support from Mercia or Northumbria, but the position was still a strong one. Even today it is possible to stand on the abbey terrace and see the battlefield sloping away from the English line: though the building of the abbey has levelled the top of the hill considerably (especially in the area where Harold stood) it would still be a big impediment to heavily armoured horsemen.

The Battle of Hastings

The battle began at the third hour (9 am) by which time William had deployed his army along the north side of the brook in the depression below the English position under cavalry and archery cover. The size of the armies is unknown, but there is some reason to think the Norman army could have been 7000 or 8000 strong. The French and Flemings were on the right, the larger Breton contingent on the left, and the Norman – stronger than the other two combined – in the centre. We have no means of knowing the size of the English army, though if the *Anglo-Saxon Chronicle* and Florence are correct about Harold's parlous state when the battle opened, it is not impossible that he was outnumbered, at least at the start.

The battle began with the Norman archers moving up to within a hundred yards of the English line and opening fire with their short bows to shake up their opponents' formation and morale. In this they were not successful, most of their arrows being taken on the housecarls' shields. When the supply of arrows gave out, they were withdrawn and the heavily armed infantry brought forward. These troops were to open up the English line prior to the planned third phase, the assault of the cavalry who would exploit the breaks and drive the English into flight. But when the Norman infantry advanced, they were met by a hail of missiles of all kinds which shocked the attackers by its sheer weight and ferocity. When the lines came together, the English and Danish professional frontline troops handed out a heavy beating to the Normans, whose mail and shields could not resist the two-handed axes. On the western sector, where the slope was gentlest, the Bretons, who probably reached the English first, panicked and fled back into the marshy valley bottom, carrying with them the cavalry units waiting behind them. At this point, seeing their enemies recoiling in confusion, the troops on Harold's right wing, which may have been, as the Tapestry suggests, ill-armed fyrdmen, raced after them. For a moment the Norman army fell back and the tremor of fear spread to their baggage guard.

The battlefield of Hastings from the valley where William lined up his army. The English were on the ridge where the abbey now stands. Harold's standards were set on the highest point just behind the right-hand building in the photograph.

225

But William, showing himself to his troops, brought in cavalry from the centre and cut off the pursuers, most of whom were cut down in the open field between the marsh and a prominent hillock below the English position which is shown on the Tapestry and which can still be seen on the battlefield. Some of the trapped fyrdmen climbed onto the hillock and defended it for a while before being overwhelmed, an incident again depicted on the Tapestry. In fact the Tapestry suggests that this incident was more serious to Harold than even the severe weakening of his right wing, for with this stage of the battle it associates the deaths of both Gyrth and Leofwine, the king's brothers, who were killed in a melee fighting on foot against mounted Norman troops. The loss of Gyrth and Leofwine and some of their hearth troops was a disaster, and for the rest of the day the crippled English army hung on as reinforcements trickled in and deserters withdrew into the weald.

The great cavalry attack: 'Here English and French fell together in battle'

William had to decide what to do next, for things had not gone at all according to plan. His decision may have come as a surprise to everyone, not least the battle-hardened mercenary commanders in his host. He determined to launch a full-scale attack on the unbroken English line with his main cavalry force, which would normally have been retained for the pursuit. All along the line squadrons of mounted knights climbed up the hill, gritting their teeth and spurring their frightened horses as they came within range of the renewed hail of

The English shield wall meets Norman knights: their identical armour may be a mistake on the part of an English artist who was better informed about his own countrymen's equipment.

spears, throwing axes and stone-headed clubs. William's were not authentic cavalry, they were mounted spearmen who jabbed or threw their javelins rather than using them couched as lances. Consequently the combination of the slope, the storm of missiles and the longswords and axes of the housecarls deprived them of any impetus and after a desperate struggle to close with the English line, in which they suffered heavy losses in men and horses, the Norman cavalry fell back in disarray. Once more, however, part of the English line went after the Normans, and Duke William was able to bring a cavalry unit against their flank and wipe them out. After these ill-advised sorties, the English line became so weakened that it was no longer possible to hold the whole ridge, and the army became concentrated around the standards on the top of the hill.

The last stand

As the battle wore on into the afternoon William used his archers, and his mounted and dismounted troops in conjunction. By now the Norman army had probably forced its way onto the flanks of the ridge and the English position had contracted to the area where the abbey stands today. The housecarls maintained their discipline, according to Norman writers who were clearly impressed by their fighting skill and steadfastness. But now William was able to support his attacks with his archers, whose supply had been replenished from wagons which are shown on the Bayeux Tapestry, and they could now get up close and fire up into the air over their own cavalry onto the heads of the defenders. That this added a final and decisive torment to the already desperate defenders seems clear. The Tapestry margins in this phase are full of archers moving forward with arrows on their bow strings, and the main narrative plainly shows several men in the English army suffering face wounds just as in the English flight fyrdmen are seen running away clutching arrows in neck and eyes. According to a now immutable legend, Harold himself was one of those struck in the eye. The evidence for this was written later and is possibly dependent on a famous scene in the Bayeux Tapestry which shows a man holding an arrow in his eye above which the commentary reads 'Here King Harold was killed'. But is this man Harold? Or is the king, as modern scholars think, the figure next to him who falls, struck on the thigh by a Norman horseman? It now appears that modern scholars are wrong and the old story right after all. The Tapestry artist is invariably clear in labelling his figures, and the name Harold comes exactly above the man pulling the arrow out of his face. Elsewhere the artist also portrays the same figure twice in one scene, as is apparently the case here. It seems too that the arrow-

227

Harold's death. The man on the left and the falling man are both meant to be Harold. The lettering above – 'Here King Harold was killed' – is crammed in to make the point.

in-the-eye story was current in England in the next generation independently of the Tapestry. In this case we should accept the story of Harold's wounding, one of the best-known traditions in British history. In this scene the Tapestry artist is probably showing us Harold both struck by the arrow and then being cut down by the Norman horseman.

As the mid-October afternoon grew darker the English centre was attacked from both sides. Still the housecarls fought on doggedly, but eventually they were so weakened that a party of Norman knights was able to break through to the king himself. Tradition differs as to who they were: William of Poitiers (*On the Deeds of Duke William*) names Guy of Ponthieu, Walter Giffard, Hugh de Montfort and Eustace of Boulogne. Guy of Amiens (*Song on the Battle of Hastings*) may have a more authéntic version when – alone among historians of the battle – he names William himself instead of Montfort. The desire to exclude William himself in later records may have been prompted by the barbaric manner of Harold's death. It appears that the knights came upon the king lying or crouching wounded between the standards and there they hacked him to bits. One stabbed him in the chest, another cut off his head, another disembowelled him, and the last cut off his leg at the thigh and carried it away. According to William of Malmesbury the Duke thought the last of these deeds was ignoble and cashiered the man who did it, which suggests that the word 'thigh' is a euphemism, and that in this dreadful moment, one of the Normans, crazy with blood-lust, cut off the king's genitalia, a piece of atavism almost but not quite unthinkable in the brutal Norman world of the mid eleventh century.

228

The site of Harold's death today, a garden around the ruins of William's church, belying the terrible events of the battle.

Harold died on the spot where the high altar of the abbey was later erected in memory of the dead. When the sun set at around 5 o'clock the housecarls were still offering a depleted but organised resistance, some so densely packed, according to Poitiers, that the dead could not fall. But once the news of Harold's wounding and death had spread, many fled, 'some on horseback, some on foot, some taking to the main roads, most on by-paths'.

The battle was lost, and as at Ashingdon, the flower of the English had fallen. The casualties among the ordinary soldiery cannot have been decisive; those among the leadership certainly were. But even in this extremity, as darkness came on, the English household troops had a sting in the tail. Part of their force regrouped in a rearguard position, a steep bank cut with ditches and overgrown with brambles and bushes at a point where an ancient causeway crossed. Between five and six o'clock some Norman cavalry attempted to attack this body and charged into the ravine where they were slaughtered. Only after further losses was the position taken. The site of this disaster was later known as 'Malfosse', 'Evil Ditch', and a recent search in the Battle Abbey records has identified the place as Oak Wood Ghyll, a quarter of a mile north of Caldbec Hill.

As Charlemagne had often done, William erected a cairn of stones, a mountjoy, to commemorate the battle; this must have been on the highest point of Caldbec Hill itself, at the site of the hoar apple tree, for this locality has always been known as Mountjoy. (Presumably the concrete Ordnance Survey datum marks the spot.) The body of Harold, or rather, its pieces, were identified by his mistress, according to Norman tradition, and it is claimed that they were initially buried on the seashore. If this was ever actually done, the king's remains were certainly moved later to his own foundation at Waltham, where the site of the grave is still shown today.

The Conquest of England: 'the French had possession of the place of slaughter, as God granted them because of the nation's sins'

It is rare that a single battle proves so decisive. Although William had to fight hard over a period of years to secure his hold on England, there was never really any doubt that he would do so, for as a poet wrote a century later, 'the Normans are good conquerors, there is no race like them'. Clearly there were military factors which go some way to explaining the extraordinary importance of Hastings. The English forces had been badly weakened by the battles in Yorkshire and this made unlikely the raising of a fourth army within such a short time. The leadership of course had been shattered at Hastings. But ultimately it is the dynastic failure of the Anglo-Saxon royal family which lay at the root. The blood line of Cerdic and Alfred had been dissipated and there was no longer now a tightknit royal kin husbanding the patrimony as we saw them do in Alfred's and Athelstan's time. It was impossible that a moderately well-born, if extremely powerful, earl such as Harold could command the allegiance once owed to the Cerdicings.

The chief lay and church leaders met William at Little Berkhampstead north of London and surrendered the kingdom to him. On Christmas Day, amid scenes of riot, he was crowned by Archbishop Ealdred of York at Westminster Abbey in the Confessor's new church. The coronation service used for his anointing was that of Athelstan and Edgar. But if the English church establishment thought that William might be another Canute, malleable and deferential, content to rule the old way, they were in for a shock. The next twenty years saw a massive redistribution of wealth in England, as the warriors and above all the magnates who had backed William in the expedition were rewarded by lands and revenues previously received by the Anglo-Saxon aristocracy. The land of the thegns who fell in the battle of 1066, of those who rebelled against him, and especially of the house of Godwin went to his supporters. In 1069–70 a great rebellion in the Midlands and North was put down with devastation and unparalleled ferocity, and more land fell into Norman hands. By William's death in 1087 it is estimated that only eight per cent of land was still held by the Anglo-Saxon thegn-hood.

William as King of the English, c. 1068. The coin is virtually identical to Harold's. The passing of the country under a foreign conqueror is unmarked in the coinage.

Domesday Book

> 1085 . . . The king spent Christmas with his councillors at Gloucester, and held his court there for five days . . . after this the king had important deliberations and exhaustive discussions with his council about this land, how it was peopled, and with what sort of men. Then he sent his men all over England into every shire to ascertain how many hundreds of hides of land there were in each shire, and how much land and livestock the king himself owned in the country, and what annual dues were lawfully his from each shire . . . and what or how much each man who was a landholder here in England had in land or in live-stock, and how much money it was worth.
>
> *Anglo-Saxon Chronicle*

Domesday Book is the product of that inquiry: a general survey of land property and lordship, as it had been in 1066 when King Edward was still alive, and as it was in 1086. In real terms it is a record of the Norman Conquest. *Domesday Book* consists of two volumes in the Public Record Office in Chancery Lane and a related book now in the Cathedral Library in Exeter. The Domesday survey has been seen as the first great achievement of Norman government in England. It might equally well be considered as the last testimony to the sophistication and efficacy of the late Saxon government. Indeed the main volume, the *Great Domesday*, is in a single English hand, and it has been conjectured that this

231

unknown man, grown old in the service of Edward and William, could have been the hand of 'the master mind of the enterprise, the man who worked out the detailed organisation of this elaborate and impressive scheme' (Christopher Brooke). If so, he may have been the last of a long line of gifted clerics who from Athelstan's time had run the royal secretariat.

For the purposes of the investigation England was divided up into seven or nine circuits to each of which was allotted a separate panel of royal commissioners. The examination was made twice: a second series of investigators followed the first, only into regions they did not know, 'so they could check the findings of the first survey', wrote Bishop Robert of Hereford, who was there that Christmas at Gloucester, 'and if necessary denounce its authors as guilty to the king. And the land was vexed with much violence arising from the collection of the royal taxes.'

Everything of importance was to be recorded concerning every estate: how many labourers, poor tenants, slaves, how many freemen, how much woodland and pasture; how many mills; how many fisheries: all to be recorded three times – how much the estate was worth in 1066 when King Edward died; how much when William gave the estate; and as it was in 1086. 'And it was also noted,' adds an Ely document, 'whether more could be taken from the estate than is being taken now' (that is, in revenue and produce). In all this the stark and grasping mind of the Conqueror is inescapable. The result though is our first and greatest public record.

Here is a typical entry, that for Roger de Montgomery's land at Montgomery:

> At the castle of Montgomery the earl himself has four ploughs, and he has six pounds of pence from a certain district of Wales belonging to the same castle's district. Roger Corbet has two ploughs there and from Wales he and his brother have forty shillings. The earl himself built a castle called Montgomery to which adjoin 52½ hides which Sewer, Oslac and Azor held of King Edward (the Confessor) quit of all geld. They had these hides for the chase. . . . These lands three thegns held. Now earl Roger holds them. They are and were waste.

The English thegns

What happened to thegns like Siward, Oslac and Ozurr, who held the estates around Montgomery in 1066? The redistribution of land after the Norman Conquest has been called a tenurial revolution of the most far-reaching kind and a catastrophe for the higher orders of English society from which they never recovered. The record of *Domesday Book*, completed only twenty years after Hastings, shows that though some Englishmen still held considerable estates, very few held any position of influence. It has been estimated that only eight per cent of the land was still held by English thegns in 1086. Only two, Thurkill of Arden in Warwickshire, and Colswein of Lincoln, held important tenancies from William (out of around 1500 tenants-in-chief). These men are survivals of the long and deep-rooted aristocracy which had provided the backbone of military power for the great West-Saxon kings of the tenth century. Now that society was effectively shattered. The lower reaches of society, the peasants and free farmers, were less hard hit – they carried on paying their rents to a new master; indeed the Normans never attempted to impose a uniform system of estate management to the conquered land. For example the different forms of social, legal and administrative custom in the Danelaw, which dated from Alfred the Great's time, were just as marked in 1166. But for the top men, their world had been upturned by foreign invaders, and they had no place in a new order which had to find rewards for upwards of five thousand Norman and French nobles and soldiers of fortune who wanted a cut of the cake.

In 1066 the numbers of English landowners who held manors and who might be called thegns can be reckoned in thousands. The fate of very few is known. Here and there *Domesday Book* names men who died in the battles of that year. And indeed with three such severe battles many hundreds of thegns must have perished even before the Norman triumph. This is especially true of Hastings, an eight-hour battle which ended in the total destruction of the English army. The English losses were remembered for generations. An Abingdon chronicler writing just a century after the Conquest refers as a matter of course to the thegns who were former tenants of his house who fell at Hastings. The sporadic but bitter fighting between 1068 and 1071 with notable risings in Western Mercia and Northumbria probably accounted for further heavy loss to the Anglo-Saxon landed nobility. It was a shattered aristocracy which the Domesday clerks recorded in 1086.

Of those who survived the grim period of the late sixties and early seventies, many saw no reason to stay in England once the Conqueror's grip was assured. There is much evidence for a widespread emigration of Englishmen into other countries, into Denmark, into Scotland and, most remarkably of all, to Greece and the Byzantine empire where there is good contemporary evidence that large numbers of Englishmen took service with the emperor in Constantinople in the generation following Hastings. As for those who stayed behind and came to terms with the Conqueror, most found themselves as subtenants on their native land, 'public servitude' as a late eleventh-century writer called it. The conditions of their lives, their very existence, depended on the extent to which an alien king (who never even learned their language) could control his alien followers. Behind the bureaucrats' prose of *Domesday*

Book, the sorrow of individuals sometimes comes to light: Aelfric of Marsh Gibbon who held his land freely in King Edward's time now holds it from William, son of Ansculf, 'at rent, heavily and wretchedly'. The process is generally unrecorded by which the Normans were eventually assimilated into English society and became English, rather than the other way around. It took a long time for English conception of England to pass into the Norman consciousness, and such thoughts were far away in 1086.

'Penitence for all the blood I shed'

Towards the end of 1086 William crossed the Channel for the last time. In the summer of the following year he launched a retaliatory offensive against the French king down the Seine towards Paris. At Mantes in the Vexin, only thirty miles from Paris, when the garrison sallied out against him, he caught them in a surprise attack, broke into the town and totally destroyed it, church and all. Now sixty years old, corpulent and cantankerous, the Conqueror could no more be crossed than in his youth. It may be that this barbarous destruction was an exercise in terror as a prelude to an attack on Paris itself. If it was we will never know, for as he rode through the falling embers in the burning streets of Mantes, his horse threw him so hard against his high pommel that he ruptured his stomach. In great pain he retired to Rouen, and when it became clear that he was dying, asked to be carried to the priory of St Gervais on a hill in the western suburbs. There the man who was 'too relentless to care though all might hate him', as an English chronicler wrote, burst into floods of tears as he prayed for divine mercy, worried about the future, and grudgingly softened his heart towards his rebellious eldest son Robert. But even in that moment it was over the disposal of his treasures that he spent most thought, for this was a man 'greedy beyond all measure' (so an Englishman said). He also expressed penitence for the vast bloodshed which had been the price of his greatness. William died at dawn on 9 September 1087, asking to be commended to the Virgin Mary, 'that by her intercession I may be reconciled to her Son our Lord Jesus Christ'. He was buried at his monastery of St Stephen in Caen, the Abbaye-aux-Hommes; the tomb was destroyed in the religious riots of the sixteenth century, and today a simple stone slab records the place.

The face of the Conqueror?

Thus passed the great political genius of early English history. Tall, inflexible of purpose, fearless, 'he conquered by fire and sword and ruled by fear', writes a modern scholar of him. There is however a bizarre

The macabre portrait of William in Caen: the costume is that of a Renaissance prince, but is the face that of the Conqueror?

tailpiece to his remarkable career. In 1522, on instructions from Rome, his tomb was opened for the first time since the eleventh century, and the body examined. It was found to have been embalmed and was in a remarkable state of preservation. The papal visitors had the presence of mind to call for a local painter who copied the face onto a wooden panel, which was subsequently hung by the royal tomb. The painting survived the destruction of 1562 but soon afterwards vanishes from the historical record. However in the sacristy at St Etienne there is still to be seen today a painting of William in the costume of the period of Henry VIII; an attached note adds that this picture is a copy of an image which was displayed on one of the walls of the abbey. Is this then a copy at one or two removes from the macabre portrait, the death mask of 1522? Can we still gaze on the face of the Conqueror?

> If anyone desires to know what kind of man he was or in what honour he was held . . . then we shall write of him as we have known him, who have ourselves seen him and at one time dwelt in his court. King William, of whom we speak, was a man of great wisdom and power, and surpassed in honour and strength all those who had gone before him. Though stern beyond measure to those who opposed his will. . . .
>
> A hard man was the king
> . . . he was sunk in greed
> And utterly given up to avarice. . . .Alas! that any man should
> bear himself so proudly
> And deem himself exalted above all other men
> May Almighty God show mercy on his soul
> And pardon him his sins.
>
> *Anglo-Saxon Chronicle*

In the years since this book was first published, new discoveries and fresh appraisals have continued, as always, to augment and modify our knowledge of the Anglo-Saxon period. In particular, there have been a number of dramatic archaeological finds. The most significant in potential is still in its early stages. This is a comprehensive re-excavation of the entire gravefield at Sutton Hoo, which, as suggested in Chapter 3, is already proving to be a far more complex site than its first excavators could have guessed. Late in 1986 a Coptic bowl of the kind described on page 73 was found nearby, adding to our impression of the wide contacts of the East Anglian dynasty. New finds in local archives in Suffolk have provided place-name evidence pointing to the site of a pagan religious sanctuary between the ship burial and the river Deben: in Tudor times it was the site of a gallows (ancient execution sites often mark traditional places of heathen ritual). Other local place-names may help investigators pin down the whereabouts of the presumed royal residence at Sutton, and of the pagan cemetery for the royal staff. Excavation of the fields around the ship mounds has already shown that occupation of the site goes back through the Bronze Age to Neolithic times. Historical investigation has already established that the events which took place at Sutton Hoo in the early seventh century had a deep and lasting effect on the landscape and on subsequent settlement of the neighbourhood. How much this was in turn affected by the Roman, Iron Age and prehistoric history of the place remains to be discovered. Finally, as for the Sutton Hoo Man himself: was the mound opened in the mid seventh century and the body removed from the pagan burial site to a Christian church (at Sutton?), after which the wooden coffin rotted, leaving its impression, but no body?

Perhaps the most significant development in recent years in historical studies of the early Saxon period has been a revaluation of ideas about kingship, and especially of overlordship. In particular there is the notoriously thorny question of the 'bretwaldas'. Recent scholarly work has tended to emphasise that Bede's famous list of kings who held the *imperium* (see p. 63) should be seen more as a literary reflection, as an attempt by Bede to give a 'potted' history of great Anglo-Saxon rulers, than as a list of successions to a recognisable political office. The nature and extent of their power must have varied greatly according to individual circumstance, and accordingly it would be a mistake to see the *imperium* literally as an 'office' of overking with rights and duties. The chronicler of King Alfred's day who added Egbert of Wessex to the list as 'the eighth king who was Bretwalda' may be interpreting Bede's kings in a way he never intended, just as modern historians have perhaps been too hasty in reading into this poetic term an institutionalised 'bretwaldaship'. At the same time, the survival of such documents as the *Tribal Hidage* (see p. 82) and a late copy of a remarkable seventh-century tribute list from Dal Riada (the early kingdom of the Scots in the Clyde valley), which was probably drawn up for one of the Northumbrian overkings named by Bede, suggests that Bede was still right to list certain kings who held power as 'wide-rulers' and claimed *imperium* over other kings.

One of those *imperatores* was Offa's predecessor Aethelbald of Mercia (see p. 80) who Bede notes was the pre-eminent king in England south of the Humber at the time he (Bede) was completing his *Ecclesiastical History*. Recently, exciting finds at Repton in Derbyshire have confirmed the importance of that place to the Mercian royal family (see p.102). Close to the mausoleum used for royal burials, fragments of a standing cross have been found bearing a tremendously striking – and grimly realistic – image of a mounted warrior king, heavily armoured and bearded. It has been suggested by the excavator that this is a 'portrait' of Aethelbald himself in still vigorous old age, depicted in the manner of imperial Roman equestrian portraiture.

The Repton dig has also brought to light sensational new information about the onslaught of the Viking 'Great Army' on Midland England in 873–4. The semicircular ditch of the Danish winter camp that year has been excavated with a dock for repairing the Viking longships which had been sailed all the way from the Humber up the Trent into the heart of Mercia. Inside the ditches, under a mound covering a half demolished funeral monument, were found the disarticulated bones of about 250 men, many of them bearing the marks of old wounds. Presumably these were members of the 'Great Army' who had died of disease or in skirmishing during the occupation of Mercia in 873. A local antiquarian's journal reveals that these burials were first exposed and then reburied in the eighteenth century: originally the bones were laid in neat rows around the central chamber, in which there was a single body, perhaps a Viking king or chief. Further mounds await investigation.

Alfred the Great's response to the threat posed by the 'Great Army' and its successors is becoming much better understood. A recent revaluation of the *Burghal Hidage* (see p.120) has suggested that in its original form it may be dated from before 886, in which case it represents the defensive measures taken by Alfred to protect Wessex against Viking attack in the eight years after his triumph at Edington. This massive reorganisation involved the movement of thousands of settlers to provide garrisons and entailed the creation of a network of support in the surrounding countryside to feed the new 'urban' dwellers. Also implicit in the burghal system is provision to allow members of the burh garrisons, *and* of the mobile field army, to be absent from the normal duties of agriculture for long stretches at a time. Such far-going reorganisation probably demanded an even more drastic reshaping of society than has been thought. It is likely that the pressures of war during Alfred's reign accelerated the decline of an 'independent' peasantry in southern England, and the spread of nucleated villages under strong lordly control, with the growth of the classic form of crop rotation and communal farming, the 'three-field system'. Recent archaeological and documentary investigations strongly support the hypothesis that here, as elsewhere, the reign of Alfred was a watershed in the development of Anglo-Saxon kingship.

The models for Alfred's 'hidden' revolution can be found in Carolingian kingship on the continent, both in its practical achievements and in the wealth of theoretical material generated by its experts on ideology and political theory in the ninth century. There had been connections between the West-Saxon dynasty and the Carolingians from the early ninth century, but in Alfred's reign they were particularly close, and two of his chief intellectual advisers were continental scholars – Grimbald from St Bertin in Flanders, and John 'the Old Saxon' from the Rhineland. One practical result of the influence of such men may have been the creation or extension of the system of hundreds and 'tenths' (tithings) over southern England. Though we have to wait till the early twelfth century for a definite statement on this (in William of Malmesbury's *Gesta Regum*), the system of local government groupings of units assessed at 100 hides, each of which had its own court for administration and justice, seems to have developed between the late ninth century and c. 940; the idea was adopted from current Frankish practice, and bears out our numerous hints that underneath the idealised picture of Alfred as the 'Truthteller' and 'England's Darling' lies the dimmer, more elusive image, far more complicated and subtle, of a politician who could be a far-sighted and even ruthless administrator, consciously juggling deeply felt secular and spiritual responsibilities – to God, to his kinsmen and people, to his dynasty (past, present and future) and even to English people in the wider territories occupied by the *gens Anglorum*: as one eminent scholar has said: 'The gulf between the theory and practice of Christian kingship was never narrower than during his reign.'

If Alfred has scooped the praise of posterity, his son Edward the Elder is a most significant figure whom we are unlikely to know better because of the dearth of sources for his reign. Instead, it was Alfred's grandson Athelstan who was able to bask in the glory. By his death in 939 the 'hidden revolution' in English government was complete. Under Alfred, his son and grandson, English administrative history was much more radically reshaped than it would be after 1066. The broad lines of the political fabric detailed in the Conqueror's *Domesday*

Book of 1086 were already present by 939, laid down by what looks like a 'family plan' pursued by the Alfredian dynasty over at least three generations. The laws of Athelstan show that by his time the government could assess the whole of the country south of the Humber in terms of ploughs and ploughlands – the essential units of the Domesday survey. Presumably such information was gathered from the hundred courts by the 'shire reeve' (sheriff – an office which first appears under Athelstan).

In this light it is worth considering how the accident of survival of government records from the Anglo-Saxon period has influenced our view of their achievement. Until Norman times – indeed until well into the twelfth century – a huge quantity of archival material from the Old English period was kept in the royal treasury in Winchester. What survives today, in addition to the royal law codes and around 2000 charters, are mere fragments: estate lists, inventories of stock and serfs from great abbeys, documents such as the *Burghal Hidage* from the central administration. Some local pieces, such as a list of places owing service to repair Rochester Bridge, a memorandum on contributions to ship crews, or an assessment for an entire shire, Northamptonshire, give an indication of the breadth and detail of the material which existed formerly. The pre-Conquest kings of England used literacy in their rule as much as the immediate post first Norman kings: but they used the vernacular across their kingdom as a means of transmitting their will down to the local courts of the hundreds, and as Old English ceased to be used in official circles under the Normans, the vernacular archives were eventually thrown out.

So these fragments are all that remains to testify to the sophistication of the Old English administration created by Alfred, Edward and Athelstan: such a paucity that earlier generations were tempted to underestimate the Anglo-Saxon achievement and ascribe to the Normans the great advances in government which seemed to be revealed in *Domesday Book*. In fact the survey of 1086 was in the Old English and Carolingian traditions, and the mechanisms which made it possible were in existence by 940. Recent work on *Domesday Book* has shown that the Conqueror's surveyors relied not only on the sworn testimony of the local juries but on written material, 'ancient rolls in the royal treasury still preserved with the [Domesday] survey of all England' as a twelfth-century historian put it. These 'Winchester rolls' may have gone back as far as Athelstan's day.

Politically, it has been said, the Normans were masters of their world. But the foundations of their England were Anglo-Saxon. Just as *Domesday Book* can be seen as a product of the Old English system of local government and the Old English royal administration, so the England it portrays is Anglo-Saxon England, the society built up on the ruins of

Rome over 500 years and decisively shaped by Offa, Alfred, Athelstan and the others. It was, for its time, a remarkably unified country (at least south of the Humber) with a vernacular literature unmatched in Europe, a standardised form of Old English, and sophisticated machinery of government, chancery, coinage and law. It had created, too, under royal patronage, a great Christian Latin culture whose artists included the anonymous masters of the wonderful books from eighth-century Northumbria or late tenth-century Winchester and Ramsey. In Bede it not only produced the greatest historian of the Middle Ages, but the thinker who perhaps more than any other gave form to the identity of the English people, the *gens Anglorum*. This idea we can trace through Alfred's preface to the *Pastoral Care*, Althelstan's laws, and the Anglo-Saxon chronicler of Ethelred's day with his identification with the English people as a whole, *eall Angel cynn*. This idea of English identity survived the Norman Conquest and of course continued to exist under Norman occupation in the language spoken by the peasantry in the countryside: indeed it is likely that the language itself had been a powerful maker of unity before 1066. During the thirteenth century the communal idea of the body politic expressed in Magna Carta may owe something to this: a 'commune of the whole land' bound together by mutual oaths – not to the Norman feudal lord, but to each other in the manner of Old English law. Sixty years later, in the Barons' Revolt of 1265, we can glimpse such ideas working at the grass roots in the village of Peatling Magna in Leicestershire when some locals, 'foolish men of the village', tried to arrest men belonging to the marshal of the king's household on the grounds that they were 'going against the commune of the realm', *communitas regni* according to the government record; *this landes folk* was perhaps what they actually said in English. So, five or six generations on from Domesday, the descendants of the Anglo-Danish free peasantry of Leicestershire, perhaps illiterate, had grasped the idea of a national community: very likely it had been handed down to them.

These speculations provoke a final question about the Anglo-Saxon legacy. Do some of the distinctive qualities of English – Anglo-Saxon – civilisation, which have been bequeathed to the English-speaking world as a whole, go back to ideas evolved in Anglo-Saxon England? Ideas about common law, property, marriage, inheritance, the role of women, personal freedom, and so on. Was 'English individualism', as it has been termed by modern scholars, already shaping itself then? And why is it that the structures of Anglo-Saxon local government, the shires, hundreds, sokes and tithings, were so effective and so long-lasting (many surviving unaltered until the so-called reforms of 1974)? Did English democracy depend in no small measure on these local institutions bound by the common oath? In the Victorian period it was widely believed that many of their institutions went back to Anglo-

Saxon times. Subsequently such ideas were dismissed as nineteenth-century romanticism. But now many scholars are seriously reconsidering this judgement as the whole of the Old English period is revalued. The lineaments (and the thought world) of the state created by Alfred, Athelstan, and their successors, may have been much more long-lasting than we have suspected.

Additional Notes for 2001 Edition

For additional information on the topics covered in this book, I can recommend the following:

First of all a valuable reference work is *The Blackwell Encyclopaedia of Anglo-Saxon England* (1999).

On Sutton Hoo – *Sutton Hoo: Burial Ground of Kings?*, Martin O. H. Carver, British Museum (1998). There is also a series of essays edited by the same author: *The Age of Sutton Hoo*, The Boydell Press (1994).

On the rise of the Anglo-Saxon Kingdoms, see now *Northumbria's Golden Age*, ed. Jane Hawkes and Susan Mills, Sutton Publishing (1998) and the forthcoming *Mercia*, ed. Michelle Brown, Leicester University Press (2001), an exciting synthesis of new material on a very important and until now strangely ignored area.

On Alfred the Great, there have been two recent biographies by David Sturdy, Constable (1996) and Richard Abels, Longman Higher Education (1998). There is an interesting study of Alfred's towns and forts: *The Defence of Wessex*, ed. David Hill and Alexander R. Rumble, Manchester University Press (1996).

On Canute, see now M. K. Lawson *Cnut: the Danes in England in the Early Eleventh Century*, Longman Higher Education (1993) and *The Reign of Cnut*, ed. Alexander Rumble, Leicester University Press (1994).

For a wide ranging view of the English state before 1066, see James Campbell's *The Anglo-Saxon State*, Hambledon and London (2000).

And finally in my recent set of essays *In Search of England*, Penguin (2000) I have looked again at a number of these stories, including the Arthur legend, Alfred the Great and the Norman Conquest, paying special attention to the reign of King Athelstan.

Those readers who may wish to follow up some of the stories in this book may be interested to know of the main modern works which are generally available. On Boudica the best modern study is *Boudica* by Graham Webster, Batsford (1978), though the short account by Ian Andrews, *Boudicca's Revolt*, C.U.P. (1972), is excellent, especially for schools. On the Roman conquest there is G. Webster and D. Dudley, *The Roman Conquest of Britain*, Pan (1973). Tacitus' *Annals* and *Agricola* are both available in Penguin paperbacks; Dio's *Roman History* is in the Loeb Classical Library (Book LXII).

The chief sources for the Arthurian era – Gildas, Nennius, the Welsh Annals, and the material on St Patrick – have all been published in new paperback editions by Phillimore. *The Anglo-Saxon Chronicle* is in an Everyman paperback edition by G. N. Garmonsway (1972). Bede's *Ecclesiastical History* is in Penguin, but its introduction takes no account of recent scholarship on Bede's milieu, his sources and his text. There are good modern works on the Arthurian period by Leslie Alcock, *Arthur's Britain*, Penguin 1971, Charles Thomas, *Britain and Ireland in Early Christian Times*, Thames and Hudson (1971) and Stephen Johnson, *Later Roman Britain*, Routledge (1980). There are stimulating general surveys of the Late Roman world by Peter Brown, *The World of Late Antiquity*, Thames and Hudson (1971), and Perry Anderson, *Passages from Late Antiquity to Feudalism*, Verso Editions (1978).

On the Anglo-Saxon period a great amount has been published in recent years. The main documentary and narrative sources are printed in *English Historical Documents* I (1979 ed) by Dorothy Whitelock, an indispensable collection marred only by its omission of the Celtic material. A handy paperback edition of some of the legal, documentary and literary prose is *Anglo-Saxon Prose* by Michael Swanton, Everyman (1975). The outstanding general survey is still Sir Frank Stenton's *Anglo-Saxon England* (3rd ed, 1971), O.U.P., though there are valuable shorter ones by Henry Loyn, D. J. Fisher, H. P. R. Finberg, and Peter Sawyer, all of which are in paperback. Henry Mayr-Harting's *The Coming of Christianity to Anglo-Saxon England*, Batsford (1972), is full of good things. A most stimulating introduction to the whole Anglo-Saxon period, with excellent illustrations, is *The Anglo-Saxons* by James Campbell, Eric John and Patrick Wormald, Phaidon (1982).

On the coins the starting point is Michael Dolley's *Anglo-Saxon Pennies* (1964), British Museum. Margaret Gelling's *Signposts to the Past*, Dent (1978), is a fascinating introduction to the study of place-names.

There are several good biographies including Henry Loyn's *Alfred the Great*, O.U.P. (1967). Frank Barlow's *Edward the Confessor*, Eyre and Spottiswoode (1979 ed), and David Douglas' *William the Conqueror*, Eyre and Spottiswoode (1964 ed), are classics. Christopher Brooke, *The Saxon and Norman Kings* (Fontana paperbacks), is a fine introduction full of exciting insights.

General surveys of the archaeological material are in David Wilson, *The Archaeology of Anglo-Saxon England*, Methuen (1976), including a chapter on the development of the towns with copious references to local publications. Particularly valuable for its illustrations is *Barbarian Europe* by Philip Dixon, Phaidon (1976). A most significant addition to the study of early England is David Hill's *An Atlas of Anglo-Saxon England, 700–1066*, Blackwell (1981).

INDEX

References to photographs are printed in bold type. Numbers in italics refer to drawings or maps.